Ronald T. Potter-Efron, MSW, PhD

Handbook of Anger Management

Individual, Couple, Family, and Group Approaches

Pre-publication REVIEWS, COMMENTARIES, EVALUATIONS . . .

"This handbook provides exceptionally valuable information that will greatly assist psychotherapists and counselors in helping their patients and clients deal with anger-related problems. The book begins with a detailed discussion of the nature of anger and provides information on the psychological assessment of anger, hostility, and related constructs. The information on anger assessment focuses on developing interventions and specific treatment plans that will help anger management counselors work more effectively with their clients. The book's examination of the pros and cons of individual versus group counseling approaches, couples counseling, and treating angry children, adolescents, and families also provides excellent guidance for effective treatment. The chapters focusing on how people develop patterns of resentment and hatred and on the role of forgiveness as an antidote for anger are especially informative."

Charles D. Spielberger, PhD, ABPP
Distinguished Research
Professor and Director,
Center for Research in Behavioral
Medicine and Health Psychology,
University of South Florida

More pre-publication
REVIEWS, COMMENTARIES, EVALUATIONS . . .

"Mediators are trained to be unbiased, impartial, and some would say, dispassionate, but to resolve disputes they must fully understand the underlying dialectic. Nowhere is this more important than in dealing with couple and family disputes in which underlying anger can easily subvert the dispute resolution process. The material is well designed and easy to read with to-the-point summaries and case studies relating to each chapter. Ronald Potter-Efron's handbook will prove invaluable both for psychologists and counselors who are called upon to treat this anger using their medical and psychological expertise, and also for professional mediators wanting to understand and appreciate the core concepts of the anger involved in family law disputes, thereby enhancing the opportunities for settlement."

Catharine Allen
Certified Mediator/Arbitrator
and President, Toronto ADR Services-Ontario ADR Services

"This is the comprehensive guide to anger treatments that clinicians have been waiting for. *Handbook of Anger Management* lays out both the issues and step-by-step interventions for treating angry children, angry families (with and without physical violence), and angry adults (including Anger-Out and Anger-In formulations). This book makes an exceptional contribution to the field by describing both individual and group treatment approaches as well as tracing the relationship between anger and the traumatized brain. This book should be indispensable for any therapist who works with angry clients."

Matthew McKay, PhD
Co-author of *The Anger Control Workbook*

The Haworth Clinical Practice Press™
The Haworth Reference Press™
Imprints of The Haworth Press, Inc.
New York • London • Oxford

NOTES FOR PROFESSIONAL LIBRARIANS AND LIBRARY USERS

This is an original book title published by The Haworth Clinical Practice Press™ and The Haworth Reference Press™, imprints of The Haworth Press, Inc. Unless otherwise noted in specific chapters with attribution, materials in this book have not been previously published elsewhere in any format or language.

CONSERVATION AND PRESERVATION NOTES

All books published by The Haworth Press, Inc. and its imprints are printed on certified pH neutral, acid-free book grade paper. This paper meets the minimum requirements of American National Standard for Information Sciences-Permanence of Paper for Printed Material, ANSI Z39.48-1984.

Handbook of Anger Management

Individual, Couple, Family, and Group Approaches

The HAWORTH Handbook Series in Psychotherapy
Terry S. Trepper
Editor

Handbook of Remotivation Therapy edited by Michael L. Stotts and Jean A. Dyer

Handbook of Anger Management: Individual, Couple, Family, and Group Approaches by Ronald T. Potter-Efron

Titles of Related Interest:

Stopping the Violence: A Group Model to Change Men's Abusive Attitudes and Behaviors by David J. Decker

How to Work with Sex Offenders: A Handbook for Criminal Justice, Human Service, and Mental Health Professionals by Rudy Flora

The Therapist's Notebook for Families: Solution-Oriented Exercises for Working with Parents, Children, and Adolescents by Bob Bertolino and Gary Schultheis

The Therapist's Notebook for Children and Adolescents: Homework, Handouts, and Activities for Use in Psychotherapy edited by Catherine Ford Sori

Intimate Violence: Contemporary Treatment Innovations edited by Donald Dutton and Daniel J. Sonkin

Your Angry Child: A Guide for Parents by Daniel L. Davis

Becoming a Forgiving Person by Henry Close

Treating Co-Occuring Disorders: A Handbook for Mental Health and Substance Abuse Professionals by Edward L. Hendrickson, Marilyn S. Schmal, and Sharon C. Eckleberry

Child Trauma Handbook: A Guide for Helping Trauma-Exposed Children and Adolescents by Ricky Greenwald

Handbook for the Treatment of Abused and Neglected Children by Peter Forrest Talley

Handbook of Anger Management
Individual, Couple, Family, and Group Approaches

Ronald T. Potter-Efron, MSW, PhD

The Haworth Clinical Practice Press™
The Haworth Reference Press™
Imprints of The Haworth Press, Inc.
New York • London • Oxford

For more information on this book or to order, visit
http://www.haworthpress.com/store/product.asp?sku=5176

or call 1-800-HAWORTH (800-429-6784) in the United States and Canada
or (607) 722-5857 outside the United States and Canada

or contact orders@HaworthPress.com

Published by

The Haworth Clinical Practice Press™ and The Haworth Reference Press™, imprints of The Haworth Press, Inc., 10 Alice Street, NY 13904-1580.

PUBLISHER'S NOTE
Identities and circumstances of individuals discussed in this book have been changed to protect confidentiality.

Cover design by Jennifer M. Gaska.

Library of Congress Cataloging-in-Publication Data

Potter-Efron, Ronald T.
Handbook of anger management : individual, couple, family, and group approaches / Ronald T. Potter-Efron.
p. ; cm.
Includes bibliographical references and index.
ISBN 0-7890-2454-3 (hard : alk paper)—ISBN 0-7890-2455-1 (soft : alk. paper)
1. Anger—Treatment. I. Title.
[DNLM: 1. Anger. 2. Cognitive Therapy—methods. 3. Aggression—psychology. WM 425.5.C6 P869h 2005]
RC569.5.A53P68 2005
616.85'82—dc22

2004020214

To the newest member of the family,
Elizabeth Leigh Berger
May she live her life joyfully
and handle her anger well.

ABOUT THE AUTHOR

Ronald T. Potter-Efron, PhD, is the Director of the Anger Management Center at First Things First Counseling in Eau Claire, Wisconsin. He facilitates anger management training seminars for professional counselors and therapists throughout the United States and Canada. He has authored and/or edited several professional books, including *Aggression, Family Violence and Chemical Dependency* and *Shame, Guilt, and Alcoholism: Treatment Issues in Clinical Practice, Second Edition*. Dr. Potter-Efron's books for the general readership include *Angry All the Time: An Emergency Guide to Anger Control, Letting Go of Anger: The 10 Most Common Anger Styles and What to Do About Them, Stop the Anger Now: A Workbook for the Prevention, Containment and Resolution of Anger,* and *Letting Go of Shame: Understanding How Shame Affects Your Life*.

CONTENTS

Preface

Anger management is an interesting field. On one hand people have been thinking and writing about it for decades. For example, Paul Hauck wrote a good general interest book on this topic, *Overcoming Frustration and Anger,* in 1974 (Hauck,1974). Furthermore, many therapeutic models have been adapted for anger management, including Gestalt therapy, cognitive therapy, and relaxation training. There is even a standard for the effective use of anger, namely assertiveness, in which people are trained to utilize the emotion of anger in an effective, prosocial manner.

However, other areas in anger management are less well developed. Foremost is the arena of domestic violence, which is still fairly primitive despite the tremendous ongoing effort of theorists and therapists. One question I will address in this volume, for example, is whether couples should ever be seen together when a history of domestic violence exists. The fact that this basic "yes/no" question must be discussed is ample evidence that we still know little about how best to treat domestic violence.

I am a full-time mental health and substance abuse therapist, so my primary interest in this book centers on the practical aspects of anger management. Thus, I provide specific suggestions in each chapter about how to help clients with problematic anger change their lives. These suggestions range from the behavioral sphere (e.g., how to take a good time-out) to the existential (how to help some angry clients describe the despair that feeds their anger). As in most mental health areas, flexibility is the key to effective treatment. The reality is that one size does not fit all. Indeed, the situation is almost the reverse: because the term "anger problems" covers a tremendously wide array of concerns, the most effective counselors will be those who make the fewest assumptions about what their clients need while being exceptionally open to discovering the nuances and details of each person's anger issues.

Let me add that I have found anger management to be a very satisfying work focus. People can and do change, sometimes dramatically. Chronically angry individuals learn both to quit being so hostile toward others and how to treat people more positively. Fortunately, most clients find this transition very rewarding. Frankly, I think that is because people whose emotional lives center on anger are usually quite unhappy. After all, who would volunteer to wake up angry almost every day, essentially scan the environment continually for reasons to justify anger, grumble or explode several times during the day, and then go to bed mad? An angry life is usually a miserable life.

To explain to clients the trap of living in anger I ask them to envision that they are driving a bus and all of their emotions (anger, sadness, etc.) are riding along. Then anger hijacks the bus, sits in the driver's seat, kicks off all the other emotions, and aims at every pothole in the road. Anger, hostility, and aggression become typical responses to nearly every event—even perhaps to someone saying, "I love you." This bus ride obviously produces a very unpleasant and unsatisfying life.

So, then, what are the treatment goals? Some clients want to kick anger completely off the bus. However that would be a mistake. Anger has many uses. In particular, it signals strongly that something is wrong and needs immediate attention. Anger also provides people with the energy to change the environment. Instead, I suggest two primary goals: (1) the client needs to get back in the driver's seat; and (2) the client needs to retrieve his or her other emotions. Basically, these are the goals of the *Handbook of Anger Management.*

Acknowledgments

Terry Trepper, the overall editor for the handbook series, helped me make the transition in my mind from writing a more specialized book on individualized anger treatment to the present format. His enthusiasm for the finished product format is greatly appreciated.

The editorial and production staff at Haworth Press are talented professionals. These persons include Jillian Mason, Amy Rentner, Peg Marr, and Linda Mulcahy.

Eileen Immerman designed many of the tables and figures in this book. I have worked with her on a number of projects, and always am impressed with her skills and creativity.

I have discussed aspects of this book with many of my colleagues, all of whom have made valuable suggestions that have improved the text. I would like to thank in particular Patricia Potter-Efron, Joshua Potter-Efron, Charles Rumberg, Ed Ramsey, Carla Peterson, Charles Spielberger, and Jerry Deffenbacher.

Chapter 1

Introduction

DEFINITIONS AND BASIC APPROACH

The treatment of anger problems is a complicated subject. Here, for starters, are just a few important questions that need to be considered:

What is anger? How can it be defined in operational terms?
What constitutes an anger problem?
What is the relationship between anger and aggression?
Is there such a thing as healthy anger? If so, what does it look like?
To what extent is problematic anger a function of social learning?
What is the relationship between anger and domestic violence?
What goals should be set for individuals with anger problems?

These questions, along with many others, will be considered in this book.

The primary audiences for this book include anger management counselors, domestic violence counselors, psychologists and mental health therapists, educators and other professionals in the healing community such as members of the religious community (who must often deal with their parishoners' need for giving or receiving forgiveness).

The following are my definitions for some frequently used terms:

Anger: An emotional state that can range in intensity from mild irritation to extreme rage (Spielberger, 1999).

Rage: The strongest form of anger, very physical, threatening the individual with possible lack of control over his or her actions.

Aggression: Actual behavior, as contrasted with the feeling of anger that is intended to achieve one's goals or eliminate frustrating obstacles, regardless of the effect upon others. Anger does not automatically lead to aggression although the two frequently occur together.

Hostility: An attitude toward specific individuals or the world that includes seeing others as enemies and a readiness to be angry with others.

Resentment: A process in which anger is stored, usually accompanied by a belief that the individual has been injured by others.

Hatred: The end product of the resentment process. Hatred is "frozen" anger that results in an intense and unchanging dislike of another.

Anger Avoidance: A pattern of thinking, acting, and feeling in which a person avoids, ignores, and suppresses anger.

Chronic Anger: A pattern of thinking, acting, and feeling in which a person seeks, embraces, and prolongs anger experiences.

The bulk of this book deals with clients who have chronic anger problems. These individuals often lead miserably unhappy lives. Anger so completely dominates their affective experience that they can seldom feel joy, contentment, or other positive emotions. Few of these persons believe that they have willingly chosen to feel angry, irritable, annoyed, and mean-spirited. Rather, they usually either fail to realize how angry they are or believe that, given their life histories, they had no option other than to become chronically negative and hostile. One critical therapeutic task, then, is to help these clients discover that they can indeed turn away from chronic anger and toward a more satisfying lifestyle. The core assumptions about anger and anger problems which constitute the foundation for this book emerge from this goal:

1. Most chronically angry clients desire at some level of awareness to become less angry.
2. Counselors first need to help chronically angry clients give voice to this desire for change.
3. Counselors then need to assist their clients to learn the behavioral, cognitive, affective, and existential/spiritual skills that make such change possible.
4. The three most immediate goals of anger management include
   - decreasing the number of angry/aggressive episodes;
   - decreasing the intensity of these episodes; and
   - decreasing the severity of these episodes.
5. Both therapists and clients must keep in view positive alternatives to anger so that the goal then becomes that of substituting new, more positive habits of acting and thinking for older, anger-provoking thoughts and deeds.
6. If possible, this positive change focus can and should be pursued not just for the individual angry client but for all members of that person's family since angry individuals tend to live in angry families.
7. These changes should be enduring both for the individual and his or her family rather than short-lived and ephemeral.

Chapter 2 describes an assessment process that will help therapists gain a tremendous amount of useful information from their clients about how, when, with whom, and why these individuals become angry, as well as exploring the consequences of their anger and aggression. I have provided a detailed assessment questionnaire that requires as little as thirty minutes to as much as two or three hours to complete (depending on how talkative the client becomes and how much the counselor utilizes the questions to initiate a treatment dialogue). I also describe Charles Spielberger's State-Trait Anger Expression Inventory (1999) and my own Anger Styles Questionnaire, two instruments that help differentiate a client's anger thus allowing the development of more specific treatment plans. In addition, I describe and elaborate upon a typology of five anger diagnoses originally developed by Eckhardt and Deffenbacher (1995). Several domestic aggression typologies are designed to distinguish, for example, generally antisocial batterers from batterers with other concerns such as borderline personality traits. Finally, I include a discussion of adult psychological conditions, such as alcoholism and major depressive disorder, which are frequently associated with problematic anger.

Chapter 3 presents four major intervention areas that singly or in combination can help clients become less angry. Anger management counselors can then select where to focus their energies with each client based on their assessment of which intervention areas would be most helpful for the particular client. These four arenas of change include (1) behavior (changing one's actions); (2) cognitions (gaining new thoughts and anger disputation skills); (3) affect itself (lessening anger and substituting other emotional awareness); and (4) existentialism/spirituality (discovering the deeper meaning of one's anger). Specific interventions are suggested in each sphere.

Chapter 4 discusses group and individual approaches to anger and aggression management and considers the pros and cons of group versus individual counseling approaches. I then specifically describe three twelve-week group formats, one each for minimally aggressive angry individuals, more severely angry persons, and male domestic abusers. A specific rationale for individual anger management is also offered.

Chapter 5 asks the reader to consider this question: Under what circumstances, if ever, would you provide couples counseling to partners in which an ongoing threat of domestic violence exists? Attachment theory is utilized in this chapter to explain some of the nuances of domestic aggression and jealousy. Guidelines for couples work are provided.

Chapter 6 touches upon the broad topic of treating angry children, adolescents, and families. I use systems theory here to provide a basic approach to working with family units whenever possible, with the goal of dethroning anger from its place of emotional dominance within the family.

The final three chapters deal with more specialized but critical aspects of anger. Chapter 7 explores how people develop patterns of resentment and hatred. Since forgiveness is usually considered the antidote for hatred, this difficult process is described. Finally, I discuss the often-neglected issue of self-forgiveness, a skill that is even more difficult for many clients to achieve than forgiving others.

Chapter 8 covers another frequently neglected topic: anger turned inward. This process is defined and described in detail, along with appropriate therapeutic interventions. Description (and treatment ideas) are provided for five self-damaging behaviors that I believe develop when anger at oneself is fused with shame: self-neglect, self-sabotage, self-blame, self-injury, and self-destruction.

Chapter 9 discusses some of the neurological aspects of anger. Since the brain's fear-signaling system seems to be the best researched and understood of the brain's emotional communication and action systems, I describe that circuitry in some detail and then attempt to apply it to the brain's anger signaling system.

Chapters 2 through 9 include one major case study to illustrate and highlight the discussions of anger management theory and practice. Although each case study is based upon actual clients with whom I have worked, many of the details have been altered and in some situations the stories of two or more clients were merged to protect client confidentiality.

Chapter 2

Assessment for Anger, Aggression, and Domestic Abuse

INTRODUCTION

Assessment for anger problems is a particularly difficult task because of the great variety of issues that can be subsumed under that term. Thus, the Buss-Durkee Hostility Inventory (1957) measures one particular aspect of anger, cognitive hostility, while the Minnesota Multiphasic Personality Inventory (Green, 1991) can tap such features as sociopathic tendencies, resentment, and "overcontrolled hostility." I have selected for presentation here three assessment questionnaires that are particularly useful from a practical perspective. The common denominators are that they are easily understood by the respondent and that they help therapists devise effective treatment plans. These three are (1) an assessment questionnaire I designed to help counselors identify the main anger concerns of their clients; (2) the State-Trait Anger Expression Inventory designed by Charles Spielberger that measures such variables as anger expressiveness and anger control; (3) my anger styles questionnaire that taps ten anger styles. In addition I will discuss two typologies, one that describes five possible diagnoses of angry individuals and another that distinguishes between four categories of domestically abusive men. Finally, I present material on two selected dual-diagnosis concerns: the overlap between anger problems and psychological diagnoses and the overlap between anger problems and problems with alcoholism and drug abuse.

Questionnaires and tools that can be utilized for the purpose of assessment are also included in two other chapters. These include an anger turned inward questionnaire that identifies both the existence of excessive inwardly directed anger and the client's accompanying belief system, and two adult attachment styles identification tools that may be particularly useful with jealous and insecure aggressors.

THE ANGER/AGGRESSION INTAKE QUESTIONNAIRE

This set of questions is best administered in person but may also be given to clients to fill out independently. It takes roughly an hour to complete in session, depending of course on the verbosity of the client and the amount of detail desired by the therapist. As with most questionnaires, its reliability depends upon the truthfulness and completeness of the respondent's answers. Therefore, every effort should be made to gather collateral information from the respondent's family, counselors, employers, and criminal justice personnel.

Although the specified purpose of this intake questionnaire is to gain assessment information, it also serves as a bridge to and motivator for treatment, since answering these questions often helps clients recognize the extent of their anger difficulties.

One important note: many opportunities arise while using this questionnaire to initiate discussions about the goals of anger management and the processes involved. I will highlight these opportunities after providing a synopsis of the questionnaire. (Appendix A provides the same questionnaire in a handout format.)

I. Please tell me about any concerns you or others have about your anger.

II. Describe your *most recent* event involving your anger or aggression:
   - A. When did this occur?
   - B. With whom?
   - C. How did it start?
   - D. While this was going on, what did you
     1. think?
     2. feel?
     3. say?
     4. do?
   - E. How did it end?
   - F. Were alcohol or drugs used by anyone involved?

G. Were physical violence, force, threats, etc., used?
H. What effects (immediate or long term) did this event have on you?
I. What effects (immediate or long term) did this event have on others?

III. Now please tell me about the *worst* incident you've ever had involving anger or aggressiveness:
A. When did this occur?
B. With whom?
C. How did it start?
D. While this was going on, what did you
1. think?
2. feel?
3. say?
4. do?
E. How did it end?
F. Were alcohol or drugs used by anyone involved?
G. Were physical violence, force, threats, etc., used?
H. What effects (immediate or long term) did this event have on you?
I. What effects (immediate or long term) did this event have on others?

IV. Frequency of problems.
A. How often have you had trouble with your anger:
1. This month?
___Never
___Once or twice
___Weekly
___Several times a week
___Daily
___More than once a day
2. Over the past six months?
___Never
___Once or twice
___Weekly
___Several times a week
___Daily
___More than once a day

3. Previously as an adult?
4. When you were a teenager?
5. When you were a child?
6. Would you say that lately you become angry
   ___more often than a year ago?
   ___less often than a year ago?
   ___about the same as a year ago?
7. Would you say that lately when you become angry you have
   ___more control than previously over what you say and do?
   ___less control?
   ___about the same amount of control as before?
8. Would you say that lately when you become angry you do
   ___more damage than before?
   ___less damage?
   ___about the same amount of damage?
   ___not believe your anger/aggression is damaging?
9. When upset are you more likely to become angry at
   ___others?
   ___yourself?
   ___both yourself and others?

B. With whom do you become angry and how often do you become angry with them? (D = daily; S = several times a week; O = occasionally)

1. Partner/boyfriend/girlfriend	__D	__S	__O
2. Parents/stepparents	__D	__S	__O
3. Your children/stepchildren	__D	__S	__O
4. Other relatives	__D	__S	__O
5. Employers/co-workers/ employees	__D	__S	__O
6. Teachers	__D	__S	__O
7. Friends	__D	__S	__O
8. Strangers	__D	__S	__O
9. Others (whom?)	__D	__S	__O

V. Immediate stressors.
   A. What has occurred in your life now or in the past several months that has caused you stress, concern, or anxiety?
      1. Financial troubles: ____________________
      2. Relationship problems: ____________________
      3. Health concerns: ____________________
      4. Job or school difficulties: ____________________
      5. Legal issues: ____________________
      6. Emotional problems: ____________________
      7. Concern about someone else: ____________________
      8. Religious or spiritual crisis: ____________________
      9. Other (specify): ____________________
   B. How have these troubles affected your mood or behavior?

VI. Anger history.
   A. Family of origin.
      1. Describe what the following people did or do with their anger, especially when you were growing up:
         a. Your father/stepfather
         b. Your mother/stepmother
         c. Your brothers and sisters
         d. Other relatives
      2. Is there any family history of bad temper, assaults, homicides, or suicides?
      3. Were you spanked as a child? What do you think about that?
      4. Were you physically or sexually assaulted? If so, how do you think that has affected you, especially in terms of anger?
      5. In general, what did you learn about anger from your family?
   B. Friendship groups, culture, religious training, etc.
      1. Describe how your attitudes toward anger and aggression have been affected by messages you received from members of the following groups.
         a. Your gender:
         b. The opposite gender:
         c. Your nationality:
         d. Your race:

e. Your religion:
f. Social groups or gangs to which you belonged:
g. Other people or groups:

VII. Possible medical and/or psychological factors.

A. Do you have any current problems or past history of problems with the following?

___Alcohol or drug abuse
___Antisocial personality disorder
___Anxiety disorders
___Attention deficit disorder (with or without hyperactivity?)
___Bipolar disorder
___Borderline personality disorder
___Brain injury, concussions, seizures
___Chronic illness
___Dementia
___Depression
___Diabetes or hypoglycemia
___Disabling injury
___Paranoia
___Post-traumatic stress disorder
___Premenstrual syndrome
___Schizophrenia
___Other major illness or condition (specify):_________

B. Are you currently taking any medications? If yes, what?

VIII. Legal history relating to anger and aggression.

A. Any current problems with the law?
B. Are you on probation or parole?
C. Are you coming here as part of a criminal diversion program?
D. Any past anger- or aggression-related legal difficulties?
E. Any brushes with the law because of your anger or aggression that did not result in charges being filed?
F. If yes to any of these questions, please give details.

IX. Use of alcohol/drugs (Current or recent use, past use, and frequency):

___ Alcohol: ____
___Amphetamines: ___________________________________

___Barbiturates:___________________________________
___Cocaine:______________________________________
___Inhalants:_____________________________________
___Marijuana:____________________________________
___Prescribed medications:_________________________
___Opiates:______________________________________
___Other (designer drugs, etc., specify):_______________
___Drug combinations (specify): ____________________

X. What connections could exist between your use of these substances and your anger or aggression?
   A. When I use ____________ I often become more angry than usual.
   B. When I use ____________ I can become violent.
   C. When I use ____________ I get argumentative.
   D. When I use ____________ I become controlling or demanding.
   E. When I use ____________ I have poor judgment.
   F. When I use ____________ I get jealous or paranoid.
   G. I only get in trouble with my anger when I use_________ ____________.
   H. Others tell me I get angrier or more violent when I use____ ______________.
   I. Mixing ____________ and ____________ makes me more aggressive.
   J. I often use ______________ to try to cool down.
   K. Another connection between my using and my anger is ____________.
   L. ____ I don't see any connection between my use of alcohol or drugs and my anger or aggression.

XI. How have you attempted to control your anger?

_____ I never have.
_____ I talk to myself. What do you usually say that helps you cool down?
_____ I leave the scene. Where do you go? What do you do?
_____ I talk with people. With whom?
_____ I go to a self-help group such as AA.

_____ I do something physical. What do you do?
_____ I do something else. What do you do?

XII. What do you think is the first thing you need to do to help you control your anger or aggression?

XIII. What else do you need to do?

XIV. How hopeful are you that you can become less angry or aggressive?

XV. Can you tell me anything else that might help me understand your concerns about anger and aggression?

Discussion of the Anger/Aggression Intake Questionnaire

The first and last questions are open-ended, designed to help clients feel somewhat in charge of a mutual exploration process. Starting out less programmed also gives the counselor an opportunity to gauge the client's motivation. Imagine the difference in a respondent who responds to the first question with "Actually, I don't think I have an anger problem. My probation officer is hung up on it, though. She claims I'm angry but she says that about everybody" versus one who states, "My anger's getting worse and worse. I'm scared I could kill someone one of these days. I need help."

The second and third sets of questions ask informants about the details of two anger/aggression episodes, their most recent and worst incidents. If the most recent episode was also their worst then the questioner can instead ask for a "typical" incident to augment this incident. These items prepare clients to think about anger in two ways: (1) that anger and aggression episodes frequently occur in discrete, describable units; (2) that each episode involves cognition, affect, and verbal and/or physical actions. A third aspect of these questions is an immediate probe for alcohol or drug use (to be extended later in the questionnaire). The inquiry about immediate and long-term effects of the anger episodes helps the questioner determine how much insight the respondent has about his or her behavior. Finally, item "i" is a first check for empathy: does the respondent show any remorse or even awareness of how his or her anger/aggression affects others such as the immediate recipient of that anger or witnesses to it such as children?

The fourth set of questions helps determine the extent and target of the client's anger. It is important to know how often the client gets angry. Just as critical, though, is gathering information about the client's movement over time with regard to this material. In other words, has the client been getting angrier over time, less angry, or staying about the same? If the client does report significant change here, moving toward more or less anger, the counselor should ask the respondent how and why that has happened. This fourth set of questions also sets the stage to introduce three *goals* for anger management: (1) to get angry less often; (2) to stay in better control even when angry; and (3) to do less damage to oneself and others when angry. The last question in the "a" subset is an initial inquiry into the direction of the client's anger: inward, outward, or both. I will discuss this issue in more detail later in this chapter. Subset "b" recognizes that people frequently are highly selective about the targets of their anger or aggression. Although some informants state that they become angry with just about everyone over just about anything, most report that their anger is more limited. One person may become angry only at a spouse and children, another primarily targets employees, still a third targets "authority figures." The implication here is that these individuals have all the tools they need to manage their anger, since they demonstrate they can do so over and over again in many settings. The interesting question, then, is how can they take those skills and apply them with their spouses, children, co-workers, authority figures, etc.?

The fifth question regards the client's immediate stressors. I believe that people break down under the weight of stress and that the greater the number of significant stressors in someone's life, the more likely he or she will break down. Although some people become anxious or depressed under those circumstances, others, perhaps including the immediate respondent, do become more angry and aggressive when stressed. If this occurs, then counseling should begin by focusing upon how the client can lessen the amount of stress he or she is enduring. Also, individuals who indicate they are highly stressed become good candidates for relaxation and stress management training.

The sixth set of questions represents inquiries into the client's history, in particular family of origin. How was anger handled then? Were positive models available to demonstrate how to deal effectively with conflict, or were the client's parents unfortunate models of losing control, becoming abusive, being excessively critical, etc.? Please note the last family of origin question: "In general, what did you learn about anger from your family?" This question implies that what was once learned can now be challenged. This set also asks about broader early life influences that may have shaped the respondent's beliefs about anger and aggression. Note that the phrasing is intended to put the client in control. Nobody is insisting that the client was affected by race, religion, or gender, but he or she may indeed ascribe some attitudes, beliefs, and actions to these influences. If so, these should be discussed and perhaps challenged.

Question set seven screens for possible significant medical and psychological conditions often associated with anger and aggression. These conditions may sometimes be the primary *cause* of a client's anger. One example would be someone who reports never having an anger problem until afflicted with depression. Another possibility is that medical or psychological conditions may *exacerbate* an existing anger problem. For instance, someone may say, "I've always been pretty angry but since I hurt my back it's been a lot worse." Finally, one's anger may be functionally *independent,* even of a serious condition such as alcoholism, as someone who says: "Yes, I get angry when I've been drinking. But I get just as mad just as often when I'm sober." Thus, a therapist must identify ongoing medical and psychological concerns and then look carefully at their relationship to the client's anger issues. This question set also asks about medications the respondent consumes. This serves three purposes: (1) sometimes clients do not know the names of conditions for which they take medications; (2) the medications may hint at a client's anger-related conditions, as with someone who takes antipsychotics; (3) it is important to screen out the possibility that a client's anger or aggression may be the result of mismedication or overmedication.

The eighth set of questions concerns legal problems related to aggressive outbursts. Some clients are reluctant to admit their past and present legal difficulties, in part because of a tendency to deny and minimize their problems.

Alcohol and drug use are the focus of question sets nine and ten. Although no substance is always associated with anger or aggression, none is entirely free from possible implication either. Therefore, therapists must ask clients who consume these commodities questions that pin down exactly what effect they have upon their anger or aggression. For instance, does the client smoke marijuana to try to cool down? Does the respondent regularly become violent when drinking whiskey? Is a particular combination of substances, such as cocaine and alcohol, especially predictive of anger or aggression? Given their answers to these questions, some clients may need to be directed toward alcohol and drug treatment. These persons must be helped to realize that all the anger management skills they develop will be useless unless they also address their alcohol and drug problems. Treatment for anger may need to be deferred in this situation, although simultaneous treatment for the two problems may also be feasible. The relationship between alcoholism, drug abuse, and addiction is discussed more thoroughly at the end of this chapter.

Question eleven allows the counselor an initial view of the client's already developed anger management resources. Does he or she know how to take a time-out? Can the client relax? Does that person have a support system of people who will help him or her cool down? Asking these questions also gives the counselor an opportunity to mention several ways people can learn to handle their anger and so makes a transition to treatment.

Questions twelve and thirteen remind clients that they are responsible for making changes and also imply that they are in control of the process ("What do you think . . .?"). This is especially useful because many angry individuals are quite oppositional and automatically resist being told what they must do.

Question fourteen asks about the client's degree of hopefulness. This question helps counselors frame their task realistically: the goals are to help clients become angry or aggressive less often, to stay in better control when they do become angry, and to do less damage to themselves and others when angry.

THE STATE-TRAIT ANGER EXPRESSION INVENTORY

Charles Spielberger's State-Trait Anger Expression Inventory-2 (STAXI-2) (1999) is a standardized, quick, easy-to-use, and easily understood questionnaire that taps several important areas of anger. Consisting of fifty-seven items, the resultant product is an individualized assessment of an individual's tendency to become angry both immediately (state anger) and as a personality component (trait anger). I have found the STAXI-2 to be quite useful both for gathering information and for developing treatment plans.

More specifically, the STAXI-2 measures these aspects of the anger experience: *State anger* measures the intensity of a subject's angry feelings and the extent to which a person feels like expressing anger at a particular time. State anger is divided into the following components:

- Feeling angry
- Feel like expressing anger verbally
- Feel like expressing anger physically

Trait anger measures how angry feelings are experienced over time, so that individuals high in trait anger are more likely than the general population to become angry and/or to stay angry on a regular basis. Trait anger is subdivided into

- *angry temperament,* which reflects an individual's disposition to experience anger without specific provocation; and
- *angry reaction,* which measures the frequency that angry feelings are experienced in situations that involve frustration and/or negative evaluations.

The STAXI-2 also has scales that report *Anger-In,* which represents the desire and ability of the respondent to suppress anger, and *Anger-Out,* which describes the person's tendency to directly express angry feelings to others. Note that these scales are independent of each other, which means that certain individuals may be high on *both* Anger-In and Anger-Out. Other scales measure *Anger Control-In,* a person's attempt to calm down and cool off, and *Anger Control-Out,* the respondent's control over the outward expression of angry feelings. Standardized tables are available for the general adult population and several subgroups, such as younger adult males, adult females, etc., making interpretation of the STAXI-2 relatively easy and meaningful for specific populations.

THE ANGER STYLES QUESTIONNAIRE

A primary unit of analysis in the behavioral assessment of anger is the discrete anger episode, a length of time that stretches from the moment a person's anger is triggered until the issue is resolved or abandoned. These episodes can take place in seconds, especially for individuals who describe their anger as impulsive and quickly over, to years, for those who cannot let go of perceived injuries.

I call the triggering event, whether from an external source or internally generated, an "anger invitation." Most people receive many anger invitations every day. Clients who develop anger problems are usually those who accept a greater number of those invitations. However, sheer quantity is only one interesting aspect related to the consideration of anger episodes. The more important issue is exactly how people respond to the anger invitations they receive. I have identified through clinical observation at least ten consistent patterns of response. These patterns are labeled "anger styles." *Anger styles are repeated, predictable ways in which people handle situations in which they could or do become angry.* Each style may be utilized appropriately in certain situations. However, people get into trouble when they overuse or misuse one or more styles, for instance when someone develops a habit of excessive moral anger and becomes outraged over minor ethical transgressions.

The following questionnaire (adapted and modified from Potter-Efron, R. and P., 1995) is designed to help counselors identify which anger styles a particular client utilizes frequently.

Directions: Please answer the following thirty Yes/No questions by circling the most correct answer based on the ways you generally handle your anger. There are no correct or incorrect answers. If you think that the best answer would be "Sometimes" then still try to select a best "yes" or "no" answer, and add the letter "S" to your response.

1. I try never to become angry. Yes No
2. I get really nervous when others become angry. Yes No
3. I feel I am doing something bad when I become angry. Yes No

4. I often tell people I'll do what they want but then frequently forget. Yes No
5. I frequently say things like "Yeah, but . . ." and "I'll do it later." Yes No

6. People tell me I must be angry but I'm not certain why they say that. Yes No

7. I frequently become jealous, even when there is no reason. Yes No
8. I don't trust people very much. Yes No
9. Sometimes I feel as if people are out to get me. Yes No

10. My anger comes on really fast. Yes No
11. I act before I think when I become angry. Yes No
12. My anger goes away quickly. Yes No

13. I become very angry when people criticize me. Yes No
14. People say I'm easily hurt and oversensitive. Yes No
15. I become angry easily when I feel bad about myself. Yes No

16. I become angry in order to get what I want. Ye No
17. I try to frighten others with my anger. Yes No
18. I sometimes pretend to be very angry when I really am not. Yes No

19. Sometimes I become angry just for the excitement or action. Yes No
20. I like the strong feelings that come with my anger. Yes No
21. Sometimes when I'm bored I start arguments or pick fights. Yes No

22. I seem to become angry all the time. Yes No
23. My anger feels like a bad habit I can't break. Yes No
24. I get mad without thinking—it just happens. Yes No

25. I become very angry when I defend my beliefs and opinions. Yes No
26. I often feel outraged about what other people say and do. Yes No
27. I always know I'm right in an argument. Yes No

28. I hang onto my anger for a long time. Yes No
29. I have a hard time forgiving people. Yes No
30. I hate many people for what they've done to me. Yes No

Each set of three questions describes a separate anger style. Specifically,

1-3: Anger avoidance
4-6: Passive aggression
7-9: Paranoia
10-12: Sudden anger
13-15: Shame-based anger
16-18: Deliberate anger
19-21: Excitatory anger
22-24: Habitual anger
25-27: Moral anger
28-30: Resentment/hate

I have found this questionnaire quite valuable in planning treatment priorities (however, please note that the reliability and validity of this questionnaire have not been researched). Basically, a client who answers "yes" to all three items in a set certainly utilizes and probably overutilizes that anger style in daily living. Even one or two positive responses merit careful probing about when, where, and with whom the client uses that particular anger style. The following paragraphs briefly describe each anger style.

The Hidden Styles of Anger

Three anger styles, the hidden styles, share a common feature: people utilizing them are partly or mostly unaware of and/or unable to accept their anger. The first of these is called *anger avoidance,* an anger style practiced by people who believe anger is bad, scary, or useless. These individuals cannot use anger appropriately in their daily lives. Instead they tend to deny, ignore, and minimize their anger. Unable to listen to the messages in their anger, these persons often become enmeshed in situations they dislike but cannot escape. The therapeutic focus for clients who are consistently anger avoidant is to help them learn how to accept and utilize their anger.

The second hidden anger style is *passive aggression.* Passive aggressive individuals often feel powerless and dominated by others. They tend to be unassertive and resentful, despising the people in their lives whom they believe are trying to control them. However, passive aggressors have discovered one tactic that defeats these powerful opponents. They thoroughly frustrate others through inaction, making doing nothing a sort of art form that they have mastered. Unfortunately, passive aggression, when overused, traps the user in a perpetual state of inertia. Masters at doing nothing, their lives stagnate and become purposeless. Therefore, treatment for passive aggressive individuals must emphasize helping them develop positive purposes and goals in life in addition to helping them become more assertive and expressive with their anger.

Paranoia, or more generally *distrust-based anger* is the third hidden anger style. Here anger is projected onto others and then defended against with "defensive" anger and aggression. The result is that paranoid individuals become hypervigilant and live in a world in which few people, if any, can be trusted and in which the danger of attack is imminent. Treatment for clients with strong paranoid tendencies should be directed first toward helping them recognize the extent of their projections and second toward helping them feel safer and more trusting.

The Explosive Styles of Anger

Four anger styles can be grouped together as the *explosive styles.* Individuals with these styles periodically demonstrate their anger through dramatic outbursts. *Sudden anger* is the most easily recognizable of these patterns, in which anger comes out as rapid, usually short-lived, intense bursts. Clients with strong tendencies toward sudden anger often respond well to classic anger management tactics such as taking time-outs that are designed to delay the expression of anger long enough for the client to regain control.

Shame-based anger is another explosive style (Potter-Efron and Potter-Efron, 1995, 1999). Here individuals rapidly convert feelings of shame into rage. They then attack their attackers, the people they believe are shaming them or might be planning to do so. The presence of debilitating amounts of shame-based anger may be associated with domestic abuse (Dutton, 1998) since intimate associates most frequently trigger (both accidentally and sometimes intentionally) their partners' shame. Clients with this style of anger are often volatile and physically dangerous. They often need long-term therapy that addresses the shame underlying their anger and aggression.

Excitatory anger represents the third explosive anger style. Individuals with excitatory anger tendencies actually seek out their anger because becoming irate and getting into arguments triggers feelings of excitement and intensity. They will need help making and keeping a commitment to calmness and moderation as well as finding acceptable social ways to meet their need for excitement.

The last explosive style can be named *deliberate anger.* Deliberate anger is purposely displayed in order to intimidate others. People who regularly utilize deliberate anger have discovered a simple two-word reality: "anger works." Because they get what they want when they get angry they keep doing so, sometimes appearing tremendously irate even though they are not really angry at all. Clients with this pattern will need to be confronted about faking their anger for instrumental gain. They also often need to learn other ways to ask for what they want and need from others since they tend to have poor social and communication skills.

The Chronic Styles of Anger

The final three common anger styles are labeled the chronic styles. Individuals who utilize these styles frequently have developed long-term anger patterns that keep them angry, bitter, and resentful.

Habitual anger is my name for the initial chronic style. Persons high on habitual anger usually think and act in ways that continually perpetuate their anger. Anger becomes their default emotion of choice, automatically appearing in situations in which another person would feel other emotions or have no affective response at all. A man with habitual anger, for instance, might respond with annoyance to being told he was loved ("Why do you say that all the time? It bugs me.") or respond with defensiveness to getting praise at work ("Oh sure, they say they like my work, but they're just trying to make me work harder."). Cognitive treatment for habitual anger is very appropriate with its emphasis upon automatic and irrational thinking processes.

Moral anger is another chronic style. People who become morally angry perceive their anger as justified and righteous, for a cause greater than their own self-interests. As with all of these styles, moral anger can be used well or poorly. Used at its best, the morally angry individual advocates for socially significant purposes. Used poorly, people wrap the cloak of righteousness around them and refuse to take it off, treating even the smallest conflicts as moral battles and turning opponents into devils and monsters. Counselors working with clients in this area need to concentrate on helping these persons become more empathic and accepting of others' viewpoints.

The final anger style is named *resentment/hate.* Resenters tend to store up incidents in which they feel maltreated instead of trying to handle each one in a timely fashion. Over time their anger becomes rigid and inflexible, building into a solidified sense of hatred. Those who have harmed them become despised and treated as loathsome and unforgivable. This anger can last from weeks to decades and is very resistant to intervention. Treatment for hatred usually centers on the concept of letting go of old wounds and getting on with life. The key term is "forgiveness," a topic that will be discussed in Chapter 6.

ANGER ASSESSMENT AS A BRIDGE TO TREATMENT

Effective assessments act as a bridge to treatment when they point out and prioritize specific topics that need work. The following questions will help counselors summarize their assessment information so that they can present clear treatment directions and priorities to their clients.

1. Prioritize these three anger goals with regard to the client's immediate need to develop skills in these areas:
   ____ Prevention
   ____ Containment
   ____ Problem resolution

Name one specific skill in top area to develop: ________________

2. Prioritize these four treatment areas with regard to the client's immediate need to develop skills in these areas:
   ____ Behavior
   ____ Thoughts
   ____ Feelings
   ____ Spirit

Name one specific skill in top area to develop: ________________

3. Prioritize people/life spheres on which to concentrate attention:
   ____ Partner
   ____ Child or children
   ____ Parents
   ____ Siblings
   ____ Work
   ____ Teachers
   ____ Friends
   ____ Driving
   ____ Legal Figures
   ____ Strangers
   ____Others (specify):______________________________

4. Name any complicating factors that must also be addressed to help the client manage his or her anger:
   ____ Alcohol or drug use
   ____ Depression, anxiety, etc. (specify): ________________
   ____ Immediate stressors (specify): ________________
   ____ Anger/aggression in other family members
   ____ Legal concerns
   ____ Other (specify): ______________________________

5. Based on the STAXI-2, which of these problems need attention (at least 65 percent on test scale):
   ____ Immediate anger (State anger)
   ____ Trait anger: Angry temperament
   ____ Trait anger: Angry reaction
   ____ Anger-expression out
   ____ Anger-expression in
   ____ Anger-control out
   ____ Anger-control in
   ____ Total anger (Anger-Expression Index)

6. Which of the following anger styles needs to be addressed (indicated by the client checking at least two of three items in designated section of questionnaire)?
   ____ Avoidance
   ____ Sneaky
   ____ Paranoia
   ____ Sudden
   ____ Shame-based
   ____ Deliberate
   ____ Addictive
   ____ Habitual
   ____ Moral
   ____ Resentment
7. What else needs to be addressed? ________________________

ANGER DIFFERENTIAL DIAGNOSIS TYPOLOGY

Kassinove and Tafrate (2002) note that there is no comprehensive diagnostic plan in the *Diagnostic and Statistical Manual of Mental Disorders* DSM-IV-TR (2000) of the American Psychiatric Association. This seems an odd omission, given the multitude of diagnostic possibilities for other affective states such as anxiety (post-traumatic stress disorder, generalized anxiety disorder, social phobia, etc.) and sadness (grief reaction, generalized depressive disorder). Indeed, the only diagnosis that specifically targets aggression is intermittent explosive disorder, the criteria for which follow:

> A. Several discrete episodes of failure to resist aggressive impulses that result in serious assaultive acts or destruction of property;
> B. The degree of aggressiveness expressed during the episodes is grossly out of proportion to any precipitating social stressor;
> C. The aggressive episodes are not better accounted for by another mental disorder . . . and are not due to the direct physiological effects of a substance . . . or a general medical condition. . . . (DSM-IV-TR, 2000)*

*Reprinted with permission from the *Diagnostic and Statistical Manual of Mental Disorders,* Text Revision, Copyright 2000. American Psychiatric Association.

Based on these criteria this diagnosis is limited in value, given its excessive breadth and lack of detail.

Anger and aggression mention can be found in aspects of other psychological diagnoses such as oppositional defiant disorder, antisocial personality disorder, attention deficit disorder, and major depressive disorder. However, the actual presence of an anger or aggressive state usually is considered a possibility rather than an absolute necessity for diagnosing these conditions. I discuss this material in more detail at the end of this chapter.

Deffenbacher (Deffenbacher, 2003; Eckhardt and Deffenbacher, 1995) has developed an interesting typology of anger states. I present this model here, with my own added treatment suggestions for each diagnosis.

Deffenbacher suggests eight distinct diagnostic categories, actually four matched pairs depending on the presence or absence of aggression. These four types reflect four different triggers for an anger episode: (1) psychosocial stress related to a specific concern; (2) repeated situational stress related to one or more classes of situations; (3) unclear or missing external sources with anger welling up within the person; (4) many and generalized triggers for anger.

1. Adjustment Disorder with Anger

Example: A woman loses her job due to downsizing. She feels quite angry for several months afterward and feels unfairly treated.

Main criteria: A maladaptive response occurring within three months of a specific stressor; the primary emotional response is anger; increased angry/irritable mood that violates cultural and developmental expectations; mild aggressiveness but not sufficient to be considered a conduct problem.

2. Adjustment Disorder with Anger and Aggression

Example: The same woman makes repeated irate or threatening phone calls to her former employer.

Main criteria: Aggressive verbal or physical behavior is present under the circumstances described previously.

The following treatments are suggested for clients with adjustment disorders with or without aggression:

1. Identify immediate stressors in the person's life that are contributing to anger.
2. Link, if relevant, with feelings of helplessness or hopelessness.
3. Help clients discover and implement immediate actions that can help restore feelings of personal control and empowerment.
4. Have client describe previous, less angry state while providing the hope and expectation that he or she will eventually return to that state.
5. Search for one or two key anger-invoking cognitions that can help restore feelings of personal control and empowerment.
6. Help prevent generalizations (such as "All men are alike, aren't they?") from forming that might lead toward the formation of longer lasting anger states.
7. Teach stress reduction and relaxation techniques if anger is comingled with anxiety.
8. Spur client's curiosity about his or her other emotions to help balance affective response to the situation.

3. Situational Anger Disorder Without Aggression

Example: Someone who regularly gets very angry in reaction to perceived criticism or negativity from authority figures such as employers, teachers, etc. However, this person rarely protests or argues with these figures.

Main criteria: A small number of situations elicit strong anger reactions but minimal aggression; the individual may become angry just thinking about these situations in the absence of immediate prompts; the individual suffers significant impairment in one or more area such as health, finances, family relationships, etc.

4. Situational Anger Disorder with Aggression

Example: The same individual regularly becomes loud, argumentative, threatening, or assaultive when relating to authority figures.

Main criteria: Aggressive verbal or physical behavior is present under the circumstances described previously.

Treatment suggestions for clients with situational anger disorders with or without aggression include all of the above plus the following:

9. Challenge already formed generalizations ("All men are like that; I'm certain").
10. Identify specific situations that trigger anger episodes and search for common denominators.
11. Focus on anger that triggers aggression.
12. Confront "automatic" anger episodes by focusing on the client's choices.
13. Basic skills training (time-out, relaxation, "I" statements, etc.).
14. Teach relational skills (empathy, negotiation, etc.).
15. If relevant, help client recognize and intervene upon shame-rage episodes.
16. In marital work, link these longer-term anger patterns with "here we go again" conflict areas and the presence of a mutually angry partnership system.

5. Anger Attacks Without Aggression

Example: A man who becomes so angry he literally "sees red" for about ten minutes about once every two weeks, but this anger is not related to specific external stressors.

Main criteria: No clear external trigger for anger; intense anger reactions or "anger attacks" over a ten- to twenty-minute period followed by a sense of relief; distressful to the individual with feelings of loss of control; although the person may want to strike out he or she does not act on these impulses.

6. Anger Attacks with Aggression

Example: The person in the previous example screams obscenities, throws objects, and/or physically attacks the people around him or her.

Main criteria: Rapid escalation of anger into violence; loss of control.

Note: These episodes may be related to, or part of conditions such as, a diagnosable psychotic condition, a dissociative flashback, etc. Neuropsychological testing is strongly recommended.

Treatment for individuals with anger attacks with or without aggression include all of the previous suggestions plus the following:

17. Refer for neuropsychological testing and possible medication trial.
18. Focus on the need to attend to warning signs that the individual is approaching an anger episode.
19. Emphasize the need to ensure everyone's safety as the first goal in treatment.

7. General Anger Disorder Without Aggression

Example: A man who becomes extremely angry several times a day and whose anger may be triggered by a wide range of stimuli that are perceived as insults, injustices, and affronts. He displays his anger at home, while driving, and at work.

Main criteria: Anger regularly experienced several times a day, more days than not for at least one year; the person has been free from frequent anger reactions no more than one month during the past year; presence of distrust of others and an expectation that the misdeeds of others are purposeful; rumination over past insults.

8. General Anger Disorder with Aggression

Example: The same individual frequently engages in verbal or physical aggression when angry.

Main criteria: Aggressive verbal or physical behavior is present under the circumstances described previously.

Treatment for clients with generalized anger with or without aggression include all of the previous suggestions plus the following:

20. Develop the theme: "Anger is in control of your life. Is that what you want?"
21. Check for highly distorted and inaccurate interpretations of others' actions and statements.
22. Identify specific anger styles (especially the chronic styles: habitual, moral, and resentment/hate) and treat accordingly. (See R. and P. Potter-Efron's *Letting Go of Anger,* 1995.)
23. Address getting angry as part of the client's self-concept ("That's just who I am—I've always been a hothead").
24. Challenge client's tendencies to become enmeshed in multiple angry systems (and his or her part in creating and maintaining those systems).
25. May need to discuss real history of abuse, neglect, betrayal, abandonment, etc., to discover and treat the sources of bitterness and anger.
26. Look for evidence of sociopathy (little empathy, guilt, or shame following aggressive episodes).
27. Initially focus on negative consequences of aggression to the client as the main reason to change one's behavior.
28. Positive gains from aggression must be addressed.
29. Identify specific anger styles (especially the explosive styles: sudden anger, shame-based anger, deliberate anger, and excitatory anger) and treat accordingly. (See R. and P. Potter-Efron's *Letting Go of Anger,* 1995.)
30. If client suffers low self-esteem, definitely discuss the shame-rage link as a generalized susceptibility with many triggers.

Although Deffenbacher's typology has not been widely adopted it has substantial merit and serves as a template for the diagnosis and treatment of anger disorders.

DOMESTIC AGGRESSION TYPOLOGY

Several authors have proposed typologies that describe different types of men who are violent within intimate relationships. These typologies all reflect the concept that not all men are physically violent within the home for the same reason. Several such typologies are noted here.

1. Saunders (1992):
   - *Family-only aggressors:* least angry, depressed, and jealous; suppressed feelings; least marital dissatisfaction; least psychologically abusive
   - *Generally violent:* most aggressive outside of home; severely abused as children; most severe violence; violence most highly associated with alcohol use
   - *Emotionally volatile:* highest levels of anger, depression, and anxiety; frequent alcohol use associated with violence; most psychologically abusive; least satisfied in marital relationship
2. Groetsch (1996):
   - *Type one:* least dangerous; normal male/abnormal circumstances; no premarital abuse; feels remorse; situational and isolated abuse; very treatable
   - *Type two:* moderately dangerous; several character defects; some premarital abuse; feels limited remorse; some use of weapons; abuse neither situational nor isolated; moderately treatable
   - *Type three:* very dangerous; personality disordered; ongoing and systematic pattern of abuse; frequent past and premarital abuse; frequent use of weapons; no remorse; not treatable; focus on consequences
3. Jacobsen and Gottman (1998):
   - *Pit bulls:* insecure; highly unstable relationships; most violence with family members; emotionally dependent; great fear of abandonment
   - *Cobras:* highly antisocial; nonremorseful; feel entitled; nonempathic; seek gratification; high alcohol and drug abuse; do not fear abandonment but will not be controlled
4. Dutton (1998):
   - *Overcontrolled:* flat affect or constantly cheerful persona; tries to avoid conflict; high social desirability; chronic resentment; overlap of violence and alcohol use; avoidant, dependent, and passive-aggressive traits
   - *Impulsive/undercontrolled:* cyclical phases; high levels of jealousy; relationship-only violence; high levels of dysphor-

ia, depression, and anxiety-based rage; fearful/angry attachment style; borderline personality traits
- *Instrumental/undercontrolled:* generally violent; antisocial history; violence acceptable; usually physically abused as child; low empathy; dismissive attachment style; macho attitude toward violence

Based on the literature and my own counseling, I suggest the following four-group typology for domestic abusers. Note that I include both genders in this typology although little research or even conceptualization regards women who act violently toward their partners.

1. *Low-level aggression/nonpathological:* This broad category includes individuals of both genders who are occasionally physically aggressive within intimate relationships but who do not suffer from significant DSM axis II pathologies and whose aggression is relatively minor. This low-level aggression is nevertheless unacceptable and should not be considered standard or tolerable behavior. Subtypes of this type of domestic aggression could include

- occasional aggressioning in a couples relationship characterized by temporary emotional overload, minor aggression, and remorse;
- Groetsch's type one aggressors facing situational problems that produce occasional but more severe violence;
- men who have learned classic "male dominance" cultural roles and whose aggression serves to maintain those roles (but who have the capacity to modify their behavior once they realize it is no longer rewarded by society); and
- perhaps Saunder's "family-only" and Dutton's "overcontrolled" men whose poor communication style and excessive desire to appear worthy are part of their perceived male role and can be altered.

Treatment for these individuals would emphasize education focused upon accepting the goal of nonviolence within relationships; stress reduction; anger and conflict management training; individual and/or couples counseling as needed. The concept of creating a nonviolent system may be as important here as that of becoming a nonviolent individual, especially when excessive anger and aggression occur within two or more family members.

2. *Needy:* These are individuals whose aggression is maintained by severe ego deficits. They have strong borderline personality traits and many could be classified as having an axis II borderline personality disorder. Their adult attachment styles are usually a combination of preoccupied and fearful. Their violence usually occurs as they experience (or anticipate the possibility of experiencing) emotional or physical abandonment. They tend to be extremely jealous and possessive. They feel empty inside and consequently cannot self-soothe. The theme of their violence is "I can't live without you so I can't let you go."

Treatment would include education focused on the rights of others to have lives of their own; relatively long-term individual therapy designed to help the individual fill the internal emptiness with a sense of self, a greater sense of safety, and self-soothing ability. Couples counseling may be appropriate but must involve helping the client gain awareness that he or she has expected and demanded way too much from his or her partner (namely, to give a feeling of wholeness) and make a serious commitment to curtail those demands. Meanwhile the partner could benefit from an increased understanding of the aggressor's psychological situation as long as he or she is strongly encouraged to separate caring for the partner from taking care of the partner. The theme of couples work would be to help the couple become less enmeshed and more interdependent.

3. *Antisocial traits:* These individuals have significant oppositional and defiant tendencies. Some merit the axis II label antisocial personality disorder. Their attachment style is usually "dismissive" but they have strong feelings of entitlement. This combination translates into "I have no interest in meeting your needs but I fully expect you to meet mine." Low empathy, high generalized violence, deliberate use of intimidation tactics, and frequent alcohol/drug abuse are concurrent characteristics. They jealously guard their partners, not because they cannot live without them but because they possess them and will not let anyone else have them.

Treatment: Many authors consider these individuals beyond hope in terms of education and therapy. Both individual therapy and couples therapy are normally excluded and partners are usually counseled to leave the relationship. Instead, the emphasis is on providing and maintaining consequences against acts of violence. However, some persons with antisocial tendencies may benefit from educational efforts that focus upon helping them develop prosocial values (guilt, empathy, respect, etc.). Some individuals may have conversion experiences when exposed to AA or religious organizations that help them value others. Group and individual counseling should not be ruled out entirely, especially for clients who do not have full-fledged antisocial personalities and who seem capable of developing beyond their entitlement concepts.

4. *Derivative aggression:* These domestic aggressors have a major physical or psychological condition that explains much or all of the person's aggressive behavior. Such conditions could include alcoholism (if virtually all acts of aggression occur while the individual is intoxicated or going through withdrawal), paranoid schizophrenia, severe depressive episodes, post-traumatic stress syndrome, chronic pain, etc. Counselors must walk a narrow line with these clients, neither totally excusing their unacceptable behavior just because they have another problem (for instance, not telling the drinker that it is the alcohol and only the alcohol that is the cause of his or her behavior) nor dismissing these concerns as unimportant. Rather, an effort must be made to understand the exact connections between the violence and other disorders to gain an understanding as to how much of the client's domestic aggression may be secondary to another condition.

Treatment here would give major attention to the contributing physical and psychological conditions that help explain the client's aggression. These conditions might be addressed before or concurrently with treatment for anger and aggression.

ADULT PSYCHOLOGICAL DIAGNOSES AND CONDITIONS ASSOCIATED WITH ANGER AND AGGRESSION PROBLEMS

As discussed previously, one very interesting aspect of assessing anger problems is the relative lack of relevant diagnoses in the DSM-IV-TR. However, many psychological conditions described in that manual do involve the presence of anger or aggression. This anger may not always be present, though. Rather, this anger or aggression may never be present with some clients, occasionally present with others with the same diagnosis, and regularly present for still others with that diagnosis. Still, some fairly predictable associations can be made between specific psychological diagnoses and certain ways that clients exhibit their anger.

Table 2.1 is intended as a guide to help practitioners recognize typical anger and aggression patterns associated with particular adult psychological diagnoses. It is meant only as a rough guideline but should help counselors notice links between certain displays of anger and aggression and possible psychological conditions or diagnoses.

TABLE 2.1. Adult Psychological Conditions and Associated Behaviors/Cognitions

Condition	Associated Behaviors/Cognitions
Adult attention deficit disorder	Frustration with routine tasks and obligations can increase tendency toward "oppositionality."
Alcoholism/substance abuse	Disinhibits normal controls over anger and aggression; may be used to inhibit/suppress anger.
Antisocial personality disorder	Intimidation tactics are used to control others.
Anxiety disorder	Anger is experienced in the face of possible loss of control over external environment.
Attachment difficulties: "fearful" and "preoccupied" states	Fears of abandonment trigger excessive vigilance, jealousy, and demands for attention.
Bipolar disorder (manic phase)	Impulsive bouts of anger occur when immediate goals are blocked.
Borderline personality disorder	Strong tendency toward "splitting" increases development of hateful feelings and inability to forgive.
Dissociative identity disorder	Angry/rageful affect may be localized within one personality state ("alter").
Dysthymic disorder	Person is easily annoyed, cynical, and sarcastic.
Intermittent explosive disorder	Sudden inexplicable bouts of extreme aggression often accompanied by inability to recall incident.
Major depressive disorder	Increased irritability, angry rejection of others, impotent rage, and suicidal ideation are common.
Paranoia/paranoid schizophrenia	Person experiences extreme suspiciousness and projects own aggressive impulses onto others.
Post-traumatic stress disorder	Overactivated terror reaction triggers defensive, dissociative episodes.
Premenstrual syndrome	Excessive irritability, oversensitivity to criticism, and overreaction to perceived attack are possible.

Thus, if the therapist notices that a client's anger often takes the form of intimidation tactics then he or she should be alerted to the possibility that the client has significant antisocial tendencies and may even merit a diagnosis of antisocial personality disorder. Another client whose anger takes the form of continuing annoyance, cynicism, and pessimism may be suspected of being dysthymic and possibly a candidate for antidepressive medications.

ANGER, ALCOHOLISM, AND ADDICTION

I briefly discussed the complex relationships between alcohol and drug abuse/addiction and anger/aggression in the intake questionnaire presented earlier in this chapter. Please consult Appendix C for more detailed information on these specific interrelationships.

A broad parallel occurs between these two sets of concerns. For example, deficits in the brain's production of serotonin and dopamine have been implicated in the development of both concerns (Volavka, 2002). In addition, anger serves many similar functions to addiction that differ from person to person. Anger can be as exhilarating as a stimulant drug such as cocaine. Alternatively, some persons develop chronic, lower intensity anger problems remindful of individuals who are habitual maintenance drinkers. Also, certain people experience transformative experiences when angry, feeling more powerful and intelligent, just as some individuals utilize mind-altering drugs such as LSD for the same purpose. Finally, anger can even have sedative effects, as noted by Jacobsen and Gottman (1998) in their description of antisocial "pit bull" batterers who actually become physiologically calmer even as they yell and scream at their partners.

One important question is how treatment of one of these concerns impacts the other. This is particularly vital because the two conditions are seldom treated simultaneously even though they certainly could be. Instead, chemical dependency counselors tend to insist that clients go through addiction treatment before dealing with their anger while anger and abuse specialists sometimes reverse the equation. Given the realities of the field, let us begin with the possible effects of alcohol and addiction treatment on the client who also has a significant anger/aggression problem. Here are four possible results of beginning with chemical dependency treatment: (1) alcohol/drug treatment may take care of the problem completely; (2) alcohol/drug treatment may help clients have fewer anger problems or to be less violent than before but not completely reduce their anger levels to normal; (3) alcohol/drug treatment may release anger that had been inhibited through substance use; or (4) there may be no connection at all—they are independent variables.

The first result, that alcohol/drug treatment may take care of the problem completely, does happen occasionally. Here clients report that they almost never get excessively angry and absolutely do not become physically aggressive except when they are under the immediate influence of alcohol or drugs. As long as these clients "keep the plug in the jug," presumably they will have no strong anger problems.

The second result, is, in my experience, more common than the first. This reflects research that consistently indicates alcoholics have considerably more chronic anger than the average population (Potter-Efron and Potter-Efron, 1991a; Walfish, 1990), even after treatment. Even a casual reading of the *Big Book* (Alcoholics Anonymous, 1976) reveals a strong concern among the writers of that book about the necessity of dealing with long-term resentments in order to avoid relapse. It seems very reasonable, then, to suggest that many clients who undergo alcohol and addiction treatment be referred to anger specialists to continue their recovery work.

The third possibility, that alcohol/drug treatment may release anger that had been inhibited through substance use, cannot be overlooked. This situation is most likely to develop with individuals who have utilized addictive processes to "stuff" their anger. These persons will often score positively for anger avoidance and passive aggression on the anger styles questionnaire described earlier in this chapter. Newly sober, these persons might get hit by a tidal wave of previously suppressed anger, which, if they have not predicted and for which they are unprepared, could easily trigger a relapse.

Finally, there may be no connection at all between a particular client's anger and addiction. The two are independent variables, so that the client might remark "Sure, I drink when I'm angry. But I drink when I'm sad, and happy, and when I'm not feeling anything at all." Clearly, all the alcohol and addiction treatment in the world will not touch this person's anger problems because the two entities are unrelated. He or she will need to be treated separately for this completely different concern.

Another important consideration is the relationship between the use of specific mood-altering substances and an individual's experience of anger. Although these experiences vary widely, some predictable correlations are found. Table 2.2 (adapted from work originally created by Michael Miller, MD, and presented in Potter-Efron, 1991a) briefly describes the overall risk that use of a particular substance will exacerbate a person's anger or aggression problems and some of the reasons why the danger is increased.

What might occur if the client first receives treatment for anger/aggression while still displaying addictive behaviors? Possibilities include (1) the client's continuing addiction problems make it virtually impossible for him or her to learn anger management techniques;

TABLE 2.2. Anger/Aggression Relationship to Alcohol/Drug Use

Drug Group	**Risk Level**	**Nature of Risks**
Alcohol	High	Societal permission/expectation; disinhibition; withdrawal; irritability; pervasiveness within society
Sedatives and barbiturates	High	Promotes irritability; assaultiveness; self-destructive attacks
Cocaine and stimulants	High	Highly associated with irritability and impulsive attacks; can produce psychotic-like personality changes with long-term use
PCP	High	Produces angry/assaultive tendencies
Steroids	Medium-high	Seems to encourage anger and aggression, especially in already prone individuals
Inhalants	Medium	Generally incapacitates users but associated with aggressive lifestyles
Opiates	Medium-low	Generally diminishes all emotions during use; aggression to procure drug money main problem
Cannabis	Medium-low	Mistakenly assumed to diminish anger/aggression; can exacerbate underlying paranoia
Hallucinogens	Low	May exacerbate underlying psychotic delusions

(2) the client can learn and even utilize these techniques well when sober but not when under the influence of alcohol or drugs; and (3) the client can learn and utilize anger management skills on all occasions, even when intoxicated and despite continuing addiction patterns. Although I have experienced the other two frequently, I find the second alternative to be most common with my clients. This may partially be due to the belief in American society that getting drunk or high allows people to take a "time-out" from normal inhibitions. However, I do not believe that is the only or best interpretation. Many anger management clients simply cannot seem to bridge the learning gap between their sober and intoxicated states. In other words, what they learn sober does not generalize to what they say and do while intoxicated. The implication of this limitation, of course, is that angry clients with alcohol or addiction patterns must be challenged at least to curtail, if not eliminate, their use of mood-altering substances.

The following sets of questions are designed to help clients understand the links between their use of alcohol and drugs and their anger and aggression issues as well as to help them recognize that they must deal effectively with both concerns:

1. How does your use of alcohol or drugs affect:
   a. how often you become angry?
   b. how strongly you become angry?
   c. how likely you are to become violent?
      i. against yourself?
      ii. against others?
      iii. against objects, pets, etc?
2. How does becoming angry affect your drinking or drug use?
   a. Does it give you an excuse to use?
   b. Does it affect your choice of drugs?
   c. Is your anger a regular part of the way you relapse?
3. Are there times you want to become angry and get high at the same time? When does this happen (e.g., shame episodes, depression, etc.)?
4. How do you plan to stop or control your anger if you don't deal with your alcohol or drug use?
5. How do you plan to stop or control your drinking/drugs if you don't deal with your anger?
6. Can you think of any way to use the energy and strength of your anger to help you deal with your drinking or drug problems?

CASE STUDY: ASSESSMENT OF A CHRONICALLY ANGRY CLIENT WITH MULTIPLE PROBLEMS

Rick, age thirty-three, works as a job estimator for a siding and roofing company. He has been married three times and has one child from his first marriage, which only lasted a few months, and two children with his current wife, Amanda. Here is a summary of selected information taken from the general intake questionnaire, the State-Trait Anger Expression Inventory-2, and the anger styles questionnaire. I also consider how Rick would be classified in terms of levels of anger and types of domestic abuse, possible relevant psychological diagnoses, and the specific effects of alcohol on his behavior. Note that numbers set in brackets refer to the number of the question on the Anger and Aggression Intake described earlier in this chapter.

[1] Rick's assessment began with this statement: "Ron, I'm desperate. I get so angry I see red. I can't stop. I want to stop. Can you help me?" And Rick meant what he said; he became so angry several times a day that blood rushing through the capillaries of his eyes caused him literally to see red. [2] As for his most recent angry incident, Rick had just yesterday shoved a potential client after "we got into a pissing contest and he said I didn't know what I was talking about." Nor was that the first time Rick had lost his temper at work. In fact, he had been fired from his previous job after repeatedly arguing with his boss.

When I asked about specific aspects of the recent episode, Rick remembered this thought: "I won't let that bastard show me up." The accompanying sensations included accelerated heart rate and rapid breathing along with a feeling of rage. What he said right before he shoved the guy was "Get out of my G—D—face, you a—h—" Finally, he shoved the man hard enough to make him fall down, told him to go to hell, and stomped off. It took him several hours to calm down, after which he went to the office, expecting to get fired. But, amazingly, the customer never called to complain. Still, Rick realized he had lost control again and that he needed help.

[3] Rick has had far worse incidents. He admitted that he beat his first two wives (but not Amanda) and that was why those marriages fell apart. The worst event he remembered occurred in his twenties when, after drinking copiously, he got into a drunken rage and destroyed his entire living room, causing over $4,000 worth of damage. The police arrived in time to stop him from killing himself with the gun that by then he was holding to his temple. He was arrested, taken to a mental health ward at the local hospital, and eventually charged, ironically enough, with malicious damage to his own property. For

that crime he served a few months in jail, went through an alcohol education class that had no effect upon him, and endured a year's probationary period.

[4] Rick gets significantly angry at least twice a day. That has been true his entire adult life, although he does say he is winding down a bit. He tends to be less physically aggressive than in the past but more "cutting" with his words. The primary targets of his wrath are his wife and kids, but nobody is exempt as he regularly becomes angry at friends, family, strangers, work associates, and drivers.

[5] Life has been particularly hard on Rick lately. His wife has been very depressed; both of his sons have been diagnosed with attention deficit disorder; the bad economy has affected his work commission so "I'm in debt up to my eyeballs." He's feeling overwhelmed, constantly irritable, and ready to snap at anything.

[6] Rick grew up in a troubled and violent household in which he witnessed his alcoholic dad beat his depressed mom. That man never hit Rick. Instead, he constantly belittled him, telling Rick he was a "worthless piece of s—" and worse. The family dissolved when Rick was nine years old. After that he lived mostly with his grandparents, whom he described as "good people who were way too old to handle us." When I asked Rick what he had learned about anger as a child, his response was "Don't let nobody ever push you around and don't trust nobody."

[7] I then went through the list of behavioral and mental problems listed in Item 7 of the questionnaire. Several possible concerns emerged, including alcohol abuse (discussed later); antisocial personality disorder based on his long history of oppositionality and aggression; borderline personality disorder because of strong traits of jealousy, insecurity, and need for relationship reassurances; and dysthymia hinted at by statements such as "I never really feel good about anything. Every day's a gray day." He also is very distrusting of others, so much so that he implied in a paranoid fashion that people were plotting against him. Rick had never been treated nor was he taking any medications, however, for any of these conditions.

[8] Rick was not currently in any legal trouble. In addition to the incident described previously Rick also has a history of relatively minor scrapes with the law including domestic abuse charges from his previous marriages.

[9-10]. Alcohol is Rick's mood-altering substance of choice although he has used other substances including marijuana, ecstasy, and amphetamines. He drinks three to four times a week, up to a twelve pack at a setting. He says that sometimes drinking actually calms him down at first but then it tends to make him more irritable, argumentative, and jealous. Later, when I asked him how he hoped to control his anger if he kept drinking, he admitted that he probably would not be able to do so and committed at first to "cutting down" and then to quitting drinking entirely, a goal that he has not been completely successful in accomplishing. He declined specific treatment for alcoholism, however, saying that he'd been through all that twice before and it didn't work. Still, he has been generally successful at reducing the effects of

his drinking upon his anger and aggression in that he no longer drinks just to give him an excuse to get mad.

[11] Rick had seldom actually attempted to control his anger since he has thought of it more as part of his personality than as a series of choices that he could make. His main effort has been just to walk away when he gets mad. However, that doesn't work very well because he spends the time away stewing over alleged insults rather than relaxing. [12] When I asked Rick what he needed to do first to help himself control his anger he said that he needed to learn how to let go of his anger instead of obsessing. [13] He added that he also wanted to learn how to be more accepting of others and to be less demanding.

[14] Finally, Rick told me that he wasn't very hopeful he could change but he was willing to try. [15] He repeated that he was desperate to change because he realized now that he was living a miserable life.

Rick took the STAXI-2. He turned out to be very high on both Anger-In (ninetieth percentile) and Anger-Out (ninety-fifth percentile) and quite low on Anger Control-In (twentieth percentile) and Anger Control-Out (fourth percentile). He placed in the upper 5 percent of adult males on the STAXI-2. All these scores describe an individual with a massively significant anger problem, one that is pervasive and characterological in nature.

Rick's anger styles questionnaire was highly positive for five anger styles: sudden anger, shame-based anger, paranoia, habitual anger, and resentment/hate. Again, high scores in this many areas indicate a broad anger problem that will undoubtedly take much time and effort to repair.

Regarding Eckhardt and Deffenbacher's diagnostic categories for anger, Rick would almost certainly be diagnosed with a generalized anger disorder with aggression. As for the domestic aggression typology described earlier, Rick would fall primarily into the "antisocial" category but with significant aspects of "needy" and "derivative" characteristics, illustrating the point that real human beings seldom can be definitively placed in one simple category.

Rick's assessment led to the following treatment plan:

1. Rick made a commitment to the goals of becoming angry less often, becoming less intensely angry, and doing less damage when angry.
2. He agreed to read two books on anger, the first with an emphasis on facing the reality of being chronically angry and the second a workbook on anger skills development.
3. In terms of anger styles, Rick chose to begin work in the area of dealing with his sudden anger, to be followed as soon as possible with the themes of shame-based anger and resentment.
4. Rick agreed to minimize his alcohol consumption and to consider making a commitment to abstinence if he could not contain his anger when drinking.
5. He agreed to a referral to a neurologist for consultation with regard to his taking antiseizure or other medications to keep him from seeing red.

SUMMARY

A thorough assessment is the first step toward successful anger management counseling. I have presented several guides toward this goal in this chapter. Specifically, I have discussed the use of a standard intake interview, the State-Trait Anger Expression Inventory, and an anger styles quiz. In addition, I have described materials intended to help practitioners in this field be better able to distinguish different levels of anger and aggression and different types of domestic abusers. Finally, the dual relationship between anger/aggression and psychological problems and another dual relationship between anger/aggression and alcoholism and addiction were considered and an assessment case study was presented.

The next steps involve designing and implementing treatment for clients with significant anger and aggression problems. That is the focus of the next chapter, in which four primary modes of intervention will be described: behavioral change, cognitive approaches, affective regulation, and existential/spiritual interventions.

Chapter 3

Intervention Approaches in Anger Management

INTRODUCTION: INTERVENTION PHILOSOPHIES AND APPROACHES

When reviewing the literature on anger management it is easy to be struck by the wide range of proposed interventions. Although certain methods, in particular cathartic ventilation techniques, have lost favor because research fails to support their utility (Tavris, 1989; Bushman, Baumeister, and Stack, 1999), many others have been shown to be effective at least with some clients in some situations. These include cognitive therapies such as those proposed by the rational-emotive techniques of Beck (1999, 1976) and Ellis (Kassinove and Tafrate, 2002; Ellis and Tafrate, 1997); assertiveness training (Alberti and Emmons, 2001); social skills training (Kassinove and Tafrate, 2002); relaxation training (Smith, 1999; Deffenbacher and Stark, 1992); and systematic desensitization (Evans, Hearn, and Saklofske, 1973). Tafrate (1995) concluded that several techniques were effective, in particular strategies that targeted self-statements, physiological arousal, and behavioral skills. Multicomponent programs, such as Novaco's (1975) stress inoculation program were also found to be effective, although not necessarily more effective than single-component programs.

These treatment modalities emerge from underlying philosophical views about the nature of problematic anger. Historically, three main philosophies have dominated psychological approaches to anger problems over the past several decades: *ventilation, reduction,* and *management.* Ventilationists tend to view the core problem in anger as emanating from people's tendencies, under societal pressure, to suppress and repress their emotions. The treatment goal, then, becomes giving permission to individuals to fully express their feelings, including anger. Hopefully, the cathartic experience produced in this manner will help clients relieve their stress, drain their anger, and get on with their lives. Classic Gestalt therapy (Polster and Polster, 1973), with its emphasis upon completing unfinished business, exemplifies this approach. Reductionists, on the other hand, focus upon people's tendencies to be too strongly emotional rather than too repressed in their emotions. Ellis's (1962; Ellis and Tafrate, 1997; Ellis and Harper, 1975) rational-emotive therapy fits this model with its emphasis upon recognizing irrational thought processes that subsequently produce excessively powerful emotional states. Finally, a balanced approach is developed in the philosophy of those who espouse assertiveness training (Alberti and Emmons, 2001) with its concept that appropriate anger expressiveness exists in a middle ground between excessive anger, labeled aggression, and deficient amounts of anger, labeled passivity.

Each of these three philosophies has value for the overall treatment of anger. Certainly, many clients do "stuff" their anger in exactly the manner described by the ventilationists. These persons tend to turn their anger inward, suppressing it, converting it into physical symptoms, or even physically attacking themselves with their anger since they themselves are the only allowed target for their aggression. I will describe treatment for these individuals in Chapter 8. However, other clients do indeed work themselves into totally useless frenzies of rage because of irrational thoughts; they desperately need help learning how to reduce their exaggerated bouts of anger. Finally, a third group of individuals needs skills training to help them express their anger in a prosocial manner that increases the probability for a successful conflict outcome. Furthermore, many clients could benefit from all three of these approaches, since sometimes they inappropriately suppress their anger, at other times they explode unnecessarily, and, in addition, they simply do not possess the skills needed to effectively communicate their anger.

The three philosophies just described reflect the ambivalence of American society toward the expression of anger. Stearns (1994), in his book *American Cool,* notes that over the past 200 years Americans have gradually given themselves more permission to express their emotions in general but with the caveat that they should not lose control of those same feelings. In other words, it is good to state one's emotions at a moderate level but not too strongly. In addition, it is definitely not acceptable to lose control of emotions. Doing so reduces one's status from full adult to that of a child. Furthermore, I would add that expressing emotion for its own sake is suspect in American society. Being emotional simply to be emotional is considered a narcissistic indulgence. Rather, the emotion of anger is supposed to be functional, specifically to communicate to others that something is wrong. It is meant to lead to effective problem resolution, not simply to being ventilated for its own sake.

Certainly this movement in American society toward disallowing the excessive expression of anger has spread across many venues, most prominently in the home, where parents are admonished not to scream at their children and spouses not to verbally or physically aggress against each other. (The development of feminist theory with its accompanying challenge to traditional male privilege, including the use of anger and aggression to maintain power and control, has also contributed strongly to this aspect of anger management.) In the workplace, owners and supervisors can no longer simply yell at their employees without fear of negative repercussions. Most anger management programs reflect this general philosophy of allowing the expression of anger in moderation while discouraging excessive anger and acts of aggression.

Three *goals* for anger management emerge from the consideration of these philosophies and traditions: (1) to help clients prevent the development or expression of unnecessary anger; (2) to promote the moderate expression of anger while containing excessive ventilation of angry thoughts or aggressive behaviors; and (3) to help clients learn appropriate conflict resolution skills. The key words I use with my clients, then, are "prevention," "containment" (or "control"), and "resolution" (Potter-Efron, 2002).

I explain that the first goal for them (with the exception of those who excessively suppress their anger) is to become less angry. In particular, I want to help them become more effective at sorting through their "anger invitations," namely, all the things they could become angry about, so that they can quit wasting their time and causing damage to others by becoming unnecessarily angry about trivial or uncontrollable issues. The second goal, containment, applies to situations in which it is reasonable to become angry. The goal here is to learn how to express anger without losing control. Their task is to tell others about their anger without losing their cool. Finally, these individuals must learn how to use their anger for problem solving. That means learning conflict resolution skills such as compromise, negotiation, and fair fighting.

The anger management program I have developed is a multicomponent model. Since anger concerns are tremendously varied, ranging from "stuffing" one's anger to violent attacks, no single set of interventions will be universally effective. Rather, practitioners will fare best by using a broad range of interventions and selecting from them those that best match the needs, strengths, and abilities of each particular client. This model is applicable both for individual and group therapy, although a limit to flexibility is practical, especially when designing and implementing anger education groups. Nevertheless, therapists should be able to use a wide range of therapeutic models and skills so that they can approach each client with personally designed intervention strategies.

This chapter is organized into four main segments, each representing a major intervention focus: (1) behavioral change; (2) cognitive reformulations; (3) affective modulation; and (4) existential/spiritual growth (see Figure 3.1) (Potter-Efron, 2004). Naturally, these areas overlap in actual practice. For example, a client who learns at the behavioral level to take a time-out when aroused will almost certainly be simultaneously challenging old automatic thoughts while perhaps also attempting to relax. Still, one client will need a more behavioral emphasis while another would do better to focus on cognitive interventions, body awareness, or existential concerns. Although most clients will probably benefit from addressing all four of these intervention areas, many may only need help in one or two spheres.

Behavior Key word: *change*	**Cognition** Key word: *choice*
Affect Key word: *control*	**Existentialism/Spirituality** Key word: *meaning*

FIGURE 3.1. The Four Windows of Change

Change is the key word when client and counselor are focused upon behavioral interventions. The goal of behavioral interventions is to help clients alter their anger- and aggression-provoking, maintaining, and exacerbating actions, which may be either physical or verbal. Taking a time-out is an example of a behaviorally focused intervention.

Choice is the key word in the area of cognitive intervention. Here the goal is to help clients learn to recognize and alter specific thoughts and thinking patterns that provoke, maintain, and exacerbate their anger. Disputation techniques, in which clients identify certain "irrational" thoughts and replace them with more "rational" ones, exemplify the cognitive approach.

The key word in the third intervention area, affect modulation, is *control*. The goal in this sphere is to help clients learn how to modulate their emotions, in particular anger, so that they do not become physically and emotionally overstimulated and then lose control over their actions. Relaxation training is a typical example of affective intervention.

Finally, *meaning* is the key word in the existential/spiritual realm. The goal is to help clients discover the greater meaning of their anger or aggression in their lives so that they can replace negativity, cynicism, and despair with optimism and hope. Forgiveness training represents one area of existential/spiritual interventions.

These four intervention areas complement one another. For instance, the likelihood for effective behavioral change is certainly increased as a client makes new cognitive choices. However, such changes may only be possible when the client learns how to control his or her bodily anger reactions, thus involving the affective sphere. However, all of these skills may feel meaningless to the client, and therefore left undone, until that person gains a sense of hope for the future and lets go of paralyzing resentments. Still, it is important to be able to decide where to focus one's energies, especially when engaged in individualized anger management. The information presented in Table 3.1 is meant as a guideline to help the practitioner decide where to place emphasis.

TABLE 3.1. Choosing the Best Treatment Modality

Treatment Focus	Client Characteristics
Behavioral	Needs immediate skills training to lessen risk for anger outbursts or violence
	Needs quickly to change actions that provoke anger and/or the anger of others
	Has anger that comes in sudden bursts that are difficult to contain
	Possesses little ability to utilize abstractions, metaphors, or analogies
	Has developed habitual and ingrained patterns of aggressive behavior
Cognitive	Needs to change thinking patterns that exacerbate anger
	Can work on anger prevention as well as anger containment
	Can move from single cognitive explanations to a more general level of abstraction
	Needs help with specific cognitive distortions such as paranoid ideation or exaggeration
	Frequently takes excessively moral, righteous, or critical stands to defend beliefs
Affective	Needs to alter bodily stress reactions to contain strong fight-or-flight reactions
	Appears to be both angry and anxious
	Needs improved awareness of bodily anger symptoms and reactions
	Demonstrates the presence of a strong shame-rage reaction pattern
	Appears to have a powerful need for excitatory, stimulating activities, including becoming intensely angry
Existential/spiritual	Needs help understanding the greater meaning of anger in terms of frustration of life goals, needs, and yearnings
	Complains of bitterness, long-term irritability, and despair
	Could benefit from an emphasis on the resentment process and forgiving others
	Needs help forgiving himself or herself
	Complains of anger at God or the presence of anger that interferes with spiritual or religious connections

BEHAVIORAL APPROACH: INTRODUCING CLIENTS TO AN OBJECTIVE CHANGE FOCUS

The immediate goal when working at the behavioral level is actual behavioral change, as against a change of attitude, seeking information, or gaining insight. Of course, most motivated clients coming for anger management already have a goal: to quit getting angry. However, that goal is quite vague. Furthermore, just stopping getting mad is really only half a goal, since no preferred behaviors are proposed to replace those the clients want ended. For these reasons I normally try to help clients expand their goal statement in two ways. First, instead of just quitting getting angry I suggest the following quantitative goals that are all targeted upon the reduction of negative behaviors: (1) to become angry less often; (2) to stay angry for shorter periods of time; (3) to become less intensely angry; and (4) to do less damage when angry through aggressive behaviors and words (either to others or to oneself). Since these are quantitative goals it is necessary to discuss at least informally and sometimes to obtain objective information about the client's actual angry behavior.

The second part of goal setting involves what I call the *substitution principle,* defined as naming what kinds of behaviors could replace the client's old angry actions. Initially very few of my clients, especially the most angry ones, can describe these more positive behaviors, perhaps because their minds are so primed to notice and react to negative environmental stimuli. Many clients need help just to name such basic behaviors as speaking in a soft voice instead of yelling, giving praise to family members instead of criticizing, smiling instead of frowning, or working cooperatively with colleagues instead of walking away.

Some readers may be concerned about possible confusion here between anger and aggression, since anger per se is not a behavior but an emotion (although the distinction between affect and action has been breaking down in the light of brain research into the complex interrelationships between physical states, actions, and feelings [Damasio, 2003; LeDoux, 1996]). This distinction implies that anger itself cannot be an object of direct measurement, at least not without sophisticated apparatus that might measure blood pressure, voice quality, etc. Although I agree with this differentiation in principle, it is important to recognize that most clients who need anger management do not make fine distinctions between their angry feelings and their aggressive behaviors. Therefore, it seems reasonable to describe under the term "behavioral interventions" those approaches that ask clients to focus upon the active elements of their combined anger and aggression. The result is an immediate emphasis not upon the "why" of their anger but upon questions such as these:

- How do you become angry? What do you say and do?
- When and where do you become angry?
- With whom do you become angry?

Perhaps the single most important question from a behavioral perspective is "Exactly how do you become angry?" Most clients do so with a combination of anger-provoking thoughts and anger-increasing actions. One way to uncover both aspects of the anger process utilizes a variant of the Gestalt therapy awareness process (Polster and Polster, 1973). I present the model to clients as having six steps related to their anger:

1. Clients initially become aware of something that they could define as bothersome, for instance, a child noisily singing to herself in the other room. This is an "anger invitation" that could be accepted or discarded.
2. They focus upon that problem and decide how disturbing or threatening it is to them, frequently becoming physiologically agitated while concluding that they are being terribly harmed and therefore have the right to become very angry.
3. They then impulsively plan what to do next, usually deciding to demonstrate their anger visibly and strongly.
4. They carry out their plan by criticizing, shouting, punishing, hitting, etc., often harming others in the process.
5. They give themselves feedback that the damage they have just done is justifiable while ignoring feedback from others that might make them feel guilty or bad.
6. Finally, they either then suddenly cease being angry and walk away from the problem without attempting to fix things or they hang onto their anger in the form of an ever-building resentment.

This six-step process can be very useful since it gives clients opportunities to reflect upon the actual behaviors they display as part of the anger episode, the cognitive processes that exacerbate their anger proclivities, the physical aspects of becoming angry, and the cognitive and behavioral choices they make that cause trouble. Furthermore, clients can then see where they need to substitute new mental and physical behaviors for older ineffective ones. They could, for example, look for the good in others instead of the bad at step one, consciously choose to calm down at step two, plan ways to address the issue rather than simply ventilate their anger at step three, take a time out if necessary during step four, accept corrective feedback at step five, and learn either to make amends if necessary at step six or to let go of their wounds.

The material just described also helps chronically angry clients realize that they become angry and then act in highly predictable patterns. Most people do not become angry in new and creative ways every time they are upset. Instead, they tend repeatedly to think the same thoughts and take the same actions. Thus, angry behavior is habitual behavior. However, habitual behavior is highly resistant to change. Chronically angry clients must accept the reality that they will need thorough behavioral retraining if they want to diminish, much less extinguish, this habit. One implication of this situation is that old behavior must be minimized and not rewarded (by others or internally by the client) while new behavior must be strongly rewarded and encouraged whenever it occurs.

The following questions often help clients realize early in counseling that they can and must make a real commitment to change if they wish to lessen their anger problems. Each question or set of questions has a specific purpose that is described after the question.

1. "With regard to controlling your anger, what are you doing now that is not working?" "What will happen if you keep on doing what you are now doing?"

   These two questions help clients recognize that what they are doing is directly and primarily contributing to their anger problems, so they must change their actions if they want to improve their lives. At a motivational level these questions help move them away from blaming others and toward taking personal responsibility for their behavior.

2. "What behaviors could you change right now?"

   This question points clients toward immediate action. In my experience most angry clients are not very patient. They want immediate results and need quick rewards to stay motivated. Focusing angry clients on the possibility of immediately changing some very specific behavior will quickly demonstrate to them that they really can gain control over their anger and aggression.

3. "What specific behaviors are you willing to change? To stop? To start?"

   Here the emphasis changes from theory to practice. Hopefully, clients will not leave even their first session until they have made a clear and concrete commitment to altering one or two very specific anger-increasing behaviors. A good commitment will include their being able to state exactly what they will attempt to cease ("I won't demand that my stepkids say they love me when I put them to bed") and a positive substitute behavior ("Instead I will just tell them I love them and leave it at that").

4. "Will you commit to these changes regardless of what others do?"

   This question is especially valuable in couples therapy. Asking it helps avoid the bargaining trap in which both persons basically say they will curtail a particular behavior if and only if their partners curtail one of theirs. In effect, agreeing to this bargain then gives the power of maintaining the behavioral changes to one's partner. If either person fails to keep his or her promise then both can revert to anger-provoking actions. For that reason each partner should commit to changing his or her behavior regardless of the other's. Even in individual or group counseling the question is important because it tweaks out the client's hidden bargains ("Okay, I'll quit yelling but she better start treating me better or I'll go back to it").

5. "How will you and others be able to see that these changes are occurring?"

   Sometimes clients talk a lot about how they are changing their attitudes. That is certainly important and should not be discouraged; however, from a behavioral perspective attitude change is only important if it results in actual behavioral change. The question here is exactly what new actions and words will people hear and see displayed by the client instead of criticism, shouting, threatening, hitting, etc?

6. "If these changes work, what would come next?"

   This question sets the stage for further success but also lets clients know that behavioral change is a gradual process that usually occurs in steps. It is not enough just to alter one or two actions, nor can everything be altered at once. Rather, clients will be assisted to make a series of changes over time that eventually will help them lead lives free from excessive anger and aggression.

7. "What positive long-term results do you expect in your life because of these changes—for yourself? For others?"

   Here clients are encouraged to visualize the final result of their considerable effort. Again the goal is not simply to have a pleasant vision of a better life. Rather, each statement that clients make about a more positive future ("I see me and my husband back together; we're not arguing; we're holding hands and really happy to be with each other") needs to be translated into operational procedures ("So what do you need to start doing right now to help make that vision real?").

Selected Behavioral Interventions

I will briefly discuss several behaviorally focused interventions in this section. (Readers wanting more detailed exercises on many of these interventions are referred to my client workbook [Potter-Efron, 2001].)

Personal Commitment to Change

This simple intervention asks clients to make an immediate commitment to curtailing their angry behavior. In order to give this promise a positive focus, I ask clients to make this pledge:

> I, ____________________________, promise to stay calm for twenty-four hours, beginning at __________ a.m./p.m. on ____________________, __________.
>
> (day of week) (date)

This promise, which as you can see borrows from the Alcoholics Anonymous philosophy of living one day at a time, presents a workable goal for clients that goes beyond their agreeing only to "stuff" their anger for a while. It leads to discussion of how they can both stop angry and aggressive behaviors and how they can maintain a physiological state of calmness.

Time-Out

This is the single most important behavioral intervention clients can learn, especially if they have an active pattern of aggression. However, I emphasize that time-outs should not be overused. They represent a fallback position when clients realize that they are feeling overwhelmed by their anger and are about to lose control. They must take a time-out against saying or doing things that are hurtful to others and ultimately to themselves. Time-outs should not be used just because someone is feeling a little anxious or annoyed with another person. Even more critically, they should never be used as a way to escape talking about important concerns or to punish one's partner.

A good time-out has four components: recognize, retreat, relax, and return:

1. Clients must learn to *recognize* the signs that they are heading toward a blowout. Some of these signs are physiological, such as a quickening heart rate or a rising voice pitch. Others are actions such as making fists. Cognitive signs, for instance, thinking that someone is a jerk, also are critical to recognize, as are verbal cues such as when a client regularly says out loud "You have no right to tell me what to do" just before losing control.
2. Clients must *retreat,* meaning that once they realize they are close to losing control they must quickly leave the situation. It certainly helps if they can tell their partners something such as this: "I'm really starting to get angry. I better take a time-out. I'll be back in a while." It also helps when the partners of angry clients allow and encourage these time-outs rather than complaining about them or, far worse, trying to keep the person from leaving.

3. Clients must then go somewhere to *relax*. The critical task is for clients to do something while away that actually calms them down, perhaps taking a walk, reading a book, or having a cup of decaffeinated coffee, as opposed to walking away but continuing to stew over alleged insults and eventually returning just as angry as when they departed. Unfortunately, sometimes this step is difficult, as when a harassed mother of three wild children knows she needs to get away but has no one to take over watching the kids. Perhaps even then she can go to her room and close the door for a short time.
4. Clients must *return* so that they can more calmly address the concerns about which they became so angry. This last step cannot be skipped. Clients must realize that time-outs are designed to help them deal with reality, not to escape it.

Normally, this entire process will take from about fifteen minutes to several hours, although some clients may need longer in exceptional circumstances. Clients should be encouraged to return as soon as they reasonably can. They should, however, check in with themselves so that they do not return before they are ready and risk getting into another argument over the same issue.

Anger Logs

Quantitative data about the frequency of a client's angry behavior can be useful to gather for three reasons:

1. Collecting information early in treatment provides a numerical baseline. A client who gets angry three times a day the first week of treatment then reduces that number to once a day by the end of treatment has significantly improved. That changes counseling from an all-or-nothing proposition in which any incident of anger or aggression is perceived by client and counselor alike as a failure, to a more realistic framework in which the goal is to effectively reduce the number of episodes of anger to manageable proportions.
2. Gathering data is an active process that tends to motivate clients toward change. Several of my clients, for example, have re-

turned from a week's charting to tell me they were astonished at how often they became angry the first few days but that they have already dramatically reduced the number of episodes.

3. Collecting this information helps clients understand that anger usually occurs in discrete episodes and that the choices they make during those incidents are critical: whether to become angry, how to express their anger, etc. This recognition sets the stage for future cognitive interventions focusing on the concept of choice.

I ask clients to collect the following information about each anger episode:

1. date;
2. time;
3. a brief description of what happened;
4. what you felt;
5. what you thought;
6. what you said;
7. what you did; and
8. what were your choices?

Normally, I collect this information only one time, early in treatment. However, some anger management programs do collect this kind of data more regularly, especially residential or inpatient programs in which the client's behavior can be closely monitored.

Praise

Although many behavioral interventions targeting the reduction of negative behavior are most useful early in treatment, those that target the development of positive actions begin to dominate later in the process. One example is helping clients learn to substitute giving praise instead of criticism. This is not easy for most clients because they have become habituated to looking for the bad rather than the good in others. They need both to retrain themselves to notice the good and then to comment on it out loud. To help them with these first tasks I provide a list of things they can praise (Potter-Efron, 2002):

Accomplishment ("Good job.")
Effort ("Good try.")
Thinking ("You figured it out.")
Appearance ("Nice smile.")
Creativity ("That's interesting.")
Morals/values ("Thanks for being honest.")
Concern for others ("You're so generous.")
Common sense ("You're very practical.")
Taste ("You have great taste.")

Note that clients should be instructed to follow the parenthetical statements noted previously with specific information (for instance, "You did a good job changing that tire, Pat") rather than being left in a generalized form. In addition, angry clients are very likely to follow praise with criticism ("You did a good job changing the tire, Pat, *but* you put the hubcap on at the wrong angle"). They should be told not to do that since criticism that follows praise essentially negates the praise.

Fair Fighting

As mentioned previously one goal of anger management is to help clients improve their problem resolution skills. In general, angry clients are often poor at problem resolution at least partly because they simply do not possess effective communication skills. Furthermore, chronically angry individuals become more concrete and rigid in their thinking and inflexible in their words and actions when they feel stressed. Just watching people repeat themselves, saying exactly the same thing again and again during an argument, is convincing evidence for the disruptive effects of anger upon communication.

Simple and specific do and don't lists can be helpful in these circumstances. I've compiled one such list to help angry clients argue better. The "don't" list includes avoiding hitting, pushing, shoving, holding, and threatening others; interrupting; name calling; saying "always" and "never"; making faces; standing up; yelling, etc. The "do" list advises clients to stick to one issue at a time, breathe calmly, listen, be clear and specific, be willing to compromise, etc. I then ask clients to extract a smaller list of two or three main ideas from the larger group that would be most helpful for them. The idea is for them to write these ideas down and carry them in their wallets or purses at all times, consulting their personalized short list before or even during conflicts.

COGNITIVE ASPECTS OF ANGER MANAGEMENT

The majority of anger management programs that I have encountered are primarily or at least significantly cognitively oriented in that they focus upon helping clients learn to recognize and alter specific thoughts and thinking patterns that provoke, maintain, and exacerbate their anger. Kassinove and Tafrate (2002) note that here are two somewhat distinct cognitively oriented approaches. The first, developed by Aaron Beck (1976, 1999), places its emphasis upon helping clients assess their automatic thought patterns in order for them to perceive and respond to situations more accurately and realistically. The second, developed by Albert Ellis (1962; Ellis and Tafrate, 1997) and labeled rational-emotive behavior therapy, places more emphasis on helping clients develop a more flexible approach in response to daily problems.

Some key principles of cognitive therapy as related to anger include:

1. Anger will be increased or decreased by how people interpret their current situation. A person's appraisal of a situation will activate or deactivate anger.
2. Many situations can be seen as "invitations" to anger. People always have a choice to accept or decline these invitations.
3. However, angry individuals have developed "automatic" (habitual, inflexible, fleeting, and only partly conscious) patterns of thinking that lead them to accept more anger invitations than others, usually without realizing that they have options.
4. Certain beliefs consistently increase a person's anger. These include the following:
   - Beliefs that justify one's angry and aggressive thoughts and actions ("I had a right to get angry after what he said to me.")
   - Beliefs about one's personality ("I'm just an angry person and I always will be.")

- Beliefs about being helpless ("My anger takes over. I can't do a thing to stop it.")
- Beliefs that give responsibility away ("It's her fault. She deserves my anger.")
- Beliefs about the world that support getting angry ("The world's a bad place. You can't trust anybody.")
- Beliefs that anger/aggression are good solutions ("Getting mad makes you feel good.")

5. Anger-producing thoughts can be replaced by anger-reducing thoughts. Negative thinking patterns can be altered with practice.

The appraisal process, the first item in the previous list, is a central concern in cognitive therapy with angry individuals. Lazarus (1991) discovered that people increase their anger when they conclude that another's actions not only hurt them but also were unjust, preventable, intentional, and/or blameworthy. An example would be a man whose best friend "steals" his girlfriend. That man might argue that his friend's behavior was unjust because it violated the principle of loyalty to friends, that his friend could have prevented this from happening by just staying away, that his friend planned to take his girlfriend away from him, and that the offense is so heinous that his friend deserves punishment.

With regard to the third point in the previous list, Hauck (1974) describes a six-step process of becoming angry that takes place mostly at an automatic, half-conscious level:

1. I want something.
2. I didn't get it so now I'm frustrated.
3. That's awful and terrible.
4. I can't stand it. I must have my way.
5. You're bad for frustrating me.
6. Bad people ought to be punished.

Notice the leap from the fourth to the fifth stage here in which the angry person makes a moral judgment against the other. This tendency to turn the opponent into a symbol of evil increases both the angry person's total anger and the desire to attack and destroy the adversary.

The point made earlier, that clients can indeed change their thought patterns to replace anger-provoking and anger-increasing thoughts with anger-declining and anger-decreasing thoughts, represents the primary rationale for cognitive therapy. That is why "choice" is the main word I emphasize during anger management counseling. Many clients simply do not realize that they possess far more freedom to choose their pathways in life than they have thought. Once they understand their choices they often feel empowered, because now their previously automatic angry reactions can no longer dictate their lives.

Selected Cognitive Interventions

Initial Questions Designed to Increase Cognitive Awareness

The following questions help clients become more aware of the part that cognition plays in anger:

1. What thoughts do you have that seem to make you mad or add to your anger?
2. What happens to you when you think these thoughts?
3. Do you have any anger increasing thoughts you just can't get out of your mind?
4. How accurate/realistic/true do you think those thoughts are that get you angry?
5. Do you ever try changing or challenging these thoughts?
6. Would you like to start changing some of these thoughts?
7. What other thoughts could/do you think?
8. How would you be different if you really could think these new thoughts regularly instead of the old ones?
9. Are you ready to start practicing these new thoughts?

These questions do not need to be asked in strict sequence or all at once. Rather, they can be intermingled with other materials at any time during intake or counseling. Note that the third question probes for a client's obsessive thoughts, such as "That's so unfair what she said to me." These thoughts are particularly tenacious and difficult to counter. Also, they seem so obvious to clients that they may not even mention them unless asked. Nor do clients question the validity of these obsessive cognitions. The eighth question represents a bridge between strictly cognitive considerations and the more broad existential aspects of anger (discussed later in this chapter). The ninth question lets clients know that altering their thought patterns takes time, energy, and effort.

Confronting Denial

Many clients deny or minimize the extent of their anger problems. Some do so by refusing to admit that they frequently feel exceptionally angry. Others admit their anger but blame everyone else for it. The effect of challenging such denial head-on by demanding clients accept their anger problems is often disastrous. All it does is trigger oppositionality. Fortunately, many clients can be helped to accept their anger and aggression problems by getting them to list and describe the consequences of their anger and aggression. I sometimes utilize a pie chart (Potter-Efron, 1994) listing the major spheres of life most frequently affected by a client's anger and aggression. These are health, family, work, school, finances, friendships, the law, values, mood, and spirit. Clients then fill in the empty spaces in each area of the chart, either individually or as a group, writing in only their own actual negative consequences of previous anger and aggression episodes.

Notice that getting clients focused on this material creates a bridge between their behavior and their cognitions. This is especially true for clients whose behavior has damaged them in several areas of life. For instance, a single client might easily report needing stitches after smashing his fist through a window, a divorce largely attributable to his anger, doing jail time for fighting, money problems related to having to replace broken objects, etc. Also, since this material is entirely self-centered, clients do not need to be empathic (many angry persons have little empathy for others). All that matters is that their anger is ruining their lives.

Also, notice the parallel here with traditional addiction counseling, another area in which denial is strong. The first step of the AA program is "We admitted we were powerless and our lives had become unmanageable" (Alcoholics Anonymous, 1976). I tell clients that admitting the full effects of their anger is the equivalent of the "unmanageability" section of the first step. I do not ask clients to accept being powerless over their anger, however, although some clients certainly feel that way. The point is that it is difficult to maintain denial when facing reality.

Challenging a Single Anger-Provoking "Hot Thought"

Many angry individuals possess poor abstraction abilities. Therefore they will need help challenging their anger-provoking cognitions one thought at a time. The goal is to help them come up with one "cool" thought that can replace the "hot" thought. I explain to clients that hot thoughts are the ideas they think to themselves that instantly make them angry. These thoughts are usually short, vague, and over-generalized, such as "Nobody tells me what to do," "I can't take it anymore," and "How dare you say that to me." I also mention that hot thoughts have two other names. Sometimes they are called "trigger thoughts" because these thoughts act like the triggers of a gun. Another name is "automatic thoughts" because they occur so quickly in the client's mind. The goal is to help clients identify their hot thoughts. That can usually be accomplished best by helping them reconstruct their most recent angry and aggressive incidents.

The next step is helping clients develop their cool thoughts. Examples help, such as changing "Nobody can tell me what to do" to "It's okay. I'll decide what I want to do after I hear what they say." Remember that each person has his or her own unique cool thoughts. What works for one person may not work for another so each hot thought/cool thought must be individually hand crafted. The test of a cool thought is simple, though. It should help the client feel calm. If "It's okay. I'll decide what I want to do after I hear what they say" does not calm the client down, then ask what thought would.

The Disputation Process

Some clients can learn a more abstract approach to cognitive change so that they can more generally challenge their anger-provoking thought patterns. The model I utilize is my own version of materials developed by Albert Ellis (Ellis and Harper, 1975). The goal is to help clients learn the process with which they can substitute positive, non–anger-provoking thoughts for negative, "irrational" thoughts. The five aspects of this process, as I present them to clients, are:

A. The Antecedent is an anger invitation, something you might get angry about.
B. The anger-provoking Belief(s) that convince you that you have a right to be angry.
C. The Consequences of your beliefs: anger, hostility, aggression.
D. Your Disputation—A thought that substitutes for "B" and is far less anger provoking.
E. Effects (positive). Your new, less angry or aggressive behavior.

Here is an example:

A. Your boyfriend calls to tell you he has to cancel his date with you tonight.
B. You think: "That's awful! What a betrayal! How dare he do that to me."
C. You start yelling at him, accusing him of betraying you.
D. New thought: "Wait a minute. He's a good guy. This is a disappointment, not a disaster. I can handle it okay."
E. You calm down quickly, quit yelling, accept his apology, and make plans for another date.

Clients need to use this technique one negative thought at a time. However, once they realize that there is a consistent way they can work to change negative thoughts into more positive ones they become more adept at doing so on their own, without needing the immediate help of a counselor.

AFFECTIVE ANGER MANAGEMENT APPROACHES

Anger and aggression are usually full brain and body reactions to a threatening event (Niehoff, 1998), although the threat can be immediate or potential, real or imagined, weak or strong. As such, anger and fear responses are frequently intertwined so that any threatening situation may trigger fight, flight, or freeze reactions and sometimes the same trigger will produce different reactions at different times. However, chronically angry clients react far more often with anger and aggression to potentially threatening cues than others. In effect anger has become their habituated response. It is as if their brains were computers that had "anger" set as their default option; their initial reaction to potentially emotional events is always to become angry as opposed to feeling any other emotion.

Furthermore, chronically angry individuals tend to develop hair-trigger reaction mechanisms so that they become instantly angry, even enraged, in the face of stimuli that would not set off another person's anger response. This is particularly true for persons whose emotional reaction system has been damaged by exposure to trauma, especially in childhood. The resultant brain damage to their amygdala and hippocampus (LeDoux, 1996; Teicher, 2002; Niehoff, 1998), makes these individuals likely to react in terror or rage to what others would consider only mildly threatening situations. In essence the brains of some people have been configured for survival in a dangerous world in which they must constantly guard against imminent threat. Imagine, for instance that the anger-dominant individual is giving a talk when someone knocks on the door. Whereas most people would have either no emotional response to this event at all or perhaps feel mildly annoyed or anxious, the chronically angry person might react with fury: "I hate interruptions! Make them stop! Why are they doing that to me?" The result of this survival reaction, unfortunately, may be that this person loses credibility and is labeled a hopelessly hostile individual.

Two goals emerge from the previous considerations: (1) to help chronically angry clients gain better control over their angry and fearful reactions to threat; and (2) to help these persons develop a more flexible and versatile emotional response system. These two goals are discussed separately next.

Gaining Control

Perhaps the best place to begin is to confront the still popular myth of ventilation. This myth states that the best way to handle one's anger is to scream, yell, pound fists, throw things, etc. People are supposed to feel better after these experiences. Furthermore, their anger should be drained from their bodies so that they become considerably less angry for a long time. Unfortunately, research has not supported this theory; instead, as Tavris (1989) writes, ventilation of anger usually increases the person's anger rather than decreases it. The effect of ventilation, in most cases, is to train people to become angrier over time. Although ventilation techniques may still have value for some clients, in particular those who turn most of their anger inward, they are definitely not recommended for the aggressively angry persons who attend most anger management programs.

I do want to comment on a second myth that I have frequently encountered among both clients and counselors in this field. Believers in this myth claim that anger is not a real emotion, or that one can always discover a deeper emotion underneath any anger display. Sometimes the allegedly "real" emotion is fear, sometimes hurt. Whatever other emotion is named, the therapeutic goal becomes getting under the anger to this underlying feeling. The phrase often used with this approach is that anger is just a "cover emotion." Certainly, though, no physiological evidence supports that anger is not a real emotion or only a cover emotion. Rather, anger is a core emotion deeply rooted in the survival centers of our brains. I believe that a grain of truth lies in this assertion though, namely that the anger of very upset individuals certainly can obscure other less visible emotions. However, that is true for any strong emotion. Intense fear, for example, can temporarily prevent observers from noticing that the presenter of that fear is also ashamed or angry. Perhaps a more fitting statement would be that "anger seldom rides alone," implying that it is usually valuable to probe for the appearance of other emotions that may be somewhat hidden, especially when a client's anger display is particularly powerful. I will mention ways to help clients access these other emotions in the next section of this chapter.

Seven questions help clients challenge the myth of ventilation while directing them toward gaining better control over their anger:

1. What happens to your body when you become really angry?
2. What happens to your mind when your body feels like that?
3. What are the costs to you for losing control of your anger?
4. How important is it to you to stay in control of your anger?
5. What do you do to stay in control?

6. Have you ever tried relaxation, meditation, or any other similar ways to stay calm? If so, what happened?
7. Would you be interested in learning some new way to relax or other ways to stay in control?

One way to help clients learn to contain their emotions is to teach exposure techniques. Kassinove and Tafrate (2002) correctly note that few anger management programs utilize systematic exposure techniques, probably because these demand somewhat advanced psychological training to be effective. These authors describe their exposure methods, which include trigger review, verbal exposure, combining imaginal exposure with other interventions, and in vivo exposure. Their goal is to teach clients to stay calm in the face of aversive stimuli, such as someone saying something critical about them, that would normally and automatically trigger a strong angry reaction.

Relaxation training is another good way to help clients learn how to contain their physical reactions to anger cues. I find relaxation particularly valuable for clients who are recognizably both angry and anxious, a combination of emotions that often leads to a rage response. Smith (1999) describes six different approaches to relaxation training, a useful reminder that it is best to fine tune each person's relaxation program to meet his or her own particular needs. I personally make relaxation tapes individually for my anger clients only after getting to know them well enough to be able to utilize statements, metaphors, and descriptions of the relaxed state that match their individual vocabularies. I also emphasize that relaxation is particularly useful as a preventative tactic. Although relaxation may help people become less angry after they get upset about something, it works better in my experience when clients practice relaxation enough so that they become less likely to get angry in the first place. Learning to relax as a lifestyle works best.

The intensity of the anger experience must be contained if clients expect to gain control over their anger. One way to help clients deal with the intensity issue is to provide them with ways to gauge the importance of a situation (its threat level). The classic question, "On a scale of one to ten, with ten being the highest, how serious is this event that is bothering you?" relates to the first approach. Another approach is to provide a range of words that describe various levels of anger. The use of an "anger thermometer" (Potter-Efron, 1994; Kassinove and Tafrate, 2002) in which various levels of anger are assigned specific words ("annoyed," "mad," "furious") is effective for this purpose.

Helping Clients Develop a More Flexible and Versatile Emotional Response System

The second major goal in the area of affective interventions is to help clients whose primary emotional reaction to any stimulus is to become angry to develop a more flexible and versatile emotional response system. Clients must realize that they have become trapped in their anger, unable to respond with any other single emotion or with a combination of emotions to life's diverse events. The general questions I ask that help them recognize this reality are these:

1. How has anger taken over your emotional life?
2. Do you ever have feelings other than anger? Which?
3. Was there a time in the past when you felt less anger? Was there a time in the past when you felt more of any other feelings?
4. What other emotions might you have if you weren't angry?
5. What feelings do you avoid with your anger?
6. How important to you is it to get back into contact with those other emotions?
7. What would it take for you to let yourself begin having those other feelings again?

A more specific question regarding a particular event is simply this: "What other feelings in addition to your anger do you have about this situation?"

The purpose of these questions is to help clients realize how much their anger has taken over their emotional life. An analogy I use (Potter-Efron, 2002) is to ask them to imagine their life as a bus in which normally they would be the driver and all their emotions would be passengers on that vehicle. What happens, though, when anger hijacks the bus? First, it throws the client out of the driver's seat. Next, anger kicks all the other emotions off the bus. Anger takes the person for a wild and bumpy ride. The goals, then, become getting the client back into the driver's seat of his or her life's bus and inviting that person's other emotions back onto the bus.

One adolescent I worked with, for example, agreed to see me only if I did not try to make her quit hating her father, a man whose affair led to the breakup of her family. She certainly had reasons to be angry and even hateful. However, after a couple of sessions she allowed me to guide her into a discussion of her other emotions as well. Soon she was admitting to loneliness ("Sometimes I miss my dad"), fear ("I'm afraid they'll never get back together"), sadness ("I cry when I'm all by myself"), and even relief ("They fought all the time; at least I don't have to listen to that anymore").

The third question listed previously, "Was there a time in the past when you felt less anger?" helps clients who have gradually become angrier over time to remember their more emotionally fluid past. These clients will have less trouble broadening their emotional responsiveness than clients who recall themselves as always angry, since they have a mental model already in place of themselves feeling other emotions. The fifth question, "What feelings do you avoid with your anger?" often helps clients who avoid "soft" emotions such as sadness and love realize what they are doing. Finally, the last two questions, "How important to you is it to get back into contact with those other emotions?" and "What would it take for you to let yourself begin having those other feelings again?" return the initiative to the clients. The therapist's offer is to help clients retrieve or develop their other emotions. The clients then decide whether to accept that invitation.

EXISTENTIAL/SPIRITUAL ANGER MANAGEMENT APPROACHES

The existential realm has been relatively neglected in anger management. By that I mean little direct attention has been given, both in the academic literature and in my observations of anger management programs, to such concerns as the greater meaning of their anger in people's lives, the anxiety that attends choosing to give up the safety of an angry life for an uncertain future, the sense of isolation that often accompanies an angry lifestyle, and, most important, the general misery of being chronically angry. One existential/spiritual area that has been increasingly discussed, however, is forgiveness. The material in that sphere is so rich and varied that I have written a separate chapter on that topic (see Chapter 6).

Existential concerns are most critical for clients who have developed an angry lifestyle that centers on a hostile attitude toward the world. I believe the central components of attitude are

1. the belief that most people are bad;
2. the concurrent conviction that most people are also untrustworthy;
3. the sense that nothing good happens in life or, if it does, that good will soon be overwhelmed and replaced by the bad;
4. consequently, the conclusion that it is useless and too painful to hope for a good life;
5. anger, especially in the forms of cynicism, sarcasm, criticism, and cutting humor is then used to push people away; and
6. clients can then guard against developing what they perceive would be false hope, vulnerability to promises that will inevitably be broken, and despair.

The result is that people become mean-spirited in their attitude and actions, developing an overall hostile worldview. The effect of this worldview is to negatively filter everything that happens so that the client's depressive opinions about the world are continually reinforced.

Meanness of spirit develops slowly. Clients with this condition can usually enumerate a great number of abandonments, betrayals, deceits, injustices, and undeserved wounds they have endured. Each injury warps their personality a little bit more until they become bitter in their estrangement from the world. They often describe a feeling of *impotent rage,* an utter inability to change the things that most matter to them. A parent's death, a painful divorce, being laid off from a cherished job—these losses must be protested even though the protests are useless. The result is that these persons seem to be constantly shaking their fists at an uncaring universe. Some literally become angry at God, as I will describe in the next case study.

The questions described here help clients address the existential meaning of their anger:

1. Was there ever a time in your life when you weren't so angry?
2. What were you like then?
3. What were your goals and values?
4. How has your anger affected your spirit?
5. How has your anger changed you as a person?
6. Whom have you blamed (held responsible) for your anger? How has that affected you?
7. Who would you be if you weren't so angry?
8. What would you do with your life if you weren't so angry?
9. How would letting go of your anger affect your being?
10. How would letting go of your anger affect your connection with others?
11. How would letting go of your anger affect your work?
12. How would letting go of your anger affect your spiritual self?
13. How much do you yearn for a life free from bitterness, anger, and hate?
14. What can you do to start moving in that direction?

The first three questions in this set refer to a past that might have been much different than the present, perhaps a past filled with joy and hope. In my experience many of my most seethingly bitter clients are "wounded idealists" who once believed strongly that the universe was good. Then one or more disasters struck, or perhaps just a long series of disappointments, and these persons gradually evolved a far more negative and hostile persona. These individuals simply cannot accept the limited reality of their current lives. They may benefit from interventions or exercises (Potter-Efron, 2001) that invite them to give up their unrealistic expectations of others, themselves, the universe, or God. On the other hand they also benefit by being encouraged to reclaim some of their discarded ideals. Perhaps, for example, a client who once was generous to others could become so again even though several individuals did take advantage of his or her altruism. However, this time the client must do so knowing well that no guarantees against getting ripped off again exist. Even so, practicing generosity again may help that person reestablish a sense of belonging with others.

Questions four through thirteen help clients assess the damage they are doing to themselves by continuing to be bitterly angry. Existential anger affects every aspect of a human being: their relationships, spirit, being, character, and personality. However, these questions should be asked in a positive manner to these critically negative individuals. The "how would letting go of your anger affect your . . ." points them toward a more positive future that lies within their grasp if they care to reach for it. Question thirteen ("How much do you yearn for a life free from bitterness, anger, and hate?") is particularly potent in helping clients find within themselves a true desire to shed their chronic hostility. Finally, question fourteen ("What can you do to start moving in that direction?") reminds clients that they must take the initiative to change.

Existentially angry persons often must work hard to lessen their pattern of habitual criticism. I frequently ask these clients to look at what motivates them to be so critical. Some answers include that criticism validates their negative view of life by invalidating the more positive beliefs of others; it helps keep them in a safe position of superiority and dominance; criticism helps them avoid noticing or dealing with their own imperfections; it keeps them in control by making others feel weak, dumb, or bad; criticism simply feels good to them; it is a way to hurt and punish others; and, perhaps most telling, criticism keeps others from getting too close to them so they will not feel so vulnerable. Some clients are willing after a discussion such as this to make a commitment to abstain from being critical of others in any way for a twenty-four-hour period. This experiment, if reasonably successful, can then lead toward helping the client make related efforts to look for the good in others, look for the spirituality of others, and to substitute praise for criticism.

CASE STUDY: A WOMAN WHO IS ANGRY AT THE UNIVERSE

Helena, twenty-eight, describes herself as once having been a perky, naively optimistic, playful woman despite the early death of her mother when she was only sixteen years old. By then, though, Helena's parents had instilled in her a deep religious conviction. "God gives people only as much pain as they can handle" was part of her faith. Besides, her mother had died slowly from cancer, giving Helena plenty of time to accept that reality.

Helena married when she was twenty-one to a hardworking and equally devout man. They had their first child two years later, a girl they named Bailey. All went well until one day Helena awoke with a sense of foreboding, realizing that she could hear no sounds coming from Bailey's room. She ran there only to discover that her beautiful daughter had died in the night. The doctors pronounced that Bailey's death was due to sudden infant death syndrome and told Helena not to feel guilty. It was no one's fault, they said. Her husband and relatives all gathered around to support her. So did her minister, who tried to comfort Helena by telling her that Bailey's death was God's will.

Helena could not be consoled, though. Instead, she began feeling a desperate rage growing within. *"God's will!"* she thought. *"God's will!"* This woman, who had prayed every day, gone to church at least twice a week, and devoutly believed in God's kindness and generosity, could no longer tolerate the thought of God. "God has betrayed me," she concluded. Within two years she had divorced her husband and began drinking regularly. She was prescribed antidepressant medications but they failed to alter her increasingly angry, hostile, and bitter mood. She saw two therapists as well, one faith-based and one secular, but quickly dismissed both for being "do-gooders mouthing platitudes." Helena also developed a sharp tongue, alienating people intentionally with mean words. Five years after her daughter's death Helena had yet to return to church. "Why should I?" she argued. "I prayed my heart out and look what it got me. Nothing but heartache."

Helena was angry not just with God, though. She was angry at the entire universe and especially the people in it. She withdrew from her family and friends, calling them all "hypocrites" for failing to offer her anything more than sympathy when her daughter died. She wanted them to share her outrage, not provide sympathy. She did keep her job as an office manager, making life miserable for the five secretaries who worked under her supervision through a steady stream of sarcastic and critical remarks. Nobody liked Helena anymore but that was fine with her. She chose solitude, even giving away her pet dog Sammy because he was too much trouble to take care of. Her solitude, however, was not healing.

Then something happened that made Helena reassess her situation. A man named Norman from another department met her at a work function and, not knowing much about Helena, asked her out. Within two weeks Norman told Helena that he wanted to get serious "but why do you act so mean to everybody?" Helena heard his question and started to tell him why with all her usual bitterness, but then she stopped. She suddenly realized that she had been ruining her own life with her chronic anger. She also recognized that she and Norman would not stand a chance for a decent relationship until she did something about her rage.

Helena decided to give counseling one more try. The first reason, she explained, was that she wanted to give her new relationship a chance. The second reason was that Helena figured she might eventually kill herself if she could not feel better, either actively with medicines or passively through drinking herself to death.

As with most clients, Helena came to counseling with only one goal, namely to eliminate her "mean" behavior. Translated into behavioral terminology, that goal was listed in the treatment plan as "fewer incidents of criticism, sarcastic remarks, etc., both at work and with Norman." The positive goal that she admitted would be difficult to achieve was described as "increased incidents of praise, encouragement, etc., both at work and with Norman." As for her relationship with God, she allowed for consideration of that issue to be placed in the treatment plan but only with the clear understanding that she was under no obligation to restore or alter it.

Helena's work began at the behavioral level. She made a determined effort to reduce the number of negative remarks and to substitute praise for criticism. The place she could best practice these new behaviors was at work because her job as a supervisor gave her numerous opportunities for either praise or criticism. What amazed Helena was how firmly the habit of negativity had solidified within her. "I find myself saying something sarcastic before I even think about it. I don't like being that way." Within a few weeks Helena had altered her words to the point where the secretaries that she supervised began smiling instead of looking down when she entered their room. Norman, too, noticed and appreciated her new behavior.

The next challenge was more cognitive in nature. Helena needed to confront her belief that her family and friends were hypocrites because they refused to treat Bailey's death as an outrage. Fortunately, Helena was able to understand and utilize disputation to challenge that belief. After consultation she substituted the idea that: "They offered comfort the best they could when Bailey died. I just couldn't take it in." Helena recognized with this disputation both that these people really did care and that ultimately she was responsible for her own estrangement from them. True, they had offered Helena a gift she did not want at that time, namely, comfort, instead of joining her in her futile outrage, but now she could finally see the value in that gift.

Helena had issues that called for affective intervention as well. Most important, over the five years of her unresolved grief she had lost track of her positive emotions. Now she could finally retrieve them. To facilitate this process we did a visualization in which Helena found herself walking down a street that had a "used furniture" store on it. Entering the store, she made her way to a chest of drawers that was oddly familiar. As Helena opened each drawer she discovered a lost emotion: sadness, joy, fear, shame, etc. The last drawer she opened was labeled "love." Each emotion was there for her to retrieve if she chose. All she had to do was take them from the drawers, and that is exactly what she did during an emotionally intense session. Helena used that experience to allow these emotions to reenter her life. She kept her anger as well, resisting her initial temptation to dump that emotion into the chest. Helena knew that she still needed her anger to keep her safe, especially as she dealt with her grief. That anger acted as a refuge, a place where she could retreat when the pain of her loss felt virtually unendurable.

Finally, after three months of weekly therapy sessions, it was time to address Helena's anger at God. We could have developed this theme along the lines of forgiveness. However, by now Helena had made many changes. She found herself returning to her "premorbid" state of optimism and joy, albeit without the naive "If I pray to God twice a day nothing bad will ever happen to me" quality of the past. Indeed, the key existential change Helena made was to realize that she had to renounce her formulaic belief system that revolved around the concept that God owed her a pain-free life in exchange for her loyalty. This change in her worldview allowed her to develop a renewed sense of faith that did not depend upon her understanding God's plan (Flanigan, 1992). She decided, however, not to return to her old church, a church that she believed encouraged her old beliefs, but instead found one whose minister was less formulaic. She actually found her first Sunday in church somewhat anticlimatic: "It seemed so easy, like I'd never left." God and the church were back in her life where, from her new perspective, they always belonged.

Helena's therapy entailed change in all four major therapeutic sectors: behavior, cognition, affect, and existential meaning/spirituality. Fortunately, because she had a model of herself from earlier days as a less angry and bitter human being, her changes could take place fairly rapidly. Essentially she reconnected with her past personality. Nevertheless, her path was not an easy one. Helena frequently regressed to her hostile state. However, she gradually broke her habit of anger, hostility, and bitterness.

SUMMARY

Anger problems have been addressed with various philosophies including ventilation, reduction, and management. The goals these philosophies suggest include helping clients prevent the development or expression of unnecessary anger, assisting them to promote the moderate expression of anger while containing excessive ventilation of angry thoughts or aggressive behaviors, and helping them learn appropriate conflict resolution skills.

Anger management counselors can pursue their task through four orientations. First, they can address the need for behavioral change, helping clients both reduce negative behavior while increasing positive actions. Second, counselors can utilize cognitive therapy techniques designed to help clients choose less anger-provoking ways to think about situations. Next are efforts to help clients contain their emotional intensity while shifting attention to other emotions. Finally, the very meaning of a client's anger may be considered at the existential/spiritual level.

The next chapter describes two main approaches to anger management training. Group education and therapy formats are initially considered, given the current dominance of these approaches. An individualized approach to anger management is also detailed.

Chapter 4

Group and Individual Approaches to Anger and Aggression Management

INTRODUCTION

Anger management has become largely group focused. This is particularly true in the area of domestic abuse, in which educational groups dominate the treatment area. I will describe in this chapter a group educational and counseling approach and then present three group formats, one each for individuals who are severely and generally physically aggressive, a second for persons who are less physically aggressive but still quite angry and verbally aggressive, and a third specifically targeted for men who commit repeated acts of domestic abuse.

Anger management, however, can also be approached from an individual therapeutic perspective. A rationale for individual treatment is provided as well as ideas for implementing such an approach.

THE GENERAL VALUE OF THERAPEUTIC GROUP WORK

Before discussing anger management groups in particular, it is useful to review the concept of group work in general. The kind of groups discussed here are small (ten or fewer members if possible) and both educational and therapeutic in intent. They have professional leaders whose jobs are both to provide specific skills training for participants and to encourage group discussion, cohesion, and mutual concern.

Group work is goal-directed activity, normally with small treatment and task groups. The general goal is to meet specific identified needs of group members. This activity is directed to individual members of a group and to the group as a whole within a system of service delivery (Toseland and Rivas, 2001). The primary purposes of groups vary but usually include giving clients mutual support, providing education, allowing opportunity for personal growth, providing therapy directed at behavior change, and offering a place for socialization skill development (Toseland and Rivas, 2001). More specifically, Anderson (1997) suggests that participants can gain the following "therapeutic factors" from participating in groups:

1. Instillation of hope
2. Universality (a sense that they are not the only ones with their problems)
3. Imparting of information
4. Imitative behavior (learning through observing others modeling desired behavior)
5. Interpersonal learning
6. Altruism (mutual cooperative aid)
7. Family recapitulation (relation of unfinished family business to how members function in group)
8. Catharsis/corrective emotional experience
9. Cohesiveness (greater caring and bonding with others)
10. Socializing techniques (improved social skills)
11. Existential factors (more choices about how to love authentically)

Wickham (2003) adds three more goals: (1) the development of improved reality testing; (2) improved problem-solving skills that enable participants to take control of their lives; and (3) improved self-concept.

Not all clients belong in therapy groups. Individuals should be screened for interest and readiness to participate, their ability to function and handle group pressures, and for the likelihood that their experience will benefit them (Wickham, 2003). Clients who would normally be excluded from group participation would usually (but not without careful consideration) include those who are extremely defiant and disruptive; individuals whose social skills are so deficient as to disable group cohesion and functioning; people whose limited intelligence or learning deficits preclude them from gaining new skills in a group format; and clients whose specific needs do not match the goals that are set for the group. A client's preference for individual counseling or, for that matter, for no counseling at all, is not per se a reason to exclude that individual from a group if in the clinical judgment of the therapist that person could indeed gain from group participation.

Groups may be continually open to new members or closed to the original participants. They may be time limited or open ended. Those that are closed tend to progress through stages such as pre-affiliation, power and control, intimacy, differentiation, and separation (Wickham, 2003; Anderson, 1997). These stages allow members to create and alter a miniature social system in which they can experiment with new communication patterns, roles, emotional connections, and attachment styles. Hopefully they will then take both the new skills they have learned and an increased belief in their ability to be effective and influential into the broader world outside the group. If not, the therapy group experience will be essentially wasted in the creation of a sanctuary from the world as opposed to the creation of a bridge into it.

EDUCATIONAL/THERAPEUTIC GROUP WORK WITH ANGRY AND AGGRESSIVE CLIENTS

Anger management groups meet several needs.

1. They are cost-effective, providing client services with relatively low fees. Since many clients who need anger management services have little money, group programs provide help to individuals who otherwise would get nothing.
2. Groups may help participants gain understanding and empathy not only for the victims of their anger and aggression but more generally for all human beings. Given that angry people generally tend to be self-focused and minimally sensitive to the needs of others, any approach that increases empathy is welcome.
3. Well-operating groups help participants break through their tendencies to deny and minimize their problems. The effect of a coparticipant saying "Yeah, I used to say that same thing but it's just BS" can be very powerful, as anyone who has ever attended an Alcoholics Anonymous meeting can attest.

4. Shame issues, which add to a client's tendency to hide the truth from themselves as well as others, may be lessened when group members realize that "we are all here because we have the same problem."
5. Anger management groups are usually centered upon education rather than therapy. Educational approaches are less demanding both of facilitators and participants and, as such, may be better utilized when larger numbers of people need to be treated in a relatively brief time.
6. Most important, I have no doubt that anger management group as presently constituted have helped preserve many lives by lessening the likelihood that participants will attack others or kill themselves.

Groups generally work best when the members share similar problems, lifestyles, educational level, and motivation for change. As such, participants in anger management groups should be carefully selected for mutual fit. In particular a distinction must be made between individuals who are prone to severe violence, defined as repeated acts of aggression intended to inflict injury, and those who are minimally physically aggressive even though they have definite anger problems. This distinction may be difficult to determine, so a well-trained interviewer should undertake a careful assessment before potential participants are assigned to a designated group. In addition, designing separate groups for domestic abusers, given the specific content of that issue, is probably wise. Thus, at least three distinct anger management groups could be designed: (1) a group for generally significantly physically violent individuals, including domestic abusers with a long history of generalized aggression; (2) one for generally verbally aggressive individuals who may be occasionally minimally or moderately physically violent; and (3) a group specifically targeted for people who have committed acts of domestic violence but who are not generally violent.

Group education should be broad in scope, touching on all four major domains of intervention described in the last chapter: behavioral change, cognitive intervention, affect regulation, and existential/spiritual intervention. However, the need to control aggression must predominate in any group designed for domestic aggressors or other highly violent individuals. Therefore, *three different twelve-week group formats* are presented next: one for minimally to moderately angry and aggressive clients, a second for more for severely violent individuals, and a third for domestic abusers. Although all three groups could be called anger management groups, only the first group should properly be designated with that title, while the second group could be called a physical aggression management group and the third a domestic abuse group. Nevertheless, all three groups share many commonalities. Consequentially, the descriptions are of three separate but overlapping groups that have several sessions in common.

Suggested Twelve-Week Anger Management Program for Minimally or Moderately Physically Aggressive Individuals

This group is designed for individuals who admit to verbal aggression against others as well as to frequently harboring intense feelings of anger, hostility, and resentment toward others. They may also commit relatively minor acts of physical aggression against domestic partners and other persons when highly stressed emotionally.

The group format includes brief lectures, group discussion, and exercises. Each session lasts from one and a half to two hours. Individuals are prescreened for group compatibility in a single session interview. They also receive two individual sessions during the twelve weeks and a final predischarge interview.

Session One: How Anger Messes Up Your Life

This initial session offers an opportunity for the counselor to motivate participants by helping them discuss how their own anger and aggression causes them significant life problems. The process is to lead a discussion that focuses on the natural consequences of excessive anger. Participants share the actual negative effects of their anger and aggression on themselves in the following areas:

- Health problems (high blood pressure, anger-related injuries such as bruises from punching the wall while upset, headaches and other psychosomatic symptoms caused by "stuffing" one's anger, etc.)
- Past and ongoing *family-of-origin conflicts* (estrangements, resentments, etc.)

- Past and current *partner relationship problems* caused or exacerbated by the client's anger (separations, continual arguing, etc.)
- *Financial difficulties* related to anger (quitting jobs, running up credit card debts to punish one's partner, etc.)
- *Spiritual issues* (anger at God, religious arguments, etc.)
- *Legal involvements* related to anger and aggression (disorderly conduct, "brushes" with the police, etc.)
- *Work problems* (warnings, failure to gain a promotion because the participant is too "hot headed," suspensions, firings, etc.)
- *School concerns* (suspensions, expulsions, acts or words of defiance, etc.)
- *Value violations* ("I said I would never yell at my kids the way my mom yelled at me but I'm doing the same thing now")
- *Mood and personality changes* related to anger (loss of hope, depression, "Jekyll and Hyde" personality changes when angry, etc.)
- *Damage to friendships* (loss of friends, isolation, fighting with friends, etc.)

Session Two: Three Goals of Anger Management and Four Ways You Can Change

I explain that this anger management program is built around three goals and four change areas, each of which will be the focus of one week's work beginning next week. The theme for this week is to introduce this material and to find out how much interest members of the group have in each domain.

The three goals are prevention, control, and problem solving. *Prevention* can best be described as learning how not to get angry in the first place. The key concept here is that of anger invitations, the idea that every person is given many opportunities each day to choose to become angry and upset or to stay calm. *Control* (or containment) means not blowing up even when angry—not "losing your cool." Time-out is an example of maintaining control in the face of a potential meltdown. The third goal, *problem solving,* means that after people calm down they need to make a serious attempt to resolve the concerns that made them angry. Teaching fair fighting skills exemplifies problem-solving training.

The four areas participants might choose to change are their actions, thoughts, feelings, and spirit. *Actions* means that participants must begin to change the things they do when angry that only make their situation worse, such as yelling or pacing. The concept of *thought* change leads to cognitive interventions such as disputation. *Feeling* changes involve lessening the intensity of the anger experience and becoming more open to other emotional experiences. Changing one's *spirit* asks people to discover the deeper meanings of their anger so they can better meet their real needs.

I present these goals and change possibilities as options that participants may want to select for themselves. That process lessens oppositionality since they are not being told they must change in these ways, only that they can if they so choose. Participants also gain an opportunity to select which goals and change areas are most personally important for them to concentrate on.

Session Three: Prevention Techniques

The goal in this session is to help clients recognize that they have the power to choose whether to become angry in a situation (as well as how angry to become and how to express that anger, the subjects of the next two sessions). The concept of anger invitations, introduced the week before, is presented as central to this discussion. Clients are asked to review recent anger invitations and to discuss the choices they made. I do not to always advocate for not getting angry no matter what the situation. Rather, my job is to stay relatively neutral while listening and to encourage group members to challenge their own and their co-members' choices to become angry. Guidelines for when anger is appropriate and inappropriate should be provided.

Session Four: Controlling Your Emotions

Containment is the theme of the fourth anger management session. Here group members are encouraged to stay in control even when angry, as well as to take responsibility for keeping anger from morphing into aggression. One specific technique is emphasized: taking an effective time-out with its four components of recognizing the danger signs of impending loss of control, retreating to a safe place, relaxing until the anger has drained from one's body and mind, and returning to deal with the original concern. Other considerations in this unit include not rushing to judgment, not making bad situations worse, and challenging the myth that ventilation of anger is healthy.

Session Five: Problem Solving

Most chronically angry clients have very poor problem resolution skills. This is partly because they have misunderstood the purpose of anger, mistakenly thinking they can solve their problems with anger instead of using anger as a way to realize that they have concerns. One important message in this session, then, is that anger is a good messenger but not a good problem solver. Trying to solve problems with one's anger leads only to verbal and physical aggression. Consequently, these individuals need to develop effective problem-resolution techniques as a substitute for the ineffective ones they are now using.

A fair fighting "do and don't list" can be helpful here because it is clear and specific (see Exhibit 4.1). Also, group members can have fun practicing fair and unfair fighting tactics with one another; here they can see what they normally do wrong because they are not as emotionally or defensively involved with one another as they would be with their families.

Session Six: Changing What You Do

The first of the four change sessions emphasizes the need for behavioral change, which by now, hopefully, many of the participants have already begun. The substitution principle is paramount here: for long-term success in the area of anger management people must not only quit doing the things that add to their anger but also start doing things that add to their satisfaction with life. So the format for this session is simple: what are the most important things you must stop doing and what are the most important things to start? By the end of this session each person should be able to fill out a 3" × 5" note card

EXHIBIT 4.1. Fair Fighting Rules

DON'T	DO
Make fun of others	Tell people what you feel
Hit, push, shove, hold, or threaten to do so	Stick to one issue at a time
Stand up and yell	Sit down and talk
Make faces	Listen
Attack the other's personality	Focus on the specific behavior you want
Name-call	Make regular eye contact (but don't glare)
Get stuck in the past	Be flexible—be willing to change your mind
Run away from the issue	Breathe calmly; stay relaxed
Say "forget it," "tough," "I don't care," "so what," or anything that ignores the other's concerns	Be open to negotiation and compromise Be responsible for everything you say
Need to get the last word in	Focus on solutions, not victories or defeats
Interrupt	Take time-outs as needed
Say "always" or "never" or other generalizations	

with six items listed: three things to stop and three to start. For example, someone might list quit yelling; stop swearing; no teasing the kids; start looking for good stuff; give praise; wait one minute before answering. Participants then are asked to keep these cards on them at all times.

Session Seven: Changing How You Think

Here counselors have an opportunity to introduce classic cognitive techniques to group members. I focus on two such techniques described in Chapter 3: knowing your "hot thoughts" (the thoughts that make you angry)" and a more general disputational process that I call "The ABCDEs of Disputation":

A = *anger invitations* you could accept or reject
B = your *beliefs* that make you accept these invitations
C = the negative *consequences* of becoming angry
D = a new thought that serves as a *disputation* of the old one
E = the positive *effects* of the new thought

Group members are helped to recognize and challenge at least one hot thought during the session.

Session Eight: Changing Your Feelings

Relaxation training is a well-documented approach to anger management. Unfortunately, relaxation can be difficult for angry clients, especially in group settings where people are self-conscious. Nevertheless, I do demonstrate a fifteen-minute relaxation procedure and then encourage discussion about its possible utility. I also offer to make individualized relaxation tapes for those members who most want and promise to use them.

The other focus of this session is on helping members notice and describe other relatively hidden feelings that frequently accompany their anger ("Anger seldom rides alone."). Many chronically angry individuals need help both recognizing and expressing these emotions.

Session Nine: Changing Your Spirit

The central idea of this session is this: chronically angry people live chronically unhappy lives. Consumed by anger, distrust, hostility, and resentment, their lives often become depressing and miserable. Their anger eventually cuts them off from other people, spiritual union, and even from themselves. The question is whether they want to continue in that pattern the rest of their lives or do something about it.

Existential approaches to anger management were presented in the previous chapter. In particular, though, clients within a group setting should be encouraged to look for the good in others and to become more empathic to the thoughts and feelings of their most significant others. Empathy is usually difficult for angry individuals, though, so they will need to use the session to practice such basic skills as asking questions to draw the other person out and listening noncritically.

Session Ten: Forgiveness

Participants in anger management groups often harbor long-standing grudges that keep them from reducing their anger. These persons need to be asked to consider forgiving those whom they believe have harmed them. Although forgiving is a long and difficult process, it can be described and discussed in one session. Members who identify themselves as needing to work in that area can then be given more information about forgiveness during individual sessions. See Chapter 7 for more information about the forgiving process.

Session Eleven: Anger Turned Inward

Although many angry people primarily turn their anger outward toward others, many others instead turn the bulk of their anger against themselves. Still others, perhaps even the majority of participants in anger management programs, do both: they have excessive anger that is directed both against others and themselves. Members should have a forum in which they can discuss how they attack themselves through name calling, self-sabotage, self-mutilation, and even suicide attempts. Participants in this discussion gain greater awareness that they are often their own worst enemy. For more information on this topic, see Chapter 8.

Session Twelve: Where Do You Go from Here?

This is a recapitulation session with an added message that twelve weeks is a very short time to master anger management. Participants are asked how they plan to follow up this program formally or informally. They are encouraged to continue reading, thinking about, and practicing their anger management skills, lest they gradually lose them over time.

Suggested Twelve-Week Anger Management Program for Severely Physically Aggressive Individuals

This group program is intended for individuals with significant physical aggression problems, defined as persons eighteen years or older who admit to or have been found to have committed several violent acts during their lifetimes, both within and outside the home, such as at work, in taverns, while driving, etc. Physical aggression includes fighting, threatening, significant property damage (such as destroying one's own car in a rage), and self-attack. Strong verbal aggression, such as continuing loud swearing at people, may be part of this pattern as well.

The goals of this group are to help individuals make a strong commitment to avoid physical aggression and excessive anger as well as to teach skills that help them keep this commitment. The following twelve-week agenda is designed for these two purposes. Sessions that were described in the twelve-week program for minimally physically aggressive individuals will just be labeled and not completely redescribed.

Session One: How Anger Messes Up Your Life

Session Two: Climbing Down the Anger and Violence Ladder

Severely aggressive individuals often need very concrete illustrations to help them understand their situations. A ladder analogy (Potter-Efron, 1994) in which letting go of one's excessive anger and aggression is likened to climbing down a ladder is one example that I have found quite useful. The eight rungs of the ladder, from the top, are these:

1. Blind rage
2. Partly controlled violence
3. Chasing and holding
4. Making demands and threats
5. Swearing, screaming, and yelling
6. Blaming and shaming

7. Giving others the "cold shoulder"
8. Sneaky anger (passive aggression)

Therapists must explain to clients the differences between blind rage and partly controlled violence. There are two main distinctions. First, when people go into a blind rage their goal is to destroy anything in their path, whereas individuals using partly controlled violence want to gain something specific such as money, use of the car, sex, etc. Second, in a true blind rage people are at least partially amnestic ("I didn't know what I did; I had to ask") while they maintain full consciousness during partly controlled violence. Clients who report that they have experienced blind rages should be referred to a neurologist or neuropsychologist for testing and possible treatment with medication.

Notice that "chasing and holding" is high on the list. In my experience many very aggressive persons do not adequately realize that holding their partners by the wrist, blocking the doorway, chasing after them, not letting them sleep, or otherwise impeding them is a violation of those people's rights. Group members must be told clearly and unreservedly that such behavior is unacceptable.

The four rungs at the top of the ladder describe possible or actual physical aggression; the bottom four rungs describe forms of active or passive verbal aggression. Many aggressors find it far easier to walk down the top four steps than the lower ones. These people will need both positive affirmation for the job they have done in curtailing physical aggression and strong encouragement to change their verbal behavior as well.

Session Three: Accepting Reality

This session is devoted to challenging a basic misperception of many highly aggressive individuals, namely, that they are the center of the universe and others exist for the sole purpose of serving them. This presumption lies at the center of the aggressor's oppositionality and defiance ("Nobody can tell me what to do."), their narcissism and grandiosity ("Why should I have to do anything? People should take care of me."), their lack of empathy ("I went to an AA meeting once. Ugh. People talking about their problems. What do I care about their problems? I have enough of my own."), their demandingness ("I want what I want and I want it now."), and sometimes their strongly addictive tendencies ("Cocaine make me feel good so I use it. Why not?").

Aggression is a frequent byproduct of this misperception. Expecting and demanding too much from others, people become frustrated and then demanding and threatening. If these tactics fail they may turn to physical attack, often in the form of deliberately exaggerated episodes designed to deliver a "Give me what I want or else you will suffer" message.

Counselors must be reality focused in approaching this material. They should acknowledge that sometimes bullies get what they want. Anger works (sometimes). Aggression works (sometimes). But even while recognizing that reality, the group leader should guide members toward addressing the immediate negative consequences of these tactics ("I tried that on my PO [probation officer] and she threw my ass in jail."). Counselors might also mention the supposed negative long-term consequences of these tactics as well, but be aware that many highly aggressive clients pay little attention to such issues.

Session Four: Prevention Techniques

Session Five: Controlling Your Emotions and Noticing Other Feelings

This session combines elements from the previous Sessions Four and Eight.

Session Six: Problem Solving

Session Seven: Changing What You Do

Session Eight: Changing How You Think

Session Nine: Changing Your Spirit

Session Ten: Shame-Rage and Paranoia

Instead of addressing all ten anger styles in this session as I do with less aggressive individuals, I concentrate with this group on the two particularly problematic styles, shame-rage and paranoia. Shame-rage (Potter-Efron and Potter-Efron, 1995; Potter-Efron and Potter-Efron, 1989; Potter-Efron, 2001) is especially dangerous because people who defend against shame by attacking others often do so with the goal of totally annihilating them. Similarly, relatively paranoid persons tend to misperceive badly the motivations of others and, consequently, they desperately try to defend against nonexistent threats. The goals of this unit are to help participants recognize their tendencies toward shame-rage and/or paranoia and to give them some initial guidelines toward changing those patterns.

Session Eleven: Understanding Others Better

The purpose of this session is to get these relatively self-centered individuals more interested in the thoughts, feelings, wants, and needs of others. The group format is useful here since members can be helped to ask one another such questions as "What really matters the most to you?" or "When [a particular event] happened, what feelings did you have?" Then a transition can be made to people outside the room through questions such as "What do you think your girlfriend might have thought and felt when you stayed out until 4:00 a.m. and forgot to call her?" Enhancing this curiosity about others is necessary to facilitate the development of empathy, a process that involves stepping aside from one's own ego to enter another's world.

Session Twelve: Where Do We Go from Here?

Suggested Twelve-Week Anger Management Program for Men Who Commit Acts of Physical Domestic Abuse

The group described next is designed for males who commit acts of physical domestic abuse. These men are frequently labeled "batterers," but that term is so pejorative and raises the level of defensiveness so high that I do not recommend using it within the context of the group.

Session One: What Is Domestic Abuse? Why Do Men Hit Their Partners?

My definition of a domestic abuse incident is an act of physical aggression (hitting, pushing, shoving, slapping, pinching, etc.) and/or threats to aggress committed by one person against his or her relationship partner (boyfriend, girlfriend, spouse). A domestic abuser (batterer) engages in *repeated* acts of domestic abuse. A serial domestic abuser repeatedly has engaged in these behaviors with two or more relationship partners.

As to the question of why men attack their partners, I offer several possibilities for group consideration. First, men in American society have received generations of training in the idea that it is perfectly acceptable to physically attack their partners, with or without reason. Next comes a consideration of the idea that men maintain power and control over women though physical domination. This, paired with many men's experience that the women in their lives can outtalk and outargue them, makes it difficult to commit to renouncing aggression. The third possibility I suggest is that perhaps some of the men in the group have problems with personal insecurity, especially in relationships, so they become angry, jealous, and violent in a desperate effort to keep their partners from leaving them.

However the group members respond to these ideas, the leader must end the discussion with a clear statement that American society is quickly changing; men are neither encouraged nor allowed to physically attack their partners. They need to understand that no acceptable justification exists for this kind of violence. This may not be a very difficult case to make; after all, the very reason they are attending the group is proof enough that such behavior is unacceptable.

Session Two: Climbing Down the Ladder of Domestic Abuse

This is essentially the same session described before but with all examples drawn from the domestic sphere.

Session Three: Accepting Reality

Session Four: Prevention Techniques

Session Five: Controlling Your Emotions and Noticing Other Feelings

Session Six: Problem Solving

Session Seven: Changing What You Do

Session Eight: Changing How You Think

Session Nine: Changing Your Spirit

Session Ten: Shame-Rage, Paranoia, and Jealousy

This session is similar to the one described previously but with added material on the topic of jealousy. Distinctions should be made between normal, excessive, and irrational jealousy. Group members should be encouraged to talk about how their jealousy "makes me go crazy." All of these topics can be tied into feelings of low self-worth and the hope that gaining control over their anger will help these men improve their sense of being worthwhile.

Session Eleven: Understanding Your Partner and Children

Many chronically angry and violent individuals are poor at generalizing their learning. This unfortunate reality is especially significant for the children of domestic abusers. For example, I once visited a domestic violence group in which two members were just returning because they had been in trouble for beating their children. Both men insisted they had not struck their wives in more than a year, since each initially went through that same program. However, when I asked if either had ever thought to apply the same ideas that they had learned about anger management with their spouses to dealing with their children, they not only said no but they looked amazed at the question itself. Include at least one session on basic nonviolent parenting techniques such as how to give children warnings that their behavior is unacceptable, how to give time-outs to their children, and also how not to take too personally such statements as "I hate you" and "That's not fair" when they are spoken by their children.

Session Twelve: Where Do We Go from Here?

Appendix B has suggested specific assignments from my workbook (Potter-Efron, 2001) that may be assigned as homework for each session for all three anger management groups.

INDIVIDUALIZED ANGER AND AGGRESSION MANAGEMENT COUNSELING: AN ALTERNATIVE TO GROUP WORK

Group work is efficient and reasonably effective in the area of anger management. However, for many reasons (described later) consideration ought to be given to individualized anger education, counseling, and therapy. This is not to say that angry clients should receive only individual therapy, however. My understanding of individualized therapy is that each client's needs will be assessed separately; that every client will be perceived as having a unique set of anger behaviors, beliefs, and concerns; and that the treatment for each person will consist of the best possible balance of individual, group, couples, and family therapy as befits his or her situation.

Certainly many clinicians already utilize an individualized counseling approach with their clients. However, the emphasis within the field in the late 1990s and the new millennium has overwhelmingly been upon the creation and development of anger management groups. This is particularly true in the area of domestic abuse in which clients, almost always men, are frequently court ordered to participate in groups lasting six to twenty or more weeks.

That being said, the remainder of this chapter makes a case for individualized anger and aggression management. In particular, I will discuss some of the specific advantages of individual therapy over group counseling. However, my goal is not to advocate for replacing groups with individual treatment but to have both modes of intervention, along with couples and family therapy, readily available so that the needs of clients can be well met.

One Size Does Not Fit All

Please imagine that you (a counselor, educator, psychologist, psychiatric nurse, probation officer, or some other type of professional helper) have been asked to treat the following eight individuals *and* that you are to form them into a single anger management group:

- *Hector:* Twenty-five, a mechanic, married. Hector has been arrested for beating his wife. He has done it before. He has also been arrested on several occasions for assaultive crimes. He was kicked out of high school after attacking a teacher. Hector hates authority.

- *Melanie:* Seventeen, high school junior. Melanie's parents say that she has not been herself for about a year now. Melanie agrees, stating that she just cannot seem to control her anger. She flies into rages at the slightest affront, first swearing at her boyfriend or parents or teachers, then yelling and pounding her fists, and then bursting into sobs. She desperately hopes the people she is angry at will not leave even while she is pushing them away. A history of depression and mental illness runs in her family.
- *Gaylord:* Sixty-two, a retired executive going through his second divorce. This man is chronically hostile, critical, and cynical. Most people, even professionals, try to avoid him because of his incessant negativity. Two of his four grown children refuse to have anything to do with him. He is volunteering for counseling because he wants to learn how to be "less of a pain in the ass before I lose the rest of my family."
- *Sharika:* Thirty-five, a medical secretary who was sexually abused from age nine to fourteen by her brother. She is tired of hating him and by extension, all men. She needs to learn how to forgive so she can get on with her life.
- *Jorge:* Forty, an attorney who keeps running into trouble at work because of his short fuse. Jorge can be volatile at home where his periodic outbursts are anticipated and tolerated. However, that same behavior is not well received at the office. He has been told that he will never make partner in the firm until he learns to treat people more respectfully.
- *Theodore:* Fifty, whose wife has demanded he get treatment for his passive aggressive behavior. Theodore totally frustrates his wife by forgetting important things, not finishing jobs, refusing to talk about what is bothering him, and, above all, by saying he is not angry when she knows that he is fuming inside.
- *Erika:* Thirty-five, a real estate salesperson. Erika seems to have an anger problem only when she has been drinking. Unfortunately, lately she has been doing that every day, several hours a day. The more she drinks the nastier she gets.

- *Charity:* Twenty-eight, a woman with a dissociative disorder. One of her alters is nicknamed "The Madman" and appears to be the repository for the entire system's anger. The Madman rages when he comes out, sometimes physically attacking anybody in sight but equally frequently cutting or burning Charity's body.

Your job is to design one set of lectures and activities that will apply to all eight of these highly differentiated clients. How can you possibly do this? True, every one of the clients named can truly claim to have an anger problem. However, each person's anger problem is so radically different from the others that it would be virtually impossible to construct a single group that would suffice for them all.

As can be seen from the previous examples, the term "anger management" has grown to include a tremendous variety of concerns. Some of the individuals described are violent and should be in "aggression management" groups rather than anger management. Others have psychological problems that probably cannot be properly addressed within a group educational context. Some of these potential clients have impulse control problems while others are dealing with the buildup of long-term resentments. Group work, though, functions best when the participants are relatively similar in primary concerns, age, education, etc. It is simply unproductive to throw together a disparate collection of individuals who have little in common, and it is unlikely that groups could be designed for all the persons described. At least some of them will need to be treated individually if only because their problems are relatively uncommon.

Paradigms Can Be Stretched Only So Far

During the 1970s and 1980s, probably most anger management clients being treated in counseling situations were middle-aged men and women who had been so overtrained at being nice they could not get angry even when anger would be appropriate. Ventilation techniques such as pounding pillows became popular at that time because the main therapeutic effort was aimed at giving these emotionally restricted clients permission to recognize and express their feelings, especially anger. By the late 1990s the goals and processes of anger management changed drastically, and most effort became directed toward individuals from all classes whose primary problem was physical aggression. Domestic abuse anger management programs were designed with a very specific goal in mind: to help abusers quit attacking their partners. Certainly an emphasis upon anger ventilation was inappropriate in this situation, especially after Carol Tavris cited research that indicated in essence that ventilating anger only increased the likelihood for more anger and rage (Tavris, 1989). A new paradigm for anger management emerged, this one placing emphasis on how male domestic abusers used physical domination over their partners to maintain not only their own power and control but also more generally that of all men over all women. Psychologically oriented anger therapy faded during this period since it was considered irrelevant to the issue of power and control.

However, Thomas Kuhn (1996) notes that every paradigm undergoes a life course beginning with a breakthrough discovery, then followed by a period of combat with the old paradigm, then victory of the new one, and then expansion of the paradigm into new domains. However, Kuhn argues convincingly that every expansion of the paradigm comes with a cost; the fit between the paradigm and the newer areas becomes less and less good. One recent example of this tendency can be seen in the disease model of addiction favored by Alcoholics Anonymous. Although this model fits middle-aged males fairly well, every expansion of it to other groups offers problems. Some women, for instance, believe the emphasis upon humility in AA is inappropriate for their gender; adolescents, meanwhile, can hardly comprehend the concept of maintaining abstinence the rest of their lives. Consequently, alternative treatment models, such as harm reduction and cognitive therapy, have begun to nibble at the edges of the disease perspective. Eventually the original paradigm gets replaced by a newer paradigm that better explains the problems introduced by the older one.

I submit that anger management is going through this same process. The current dominant paradigm that focuses upon power and control as the primary motivator for aggression is quite appropriate for a certain group of male batterers. However, that model loses potency when applied to a range of other persons: women who are violent toward partners and children; people who get angry frequently but are never physically violent; individuals whose anger feels far more connected to feelings of abject powerlessness and helplessness than to their own power and control; those who seem to gain nothing from their anger and aggression but cannot stop; batterers with attachment or psychological problems whose anger stems from deep personal sources.

Into this current paradigm-stretching phase individualized anger treatment, in particular psychologically oriented anger management, has a valuable place in the spectrum of care. This approach is especially useful for individuals whose anger stems from or is commingled with ongoing psychological vulnerabilities. The anger and aggression problems of clients with attachment difficulties, jealousy issues, lingering resentments, depression, and anxiety typically will not be resolved within group settings that treat anger simply as overlearned behaviors or as relationship manipulations. Although they certainly may profit from such groups they will need a more individualized treatment plan to benefit fully.

Individualized Treatment Encourages More Specific Goals and Methods

Three primary goals characterize anger management work: *prevention of unnecessary anger and aggression*; containment of one's anger so *as not to lose control;* and *resolution of ongoing conflict* in order to reduce the buildup of more anger. Presumably most anger management groups give equal time to all three, although in my experience more effort often is placed on prevention and containment than resolution. However, individuals have greatly differing needs with regard to these goals. The man who suddenly "snaps," seemingly without warning, will need to be guided strenuously toward greater awareness of the buildup cues that predict these explosions. Thus, prevention will need to be emphasized. Another client, though, says that she knows perfectly well that she is ready to explode. The problem is that she then chooses to keep going, perhaps because she gains a certain excitement from the action. This woman will need much work in the arena of containment. Finally, another person fundamentally believes in the principle that once somebody gets on his "s— list" he should never let that individual off it. The bulk of treatment for this client will be in the area of resolution. Individualized anger management permits the design of a treatment plan that allots time proportionate to need.

Similarly, at least four different intervention methods in anger management can be identified. These are *behavior, cognitive, affective,* and *existential/spiritual* interventions. The *behavioral* emphasis describes how clients develop a habit of anger and aggression, teaches basic tools such as how to take a time-out, and offers help in developing positive, prosocial modes of communication. *Cognitive* interventions help clients understand how their "irrational" assumptions about the world, beliefs about people or themselves, and interpretations of others' words and deeds create excessive anger and prepare the way for harmful actions. *Affective* interventions are directed at teaching individuals to relax instead of becoming agitated and to locate other emotions instead of or in addition to anger that they have been disregarding. Last, *existential/spiritual* interventions attempt to place the client's anger into a larger perspective such as the meaning of anger within that person's life, the role of despair or impotent rage, and anger as a signal that some important need that has been ignored must now be addressed.

Individualized treatment permits a much greater flexibility in selecting from among these four approaches. While one client will benefit primarily from behavioral and cognitive approaches, another will do far better with affective interventions, and a third might need existential or spiritual assistance most.

The combination of three different therapeutic goals (prevention, containment, resolution) and four different methods (behavioral, cognitive, affective, existential/spiritual) results in twelve possible emphases. Individualized treatment permits therapists to select among these twelve variants the particular emphasis that might best benefit the client.

Specialized Issues Demand Specialized Treatment

Some areas of anger management stand apart from others because of their uniqueness. These areas are somewhat specialized and are best approached by therapists with appropriate training and experience. Four that I will briefly mention here are (1) the dissociative anger episodes of individuals with dissociative identity disorder and post-traumatic stress disorder; (2) the self-mutilative and self-destructive behaviors of individuals who habitually direct fierce anger inwardly against themselves; (3) the rageful outbursts that emanate from clients with significant attachment insecurities, some of whom may be diagnosed with borderline personality disorder; and (4) the seething anger, spitefulness, and vengeance seeking of those who hate and cannot forgive.

Clients such as these might benefit somewhat from standard anger management groups. Hopefully they will gain an improved ability to take time-outs, combat anger-provoking thoughts, utilize fair fighting tactics, and become more accepting of their partners. Realistically, though, these individuals will need much more help. Many of these people will quickly lose the skills they learned in group if they fail to receive extra care while others will only be able to use them at work or in otherwise less threatening situations. Without individualized care the dissociative person will still blindly defend himself against illusory attacks; the self-mutilator will "stuff" her external anger only to increase the number and intensity of attacks against herself; the person with attachment insecurities will be unable to control irrational bouts of jealousy; the person who hates will continue to turn away with disgust from past friends and family members while bathing in the pain of remembered insults.

I advocate a "both/and" or two-tier approach to anger management with these difficult and seriously impaired individuals. If possible, these clients should receive both group and individual counseling. However, if that proves impracticable and a choice must to be made between the two formats I would advocate for individualized therapy over group work. Clients can pick up standard anger management tools (time-out, etc.) through readings and workbooks. Outside materials can be assigned and then discussed within therapy sessions, enabling counselors to link that material to the specific needs of their clients. No amount of reading about dissociation, self-mutilation, attachment disorders, or hate can substitute for the combination of caring and confrontation that occurs during therapy. In each of these situations these chronically fearful and suspicious persons need to learn how to trust another human being. The gradual development of trust allows stronger and more effective challenges to the deeply held irrational belief systems that underlie the anger and aggression these clients display.

Essentially, clients with these deeper pathologies must learn to manage their anger at two levels. First, they need to learn some basic skills that allow them to participate relatively safely in the world around them. Then they must discover the links between their anger and aggression and the core insults to their honor, integrity, sense of self, spirit, wholeness, and ability to achieve a sense of belonging and intimacy with others. Individualized anger management is the key to this second tier of learning. Once achieved, many of these clients will be able to practice anger management not as a set of skills to be applied mechanically but as a way to heal their troubled lives at the level of soul and core self. Only then will they be able to achieve a state of contentedness that is implied in the promise of anger management—that clients will be able to substitute positive thoughts, beliefs, emotions, and experiences for the negative ones they have now.

An Individualized Focus Allows Treatment for Anger As a Symptomatic, Secondary, or Complementary Issue

Anger management, as presently conceived and practiced in group counseling approaches, usually stands alone as a separately targeted phenomenon. However, in many situations an individual's anger might better be treated as part of a larger problem or more compelling issue.

One example concerns clients whose anger is secondary to a major depressive disorder. True, these individuals certainly have anger problems. They frequently make negative, cynical, disparaging, and hostile remarks for seemingly little reason; they offend people by avoiding them unnecessarily; they report that they feel continually irritable and consequently short-tempered; they are pessimistic and even paranoid in their interpretations of the words and actions of their associates; they appear to pick fights just to ensure that everybody around them feels as bad as they do. Anger management counseling can help these persons curtail some of these activities, especially the most visible and public ones. However, that treatment must be folded into a larger discussion of the client's depression so that the client can be steered toward medical assistance and/or cognitive depression therapy. Obviously, the facilitator of anger management programs must be well trained in the relationship between anger and depression so that depressed clients sent for anger management can be appropriately diagnosed and treated.

Alcoholism and drug addiction is another area in which anger concerns become commingled with another major or even primary issue. Sometimes the causal connection seems fairly obvious: a person becomes verbally aggressive or physically violent only under the influence of copious amounts of an intoxicant, or someone who is already angry gets drunk in order to release inhibitions against expressing that anger. At other times, the relationship seems to circle or spiral so that separating the individual's use of mood-altering substances from his or her anger issues is impossible. This is particularly likely with people who harbor long-term resentments. These persons may say they drink to forget their misery but in reality their drinking only compounds their pain and increases their sense of victimization. Other clients use various substances, frequently marijuana, in an attempt to contain their anger. Newly abstinent, these individuals may find themselves overwhelmed with floods of anger that had been effectively held off through addictive processes.

So what comes first, alcohol and drug abuse treatment or anger management? Traditionally trained addiction experts emphasize addiction treatment, believing that the anger issue is symptomatic and secondary. Anger management specialists might argue that the client needs their services in order to be willing to participate in addiction treatment. Probably the best answer is that both issues need to be treated in whichever order the client will allow, including simultaneously. Again, as with psychological concerns such as depression, the treatment facilitators in either specialty must be knowledgeable enough about both conditions (anger and addiction) to be able to handle each client's needs creatively.

A third situation that calls for individualized attention concerns clients whose anger is primarily associated only with a relationship partner or within the family. Two examples are a very jealous person who makes constant angry accusations to his or her partner, and an adolescent who gets along well at school and with friends but argues and fights with his parents and siblings, all of whom have their own anger problems. Group work alone probably will not suffice for either of these persons. The jealousy issue is too potent and individualized to be adequately addressed in groups, and the adolescent cannot be expected to make lasting changes without family intervention that addresses the concept of systemic anger within the family. Rather, both of these persons will need a combination of group, individual, and couples or family therapy to help them understand and curtail their aggressive behaviors.

The issue of couples counseling is particularly interesting when physical aggression is evidenced within a relationship. Traditionally, couples counseling is ruled out in these situations because of the risk that comments made in counseling will be used as an excuse for further violence by the perpetrator. Instead, the couple is split into a victim and victimizer duality, with each treated separately (and often the victim is urged emphatically to leave the victimizer). Probably that is the best approach when one of the two persons has a long history of relationship violence that appears to be intractable. However, automatically ruling out couples counseling because of any history of relationship aggression can become a rigid ethic rather than a considered decision. Some couples might benefit from counseling as long as they understand that the therapist retains the right to curtail counseling if what is said during sessions is misused or appears to worsen the situation. Perhaps some clients here will benefit best from sequential treatment, beginning with group counseling intended to help the client learn generally how to deal with anger, then individual therapy that addresses the key personal dynamics that propel anger and aggression, and then couples or family work designed to help the client establish and maintain more functional, less anger-dominated intimate relationships.

Individualized Anger Styles Call for Individualized Treatment Procedures

As noted in Chapter 2, I believe that most individuals typically handle situations in which they could become angry in one or a few predictable ways. I have identified ten of these "anger styles": anger avoidance, passive aggression, paranoia/distrust-based anger, sudden anger, shame-based anger, deliberate anger, excitatory anger, habitual anger, moral anger, and resentment/hate (Potter-Efron, 1994). Each of these anger styles can be valuable at times but can become problematic if overused or misused. For example, anger avoidance is appropriate for many situations in which it is just not worth the effort to get angry. However, since problems seldom are addressed through anger avoidance, it is a poor long-term strategy especially with significant issues. Similarly, moral anger serves wonderfully in situations calling for advocacy, fueling a person's determination to see that justice prevails. However, some individuals get caught up in moral anger, in effect wrapping themselves in a cloak of moral righteousness. This stand of moral superiority may then lead to lessened empathy and the creation of rigid, unyielding positions.

The questionnaire detailed in Chapter 3 can help clients identify which anger styles they employ most frequently and which cause them trouble. Then treatment may be tailored more efficiently toward meeting their specific needs.

Most Anger Management Groups Are Really Aggression Management Groups

The term "anger management" has been used so broadly that it no longer has any clear meaning. Most critically, the bulk of anger management groups are really designed for relatively violent individuals whose behavior has caused them trouble with the law or their families. The purpose for these groups would better be labeled as "aggression management" than anger management.

This focus on aggression management excludes many individuals who might benefit from counseling focusing more upon the emotion of anger than the behavior of aggression. Certainly clients with mostly hidden anger styles will seldom be treated in aggression management groups because their anger is more internally than externally directed. Nor will many chronically angry people benefit fully from aggression management, especially those whose anger primarily takes the form of long-term resentments. Another group of potential clients that will probably gain little from traditional aggression management groups are persons who spend their time complaining, nagging, and grumbling, all low-grade forms of anger expression that seldom result in physical attack. Still another set of persons who may be misplaced in aggression management groups are those whose aggression is relatively mild, such as a person arrested for a domestic incident in a mandatory-arrest state, but who has no track record of violence and whose aggression in this incident was both minor and anomalous to his or her entire previous personal and relationship history.

Women, too, are generally underserved when anger groups focus upon limiting physical aggression. One reason is that their anger too often remains unexpressed, socially prohibited as unladylike. If expressed, women's anger is perhaps more likely than men's to be verbal than physical and more likely to be powered by relationship concerns than strictly hedonistic goals. For that matter, even if a woman does become physically violent she will unlikely be placed in an anger management group because most such groups are designed for, taught by, and populated exclusively by males.

One solution for the current limits of anger management groups is to expand their membership to include all these diverse populations. However, the danger there is that the groups would become so diluted that they would lose any clear direction. Another possibility is to develop true anger management groups in which the emphasis is much more on anger as an emotion than aggression as a behavior. I believe this is already happening to some extent. However, the sheer extent of human variety in the experience and expression of anger guarantees that not enough groups could ever be devised to meet every person's needs.

Ultimately, I believe that the best way to serve the diverse population of people who could benefit from anger management is to carefully individualize treatment, beginning with a thorough assessment process and continuing with a personalized treatment plan that might include elements from individual, group, couples, and family therapy; individual or group education programs; medication management; and involvement with the corrections institution when necessary.

Guidelines for Gauging Treatment Effectiveness: Individual Work with Angry and Violent Individuals

Working individually with exceptionally angry and aggressive individuals does have its drawbacks. Perhaps the worst problem is the potential lack of honest or realistic feedback from the client about how well he or she is containing anger and aggression. The following guidelines can minimize this problem:

1. Be sure to get signed releases immediately from these clients (while assuring them of their privacy rights and negotiating with them, if necessary, as to what the therapist can and cannot reveal); if at all possible, one release should be to allow communication with the client's relationship partner.
2. Regularly check with these persons as to the client's success with anger and aggression containment.
3. When clients report successes ask for specific details. See if they can discuss differences, both behavioral and cognitive, between how they responded in these immediate situations as opposed to what they would have done before in similar circumstances.
4. Frequently ask clients what they are doing right when they report the absence of aggression or anger. This helps them realize that change happens because they are substituting new behaviors for old.
5. Regularly inquire if anyone else has commented on either their changes or lack of changes since beginning treatment. Lack of confirmation may be a sign that clients think they are making more changes than they really are (or an unwillingness to give them credit for changing by angry, doubtful, or distrusting significant others).

CASE STUDY: A MAN WHO BENEFITED FROM BOTH GROUP AND INDIVIDUAL COUNSELING

Hector, a twenty-five-year old male, was sent to my anger management group by his probation officer even though he was actually still in jail at the time. Hector had a lengthy history of relatively petty crime (convictions for cigarette theft and disorderly conduct) and relatively minor domestic aggression. (He reportedly pushed his way past his wife, Tammy, when she tried to keep him from leaving during an argument, causing her to fall but not be injured; a talk with Tammy confirmed this report.) He was nearing the end of a six-month sojourn in jail for writing bad checks and faced another year of probation.

Hector did well in the anger group, becoming a leader on the first evening when he disputed another member's claim that nobody wanted to be there. "Well, I do," he said. "I'm tired of being angry all the time." He steadily reported success with his anger except in one area: jealousy. No matter how hard he tried, he found himself sitting in his cell at night wondering what Tammy was doing, with whom she might be speaking, if she was planning on leaving him, and, worst of all, if she was already having sex with another man. Although we discussed jealousy in the group, Hector simply could not conquer this obsession. Consequently, he asked for and received permission (and funding) from the department of corrections to attend twelve individual anger sessions with me, six sessions before and six after he was released from jail.

Hector made revelations that in individual therapy sessions he had not talked about in the group. Most significant, he described the day he stumbled upon his father having intercourse with a family friend. His father swore Hector to secrecy, but his mother became suspicious and asked Hector if he knew what his dad was up to. Hector was caught in the middle. He lied to her but felt terribly guilty. Hector believed his jealousy problems originated then. It didn't help that these events took place just as he was entering puberty. "I guess I've always believed that married people cheat on each other, just like Dad did to Mom."

Why hadn't Hector discussed these issues in group treatment? The reason, he explained, was that he was too ashamed of his family of origin. Besides, he pointed out, despite confidentiality agreements you could not count on the group members, all young men with honesty problems, to keep quiet.

Hector made good progress during individual therapy. He came to realize that the generalization he had made—that since his father cheated on his mother then anyone might cheat on a partner—was far too broad and certainly not an inevitability in his marriage. He claimed to become more trusting of her, a statement validated by his wife, who told me she had been thinking of leaving him due to his jealousy problems.

Hector gained anger management skills in both his group and individual therapy experiences. His group supplied support, general information, and motivation. Individual counseling helped him with personal issues that had kept him jealous and insecure despite his overall improvement.

SUMMARY

Both individual therapy and group counseling have their places in the treatment of anger management. Some advantages of group therapy include efficiency, socialization, role-playing opportunities, peer confrontation, an educational focus, and cost-effectiveness. Individual therapy offers greater depth, an opportunity to probe relatively unique problems and patterns, and flexibility. Many clients will benefit from either intervention mode, while some do better in one or the other. Some clients need both therapies to master the art of anger management.

One alternative to individual or group therapy is couples counseling, a somewhat controversial elective that will be addressed in the next chapter.

Chapter 5

Attachment Theory, Domestic Violence, Jealousy, and Couples Counseling

INTRODUCTION

Work with angry partners through couples therapy has been a relatively neglected area, especially when one or both persons have been physically violent within the relationship. Indeed, many counselors work only individually with physically aggressive individuals, judging the risks as too great to merit couples counseling. Certainly that is a legitimate concern. The emotional volatility of couples counseling might increase rather than decrease the risk for violence, especially in the period immediately after a session. Furthermore, some clients could be intimidated from being truthful during discussions if they believe they will be punished for their honesty. An additional risk is that physically violent individuals will attempt to use counseling sessions to convince themselves, the spouse, and the counselor of the correctness of their behavior.

Nevertheless, couples counseling within the field of domestic violence has been recommended by several authors. Neidig and Friedman (1984), for example, detail an extensive anger management program they developed for couples in which acts of domestic violence had occurred. They cite six major principles upon which their program is based.

1. The primary goal is to eliminate violence in the home.
2. Although anger and conflict are normal elements of family life, violence in the family is never justified.
3. Abusiveness is a learned behavior.
4. Abusive behavior is a relationship issue, but it is ultimately the responsibility of the male to control physical violence.

5. Abusiveness is a desperate but ultimately maladaptive effort to effect relationship change.
6. Abusiveness tends to escalate in severity and frequency if not treated.

They choose to work with couples because they concluded from their work with military men that most acts of abuse occur during periods of exceptional stress and were related to specific deficits in the areas of anger control, stress management, and communication.

More recently, Tucker et al. (2000) discuss the use of in-session "meta-dialogue" between co-counselors in couples therapy with domestic abusers and their spouses. The work they describe is an add-on to a male batterers program in which the male has perpetrated mild to moderate violence. Their goal is to develop an approach to working with such couples that attends to the systematic issues in the marriage. They do so while simultaneously keeping responsibility for the violence with the perpetrator and assuring the safety of both partners.

Holtzworth-Munroe et al. (2003) distinguish couples in which "common couple violence" is characterized by relatively mild to moderate physical aggression, often by both partners, from a more severe husband-only aggression in which the male's violence serves to control his partner. They suggest that couples counseling might be appropriate only for the former group. They also recommend conjoint treatment primarily for "family-only" male perpetrators, men whose violence is linked with stress and skills limitations that periodically predict physical aggression during escalating marital conflicts. These men are remorseful about their aggression, have low levels of psychopathology, and maintain generally positive attitudes toward women. In contrast, they do not recommend couples work with dysphoric/borderline batterers or with generally antisocial males. Couples counseling should be considered even with couples in which violence has been manifested.

An adult attachment model is very helpful in organizing couples work with angry and violent couples. The central reason is that within the perspective of this model, "Contrary to the dominant feminist perspective . . . we believe that relationship abuse is best understood within a dyadic or relationship context" (Bartholomew, Henderson, and Dutton, 2001, p. 57). If so, then the likelihood of creating a mutually safe relationship is increased through couples work at least for some violent couples. Johnson and Sims (2000) note, "From an attachment perspective the underlying cause of marital distress is the lack of accessibility and responsiveness of at least one partner and the problematic ways in which the partners deal with their insecurities" (p. 172). The attachment model implies that anger serves as a protest against separation (Dutton, 1998) and as such helps explain both relationship aggression and jealousy.

I will review the literature on adult attachment in this chapter, relate this material to domestic aggression and jealousy, and present general guidelines for working with violent couples.

MODELS OF CHILD ATTACHMENT AND ADULT ATTACHMENT

Over forty years have passed since John Bowlby (1969, 1973, 1980) began developing his model of maternal attachment. Excellent reviews of the attachment model he and Mary Ainsworth developed and tested are provided by Berman and Sperling (1994); Karen (1994); Levy and Orlans (2000); and Wilson (2001). Although I cannot review this entire process in this volume, the key concepts Bowlby developed can be summarized.

Definition

Attachment is an enduring emotional bond that involves a tendency to seek and maintain proximity to a specific person, particularly when under stress. It is a mutual regulatory system that provides safety, protection, and a sense of security for the infant. Attachment is "an intense and enduring bond biologically rooted in the function of protection from danger" (Wilson, 2001, p. 38).

Key Characteristics

- The attachment system represents an independent behavioral system. (It is not a drive but it is equally powerful.)
- It is a homeostatic process that regulates infant proximity and contact-maintaining behavior, allowing distancing and independence but ensuring the closeness of the caregiver as needed.

- Attachment is organized around specific attachment figures. Each relationship is unique, so a parent's bonding connection with one child may be very different from his or her experience with another child.
- The physical goal of the attachment process is to ensure that the infant will survive its period of complete dependency. The concurrent psychological goal is for the infant to develop an internal sense of safety and trust.
- If attachment needs are well met the infant will normally develop a sense of having a *safe haven*. He or she will feel a deep sense of belonging, that there is and will always be a place for him or her.
- If attachment needs are well met the infant also develops the sense of having a *secure base* from which he or she can explore the environment. Thus, feelings of safety encourage risk taking and exploration of the world.
- The attachment system is not always active; it is turned on when the attachment figure moves away from infant or when the child feels threatened, disturbed, or needy.
- When threatened, disturbed, or needy, the infant then behaves in ways designed to restore adult proximity (crying, calling, crawling after, etc.).
- There is a standard sequence of infant reactions to attachment figure separation: *protest, despair, detachment.* Anger is often part of the protest phase. Detachment may be thought of as a reintegration phase in which the infant reestablishes an inner sense of quiet (with or without complete resolution of the attachment crisis).
- Children gradually develop *internal working models* of their attachment world by age nine to eighteen months (Diamond and Blatt, 1994). These internal working models are mostly unconscious sets of expectations about whether and how well their security needs will be met by significant others. Internal working models include a conception of the self as worthy or unworthy and positive or negative predictions about the consequences of attachment. They also provide a context for later social relationships (Dutton, 1998).

- Four basic attachment styles have been identified based on children's and mothers' reactions to experiments in which children were temporarily separated from the mother.
  1. *Secure:* The child feels distressed, seeks out mother, feels relief, returns to play.
  2. *Anxious/avoidant:* The child feels distressed but ignores mother when she returns, acting as if he or she were indifferent to the mother.
  3. *Anxious/ambivalent:* The child exhibits high levels of distress, and a mixed approach/rejection reaction when mother returns (e.g., hugs but arches away).
  4. *Disorganized/disoriented:* The child displays no consistent pattern and/or unusual behaviors upon mother's return (e.g., fall to floor, turn in circles). This is speculated to be the result of the mother's unpredictability so that, paradoxically, the mother is both the source of insecurity and its solution.
- These attachment styles are stable over time (traitlike) and consistent with the mother's parenting characteristics and attachment style. Parental behaviors predict children's attachment style: sensitive and consistently responsive parents tend to have secure children; parents who are unresponsive and rejecting of proximity tend to have avoidant children; inconsistent parents who alternate between unavailability and intrusiveness tend to have anxious/ambivalent children; excessively disturbed parents with very unpredictable behavior tend to produce disorganized/disoriented children.
- Many positives result for children whose attachment needs are well met, including
  1. a sense of safety and protection;
  2. basic trust and reciprocity;
  3. ability to explore the world;
  4. self-regulation of affect;
  5. identity formation as competent and worthy;
  6. the ability to balance the desires for autonomy and dependency;

7. the establishment of empathy and consequently a prosocial sense of morality;
8. a positive view of others and the world; and
9. resiliency in the face of adversity, stress, and trauma (Levy and Orlans, 2000).

Adult Attachment Patterns

Although Bowlby predicted that adults should possess, maintain, and exhibit specific attachment patterns that were initially generated during childhood, little research was initially directed toward adult attachment patterns. However, the 1990s has witnessed an explosion of interest in adult attachment. A semistructured adult interview format has been developed (George, Kaplan, and Main, 1996) as well as more direct self-report measures (Brennan, Clark, and Shaver, 1998).

Adult attachment can be defined as "the stable tendency of an individual to make substantial efforts to seek out and maintain proximity with one or a few specific individuals who provide the subjective potential for physical and/or psychological safety and security" (Berman and Sperling, 1994, p. 8). Although similar in form and function, adult attachment differs from parental/infant bonding in one important way. Adult attachment is more reciprocal in that both persons can play the roles of caregiver and care receiver. In other words, they serve as complementary attachment figures, serving the dual purpose of comforting each other and preserving the dyadic unit.

Bartholomew (Bartholomew, Henderson, and Dutton, 2001) has developed an insightful model of adult attachment styles. She describes four main styles based on the interactions of two dichotomies: high or low personal self-worth and high or low perceived worthiness of others. The styles are labeled and described as follows:

1. *Secure:* These adults have basic trust in themselves and others; they tend to be resilient, flexible, and adaptive; they are able to seek and receive support when stressed; they are also able to give support to others; they have a positive view of self but can admit weaknesses and needs; they are generally interdependent in relationships; they can be comfortable with both intimacy and autonomy. Key terms: *confident, good-natured, dependable,*

understanding (here and in the following descriptions, key terms are taken from Klohnen and John, 1998).

2. *Dismissive:* These adults possess high personal self-worth but perceive others as of low worth; they appear to have little anxiety about interpersonal relationships; they tend to avoid relationship commitments; they defend against attachment anxiety by lessening need for attachment so that they appear to be quite self-sufficient; however, dismissive individuals may become very anxious when their attachments are lost or threatened if they encounter failure in their defenses against feeling; they often pull away when partner seeks intimacy, especially withdrawing when others are stressed and needy; they treasure autonomy and self-reliance; they may be overly critical and controlling when helping partners; they are often perceived as cold and hostile by others; they do not use their partners as safe havens or secure bases (Fraley, Davis, and Shaver, 1998); they deny the value of close relationships; they may have limited and overidealized memories of childhood. Key terms: *independent, competent, rational, sarcastic.*
3. *Preoccupied:* These adults have low self-worth and perceive others as more worthy than themselves; they display high anxiety but low avoidance; they seek acceptance, safety, and validation from others; they frequently become enmeshed in earlier unresolved attachments; their need for autonomy may be compromised because of a more compelling need for security; they demand emotional contact but may never be satisfied because of their unrealistically high demands ("I scare people away; I want to be so close, all the time, and they get nervous." [Bartholomew et al., 2001]); Key terms: *expressive, dependent, needs approval, self-revealing.*
4. *Fearful:* These adults perceive both themselves and others as having low worth; they are high on both anxiety and avoidance; they desire acceptance but avoid intimacy because they fear and anticipate rejection ("I'm afraid I'll say something that ruins the relationship" [Bartholomew et al., 2001, p. 47]); they need others to validate self-worth; conscious fear of anticipated rejection. Key terms: *vulnerable, doubting, timid, distrusting.*

ANGER, ABUSIVENESS, AND ATTACHMENT STYLES

From an attachment perspective, "anger is triggered when there is a threat of separation and has the function . . . of ensuring that the attachment bond remains intact" (Holmes, 2001, p. xvii). Thus, anger has a positive function, serving to signal and underscore the protest stage of a separation crisis. Even episodes of domestic aggression may represent this kind of protest: "An assaulter's abusive episodes can be seen as an adult's version of protest when attachment needs are not satisfied" (Bartholomew, Henderson, and Dutton, 2001, p. 60).

Unfortunately, adults who possess the three relatively insecure attachment styles (especially preoccupied and fearful) may well have distorted, exaggerated, excessive, and misdirected attachment needs. These persons place unrealistic demands on their partners, wanting and needing far more than can reasonably be expected from another human being. They then become irate when those needs are not met. In essence, because they need their partners to make up for a lifetime of unsuccessful attachments, they create situations in which their intense separation rage is not resolved by reunion (Berman, Marcus, and Berman, 1994). Constantly fearing abandonment, these individuals ruminate over negative interactions, become hypervigilant and jealous, display high but inflexible self-disclosure, and see even their partner's normal withdrawals as evidence of abandonment (Dutton, 1998; Roberts and Noller, 1998), perhaps using violence to prevent the partner's withdrawal.

Relationship violence has been tied to specific attachment patterns. For example, both avoidance/dismissing and anxious/ambivalent attachment styles are associated with anger, shame, fear of negative evaluation, and pathological narcissism (Mikulincer and Florian, 1998). In addition, anxious/ambivalent partners often become excessively hostile and angry during conflict resolution discussions, perceive their partners more negatively, and become most angry and hostile when discussing a major problem (Rholes, Simpson, and Stevens, 1998). Fearful and preoccupied partners often have trouble leaving abusive relationships because of low self-worth that makes them think that violence against them is justified (Bartholomew, Henderson, and Dutton, 2001).

Bartholomew, Henderson, and Dutton (2001) have linked the perpetration of abuse with adult attachment styles for both genders as follows:

- *Dismissers:* Individuals high on dismissiveness tend to be distant and callous ("Get away from me"). When they become angry in relationships they are likely to leave rather than argue due to the deactivation of their attachment system.
- *Preoccupied and fearful:* The chronic anxiety about rejection and abandonment endured by these persons leads to high levels of negative affect and anger. In general, the attachment dynamics of abusers are similar for males and females, hetero- and homosexuals. *Preoccupied* individuals, whose excessive needs for support and reassurance are inevitably frustrated leading to increasingly demanding behavior, are especially likely to be both *perpetrators* and *recipients* of abuse for both men and women. However, while men who are *fearful* are also more likely to be *perpetrators* and *recipients* of abuse, women who are *fearful* are likely only to be *recipients of abuse.*
- The majority of the most severely abusive men studied by Bartholomew, Henderson, and Dutton (2001) were preoccupied or fearful. Furthermore, the more strongly preoccupied or fearful they were, the more severe the reported abusiveness.
- Regarding women who lived in abusive relationships, 53 percent were described as preoccupied and 35 percent as fearful. In addition, preoccupied women stayed in relationships longer and had more contact after leaving, presumably because of their combination of strong attachment anxiety and an approach orientation toward conflict.
- The attachment style interactions between partners are important to understand in abusive relationships:
    a. Two preoccupied individuals often become locked in highly volatile conflict.
    b. The combination of a fearful woman and a preoccupied man best predicted male unidirectional violence. This pairing best fit the stereotypical model of a battering male and victimized female.

c. However, the pairing of a preoccupied woman with a fearful man was also common in abusive relationships and predicted both the most severe abuse and the presence of a mutually abusive relationship.

Cowan and Cowan (2001) note that insecure men with secure women partners produced the most negative and volatile relationship pattern in their research. Perhaps the men in these relationships felt a need to overpower, shame, belittle, and humiliate their partners in an effort to gain power and control over a person they correctly perceived as having greater confidence and possibly competence than they.

Finally, ". . . the pairing of two insecure individuals may prove to be a highly volatile combination, especially if one partner is scared of abandonment and the other fears intimacy" (Roberts and Noller, 1998, p. 322). This statement describes the "chase and run" pattern often seen in couples therapy in which one partner, seeking intimacy, attempts to increase closeness, only to have the other partner, seeking autonomy, simultaneously attempt to increase the physical and psychological distance between them.

ROMANTIC JEALOUSY AND ATTACHMENT

Romantic jealousy may be defined as a felt need to guard and protect one's relationship partner against the threat of a real or imagined rival. Jealousy always involves a comparison between the self and another, the rival, with regard to how attractive both may be to an actual or potential partner. Jealousy should be distinguished from "envy," which represents a state in which one person wants to take away something that belongs to another person (wealth, status, competence, an attractive mate, etc.) or, if that is not possible, then at least wants the rival to lose that asset.

Jealousy exists on a continuum from *normal* (moderate in intensity, triggered by specific cues, may be an accurate sign of relationship distancing, seeks reassurance) to *excessive* (frequent, intense, minimal or no cues, needs repeated reassurance, causes relationship distancing) to *irrational* (delusional, no claim on the other person, paranoid projection). As Pittman (1989) notes, it is normal for someone to want to guard and protect his or her most valued objects and relationships. Pittman even describes a condition he labels "relationship drift" in which jealousy is triggered not by the partner's actual involvement in an affair but because of a gradual distancing between the partners. Thus, a moderate amount of jealousy, from an attachment perspective, reflects an acceptable response to a real signal that the partnership is or could be endangered. However, many individuals seek counseling because they receive too many danger signals, many of which are inaccurate, and then they react too strongly to them. These chronically jealous persons often become violent as they attempt desperately to keep their perceived rivals away from their all too vulnerable (in their eyes) partners.

Although men and women tend to become jealous with about the same frequency and intensity, men may be particularly sensitive to women's potential sexual infidelity while women may be particularly sensitive to men's potential emotional infidelity (Buss et al., 2001). However, this hypothesis is controversial and should be considered highly tentative at this writing.

The attachment model is particularly useful in describing and understanding some of the dynamics of jealous interactions. In particular, jealousy and attachment are similar in that both (1) function to maintain close relationships; (2) are triggered by the threat of separation from attachment figure; (3) involve a range of emotions including fear, anger, and sadness; and (4) reflect both the actual current relationship concerns and the individual's internal working models of relationship stability (Sharpsteen and Kirkpatrick, 1997). Note that jealousy episodes most closely parallel the protest stage of attachment separation in that anger is more present than sadness for most people. Anger represents a protest against the perceived injustice of the situation (Sharpsteen and Kirkpatrick, 1997).

Jealousy is particularly likely when an individual fears the loss of "formative attention," which is defined as "attention that sustains part of one's self-concept" (Parrot, 2001, p. 313). This threat may induce the jealous individual to treat people as if they were property ("You belong to me") or an extension of one's ego ("You are me") or believe that a relationship represents a total merger of personalities (an "us" without two "I"s). All of these beliefs turn the partner's normal distancing into a potentially devastating threat. The implicit message of the jealous person trying to protect these needs is "I am nothing without you. I can't live without you."

Relatively jealous persons often have generally poor self-concept. In particular, they may believe they suffer specific inadequacies in a major relationship area such as being a good provider or sexual partner. Because of these deficits, they do not feel like "keepers" so they anticipate rejection. Jealousy correlates with anxious/ambivalent attachment style (White and Mullen, 1989), with fearful attachment (Dutton, van Winkel, and Landout, 1997), to sensitivity to rejection (Leary, Koch, and Hechenbleikner, 2001) and to domestic abusiveness (Dutton, van Winkel, and Landout, 1997). *Secure* individuals score lowest on jealousy measures (Knobloch, Solomon, and Cruz, 2001) but are most likely to directly express their anger toward their partners. Meanwhile, avoiders are more likely to turn their anger toward the rivals, while anxious individuals are more likely to suppress their anger rather than confront their partners (Sharpsteen and Kirkpatrick, 1997).

Jealous individuals may sense, perhaps correctly, that their partners are far less committed to the relationship than they are. Of course, they may even correctly speculate that a partner is having an affair with a rival. In addition, excessively jealous persons frequently can detail a history of past betrayals (by past or present partners, as a witness to parental infidelity, and including their memories of their own lapses), which have increased felt insecurity, preoccupation, and fearfulness.

CASE STUDY: EXCERPTS FROM AN INTERVIEW WITH A JEALOUS MAN

Saul S, age thirty-two, is an electrician with whom I tape-recorded four hours of directed conversation centering on his history of violent jealous outbursts. These episodes occurred in a string of dating and marital relationships that began with his first major relationship at age sixteen. These bouts of jealousy have continued, though in diminished form, through his recovery from chemical dependency and despite years of therapy. Clearly, Saul's jealousy is strongly affected by attachment considerations. As with many excessively jealous individuals, he demonstrates in his statements that his attachment style is a mixture of preoccupation and fearfulness. His core insecurity about relationships developed as he grew up in a chaotic household that included spouse battering, infidelity, alcoholism, and marital separations. It was then enhanced by his experiences with dating partners, the first two of whom were "unfaithful" to him. Here are some attachment-related excerpts from that conversation:

- *Becoming jealous:* "I feel threatened by other people talking or being with somebody I care about and that affects my self-worth. . . . I guess it's fear, just being afraid that they [his partners] may choose to have interest in someone else . . ."
- *The feelings that accompany jealous episodes:* "I would become tense, nervous, fearful. I always get angry."
- *Fearfulness:* "That I won't measure up to their expectations, whatever they may be. I don't know if I fit in with what they want." [Finish this sentence] "The worst thing that my partner could do to me is . . . not pay attention to me."
- *The initiation of a jealous episode:* "I start out angry and demand answers. How do you feel about me? Do you care about me? Why do you do what you do? Would you do that if you cared about me?"
- *The purpose of a jealous outburst:* "It's like I'm forcing the other person to tell me they care about me. They do love me."
- *A typical angry episode:* "Yelling and screaming, at one time I threw a coffee table through the window. Pay attention to me or I'm throwing this through the window."
- *The costs of Saul's anger:* "A lot of the time I end up pushing people away because I get angry with them. And then that seems to cause it to get worse because then I feel I don't fit in with their plans . . ."
- *The damage to the relationship because of Saul's jealousy and insecurity:* "She would tell me she loves me but I couldn't grasp it because I felt something was missing. But after a while she didn't even want to say she loved me. . . . I was pushing her away."
- *How Saul's relationships have ended:* "The first one I went to jail; the second one I went to jail; the third one I went to jail. I would rather have them take me out of there than to have to leave on my own. It doesn't matter that you called the police because I'm not going to leave because of that. Therefore, you're not going to win."
- *Insecurity and defensive anger:* "I feel I have a poor sense of self-esteem. It's just there. But I hate hearing them tell me I'm insecure. I would actually become angry with them and say how can you say I'm too insecure? How dare you?"
- *Preoccupied attachment style:* "I feel I need acceptance from the other person. That I need to feel okay with myself. I need them to tell me I'm okay, that things will be fine, some reassurance. It's like you owe this to me."
- *Fearful attachment style:* "I choose not to have many friends because the less I expose myself to other people the less I feel they would really know who I am or a chance of being rejected by others. . . . I'm always suspicious. I expect my partner to try to hurt me and I guard against it."

- *Developing distrust after Saul's girlfriend cheated on him:* "I became very distrustful, wanting to know where she was going, who she was going to see, if she was going to a girlfriend's house or what. I just always wanted to know what was going on."
- *The cost of getting all the attention Saul allegedly seeks:* "I have had that happen and actually I didn't care for it much. It was nice for a while but then it got old." [Saul actually has a need for autonomy even though that need is usually subordinated to his need for attention.]
- *Finding a sense of safety in Saul's most recent relationship:* "I just felt good to be around her. I would be happy, content. Felt like I belonged and I still felt okay when she was gone but she wasn't."
- *Getting past the core insecurity: [Finish this sentence]* "The best thing your partner could do for you is . . . to pay attention to me but I don't know if that's really the right way to say it. Maybe interact, communicate with each other, be supportive of each other."

Notice, in these last two excerpts, that Saul has indeed made significant progress in his quest to become less jealous and insecure. First, he has developed an improved ability to feel that he belongs with another person while retaining a sense of personal autonomy, a combination that better fits the concept of secure attachment than either preoccupied or fearful. Second, Saul still wants his partner to pay a great deal of attention to him but at the same time he talks about being mutually supportive, another sign of increasing security.

Attachment Theory-Related Treatment Strategies for Romantic Jealousy Concerns

White and Mullen (1989), in their excellent description of jealousy, mention several coping strategies individuals utilize to address their jealousy. These tactics include denying the problem, seeking to improve the relationship, trying to interfere with or punish the partner's actions, developing alternatives (meeting new people), derogation of the partner ("She's no good anyhow"), introspection ("What have I done?"), and demanding commitment by the partner. Some of these strategies, especially seeking to improve the relationship and introspection, might move the jealous person toward security and away from preoccupation and fearfulness. Others, including derogation of the partner and demanding commitment, might only increase their perceived insecurity.

Therapists can employ several approaches that help jealous clients address their attachment difficulties. First, they can help their clients articulate a goal, namely, to learn to feel like a "keeper" rather than someone their partners are likely to discard quickly. The analogy I utilize here is to ask the client to imagine that he or she is a seashell lying on the beach with hundreds of other shells. That person's partner or potential partner is walking down that beach, intent on selecting one and only one shell to take home and keep forever. That person reaches down and picks up the shell that represents the client, carefully examining it, seriously considering taking it home. The question is this: "Do you believe you are a keeper?" Some clients believe that they are keepers, meaning that they do indeed think a potential partner would find them attractive and want to select them. Others, especially fearful clients, doubt that they could be attractive enough to gain another person's attention, much less be a keeper. Highly jealous individuals, though, especially preoccupied ones, tend to believe that their potential partners might very well select them but that they will keep strolling down the beach, still looking for an even better shell, instead of heading home with their prize. Thus, they stay insecure no matter how long their partners are faithful. Setting the goal of learning to feel like a keeper, then, involves discussing with the client how that might happen with emphasis upon developing an internal sense of worthiness as opposed to attempting to keeping one's partner off the beach of life.

A jealous individual must learn to value his or her partner as a separate person, not as part of oneself. Highly jealous people tend to engulf their partners because they carry a flawed life formula: 0 + 1 = 2. They are the zero; the partner is the one; somehow partnership with that person is supposed to create a "two," filling in the client's tremendous sense of emptiness. That strategy might work for a while. Almost inevitably, though, it will fail because the client is all too aware of the reverse formula: 2 – 1 = 0. They believe they cannot live without the partner, that separation would once again reduce them to total emptiness. They need to recognize that the only relationship formula that really works is this: 1 + 1 = 2.

Many jealous clients have a long history of relationship betrayals that include infidelity, abandonment, and physical and sexual abuse. Therapists need to help clients process their personal history of betrayals and infidelities, focusing on the consequent loss of trust. This leads to the question of how realistically trustworthy is one's current partner. Sometimes that person is actually quite faithful, in which case the client must learn to distinguish that individual from everyone else. It is also important to challenge the jealous person to admit to his or her own infidelities; many jealous clients basically project their own sexual indiscretions onto their partners. They may also have concluded that since they cheated on their partners, certainly all their partners will at least want to cheat on them.

Another useful approach is to help clients identify their main attachment style, their partner's style, and how the two styles might interact in ways that foster jealousy and insecurity. This is particularly useful when clients have the ability to abstract beyond specific individual experiences to recognize patterns in their lives. It also helps clients realize that their engulfing behavior may be promoting increased dismissiveness from their partners, certainly not a desired effect.

Finally, the therapist may want to consider couples counseling if the relationship is stable and safe enough to do so. Mutual goals would include identifying attachment patterns, addressing any real problems with distancing in the relationship, what Pittman (1989) calls "relationship drift," discussing and deciding mutually acceptable third party contact guidelines for the relationship, and developing mutually acceptable patterns of reassurance when either partner becomes insecure or jealous.

The partners of excessively jealous persons may be seen independently as well. If so they should be informed that (1) excessive jealousy is not a sign of love so much as a sign of insecurity and possessiveness; (2) they should not allow the excessively jealous partner to control their lives by limiting their activities and relationships; (3) they should quit trying to "prove" their innocence in situations where they are unjustly accused as opposed to simply declaring that they refuse to be continually interrogated.

ADULTS WITH ATTACHMENT CONCERNS: GENERAL THERAPEUTIC CONSIDERATIONS

Therapy in the area of anger management can often be highly confrontational as clients, especially those who have a history of domestic aggression, are challenged to break through their denial and minimization defenses and accept responsibility for their actions. Although such confrontational tactics may be needed occasionally, they seldom increase the client's felt sense of safety or security. However, individuals with significant attachment deficits, especially men and women with preoccupied and fearful attachment styles, do need a sense of safety to promote personal healing, lessening of protest-related violence, and improved communication skills. For this reason the ideal therapeutic role of the attachment-oriented therapist is to help the client "contemplate and indeed re-experience his or her life story within a safe and healing context, with an emotionally available and sensitive other who gives new meaning and shape to life events and the patient's sense of self and relationship" (Slade, 1999, p. 586).

Bowlby (in Sperling and Lyons, 1994, and in Clulow, 2001) described five main roles of the therapist:

1. To provide a secure base for personal exploration
2. To encourage clients to consider how they engage in relationships and their expectations with significant figures (their working models)
3. To encourage examination of the relationship with the therapist as that relationship reveals information about the client's models
4. To foster recognition of how early parental expectations and experiences affect current perceptions and expectations
5. To enable the client to recognize that these models may or may not be appropriate in the present and future and to encourage the development of new, more autonomous models

Another difference between attachment-focused therapy and traditional anger management education and treatment is that couples work is more strongly encouraged in attachment counseling. The rationale for this emphasis is that each couple's unique pattern of anger or aggression is best addressed through mutual engagement. Couples can be helped to break through their attachment difficulties by (1) identifying problematic cycles that maintain attachment insecurity and marital distress; (2) promoting client identification of disowned attachment needs and aspects of self; and (3) fostering moments when one person can express vulnerability and attachment needs while the other person responds appropriately (Johnson and Sims, 2000). A couples therapy scenario is described later in this chapter. With regard to intimate bonds, the overall aim of psychotherapy is to help the patient find a balance between attachment and detachment (Holmes, 1996).

Creating a *safe haven* is critically important during attachment work, regardless of whether the counseling is individually, couples, family, or group oriented. This goal can be facilitated, for example, by thoroughly discussing confidentiality guarantees, disallowing physical and verbal aggression such as shaming or blaming others within the session, and by placing a strong emphasis on increasing each person's sense of safety in relationships (both within and outside of counseling sessions). Counselors should be alert for small signs of client fearfulness (hesitations, topic switching, etc.) as cues to discuss the issue of the client's sense of safety within and outside of therapy. In couples work the therapist must reach a clear understanding that couples therapy may (at the discretion of the counselor) be curtailed if violence occurs between partners inside or outside of counseling sessions. In addition, couples should be warned against using materials shared in couples counseling against each other in private or public situations. The counselor should also regularly watch and listen for any signs that either partner is feeling ganged up on, since failure to do so will usually result in that person dropping out of treatment.

Another therapeutic goal is to create a *secure base* for exploration. One way to do this is to gently push clients outside of their comfort range. For example, this may be done by responding in a noncomplementary fashion to the client's customary interpersonal strategies. Thus, dismissive clients need to be challenged to express more fully their feelings while clients with more "hyperactive" tendencies need more to be encouraged to stay calm (Dozier and Tyrell, 1998). Another useful approach, when asked for specific advice ("What can I do?"), is to give a range of specific suggestions graded by felt riskiness to the clients so they can choose which ones they want to try. Also, suggestions for change can be offered tentatively: "What do you think might happen if you were to do [this] instead of [that] the next time that happens?"

Another aspect of attachment-focused therapy is helping clients discover their *working models* of intimate connection. One way to do this is by showing them the following four brief paragraphs described by Brennan, Clark, and Shaver (1998) and asking them with which they most identify:

1. "It is easy for me to become emotionally close to others. I am comfortable depending on others and having others depend on me. I don't worry about being alone or having others not accept me."
2. "I am comfortable without close emotional relationships. It is very important to me to feel independent and self-sufficient, and I prefer not to depend on others or have others depend on me."
3. "I want to be completely emotionally intimate with others, but I often find that others are reluctant to get as close as I would like. I am uncomfortable being without close relationships, but I sometimes worry that others don't value me as much as I value them."
4. "I am uncomfortable getting close to others. I want emotionally close relationships, but I find it difficult to trust others completely, or to depend on them. I worry that I will be hurt if I allow myself to become too close to others."

These four paragraphs describe in order secure, dismissive, preoccupied, and fearful attachment styles (see Table 5.1).

I have developed a more detailed set of descriptions of the four attachment styles. Clients often state, when viewing these descriptions, that they see themselves partly in two or more of the styles and that they recognize themselves as acting differently with regard to these styles with different individuals or at different times in their lives. These remarks are useful in helping clients realize that attachment styles are not rigid and deterministic and that they partly reflect the unique aspects of each relationship. The italicized sentence at the bottom of each section describes the client's family-of-origin situation whereas the other statements in each section relate to the client's more immediate past and present relationships.

Another likely task of the attachment-informed therapist is to help clients relate their attachment styles to experiences within their families of origin and/or past or current adult relationships. Some key

TABLE 5.1. Adult Attachment Styles

Attachment Style	Client Characteristics
Secure	I feel loved and loving. My family feels like a safe place to me. I trust people close to me. I am usually comfortable when alone. I am usually comfortable with others. *Growing up, I could usually count on my parents for comfort when I needed it.*
Dismissive	I value independence a lot, even in close relationships. I don't much want people to depend on me and I don't want to depend on others. I get uncomfortable around people who are very emotional or really needy. People should be able to stand on their own two feet. *Growing up, I learned my parents would seldom or never take care of my needs.*
Preoccupied	I worry a lot about what others think of me. I expect to be rejected or abandoned by the people I love. I give a lot to others but often think that people don't give back much to me. I seem to want more closeness than people are willing to give to me. *Growing up, I had to work hard to gain my parents' emotional support.*
Fearful	I don't believe I'm worth loving. I don't trust others very much. I want to be deeply loved but doubt it will ever happen. Sometimes I feel I can't count on anybody, including myself. *Growing up, I never knew what to expect in my family. Sometimes my needs might be met, other times ignored, and sometimes punished.*

questions could be asked regarding the theme of loss and abandonment:

> Do you remember how you handled situations in which your parents left you?
> Did you get angry? Feel scared? Feel hurt? Feel little or nothing at all?
> Can you give me a few examples?

With regard to the client's specific relationship with each parental figure these questions would be helpful:

> When you were growing up, what attachment style best describes the relationship you had with your mother? With your father? With other important caregivers?
> Can you give me examples of why you say that?

Here is another set of questions that connect the client's past with the present:

> How do you think growing up that way has affected your adult relationships? Your sense of safety and trust in relationships? Your ability to depend on others and to be dependable? Your ability to give and receive love?

Next, clients can be queried about how their adolescent and adult friendship and dating relationships have modified their attachment styles:

> How have past adolescent or adult relationships affected your attachment style?
> Have they helped you become more secure? Less secure? In what ways?

It might be important to inquire about how clients play out their own parenting roles:

> In terms of parenting styles, how much are you like your mother? Your father?
> How do you want to be like them?

How do you want to be different?
Can you give some examples of how you have chosen to act differently than your mother or father in this area?

These questions help clients connect their own attachment history to their current parenting behavior while also implying that they have the ability to modify the lessons they learned as they relate to their own children.

Finally, a last set of questions returns the client fully to the present:

How is your current relationship affecting your attachment style?
Is it helping you become more secure? Less secure? In what ways?

These questions acknowledge that each close relationship has the potential to challenge and alter a person's attachment style. Successful relationships that allow the fulfillment of attachment needs gradually help clients feel more secure overall, while difficult relationships in which attachment needs are frustrated move individuals toward dismissive, preoccupied, and fearful states.

Therapy often involves helping clients expand their range of choices. In the area of attachment this concept sometimes translates into helping clients who are locked into one attachment style become more flexible. For example, dismissive clients, who basically shy away from intimate relationships, should be actively encouraged to move closer to others. One way to do so is to maintain a focus on feelings during discussions; another possibility is empathy training that would enhance the client's involvement with and curiosity about others. More abstract, dismissive clients will benefit from learning to distinguish between not having needs for intimacy and dependency versus defending against those needs with a veneer of self-sufficiency, and by suggesting the concept of "interdependence" to help dismissive individuals realize they can maintain independence while developing their capacity for intimacy.

Preoccupied clients may need to work in the areas of self-esteem and shame to gradually raise their sense of self-worth and self-respect. Simultaneously, they will need assistance to recognize that their fears of aloneness and abandonment are based on the belief that they are less worthy or lovable than their partners. The therapist must discourage desperation efforts by the preoccupied client to force others to demonstrate their love, caring, and interest in them (but do get them to discuss how their repeated efforts occasionally pay off for them since they have developed a powerful reward system based on random and irregular rewards). They should also be encouraged to move toward autonomy, for instance by giving them assignments to do things alone that they would normally do with others.

Flexibility within intimate relationships is particularly difficult for fearful clients since their distrust of others is so deeply established. For this reason it is vital to focus on the theme of trust: how trust has been broken in the past, their negative belief systems ("Nobody can be trusted, especially . . ."), and the possibility of developing trust and challenging negative belief systems in current or future relationships. Therapists should help fearful clients set goals both for autonomy and closeness since they are deficient in both areas, while encouraging self-esteem and shame work to gradually raise the client's self-worth and self-respect. Last, fearful clients need to be encouraged to become more visible in their relationships, which means regularly stating their wants, needs, and opinions even though doing so will make them more vulnerable to attack and rejection.

IDENTIFYING AND TREATING ANGER PATTERNS AND LOSSES IN CLOSE RELATIONSHIPS BASED ON ATTACHMENT STYLES

Now that some general therapy goals and processes related to attachment theory have been described, it is possible to make more specifically comment on how this model can be utilized with angry clients. These ideas have been organized around the four attachment styles as if any one individual possessed only one such style. Please bear in mind, though, that few persons identify with only one style.

Secure Attachment Style and Anger

In theory, anger will usually be associated with realistic threats to connection for clients who are basically secure. Furthermore, their anger will be proportional to the actual level of threat, serving as a signal of protest against actual or potential loss ("I don't like it when you stay out so late every night. We don't have any time with each other anymore."). Presumably their anger will soon cease after the concern has been relieved and the relationship rupture has been repaired. Consequently, the treatment focus will be to encourage individual exploration and couple discussion of realistic threats. Anger should be considered a bid for renewed contact and closeness by a client who senses that his or her partner has become so distant that the relationship itself is endangered.

Dismissive Attachment Style and Anger

The anger of dismissive individuals frequently arises whenever a relationship partner attempts to lessen the physical, emotional, or psychological distance between them. The felt threat is to the person's autonomy and the immediate reaction is to push people away with anger, especially when the ability to distance or escape appears blocked (as when the partner walks in front of the television set and demands attention). Anger often takes the form of criticism and sarcasm as befits the dismissive person's stance of superiority and the reality that constant criticism is a very effective way to drive people away. Indeed, the first reaction of a dismissive individual to a partner's actual departure may be relief as the pressure to become more intimate lessens. However, dismissive individuals may occasionally become angry and jealous when their partners actually do leave as an unanticipated abandonment crisis develops. This abandonment crisis is usually described with comments such as "I didn't know she meant so much to me until she left. I know I neglected her before but I swear I'll pay attention to her from now on if she'll only come back to me" but also as "How dare she leave me after all I've done for her? She's going to regret this."

The treatment focus with angry dismissive persons centers on explaining their anger as a defensive reaction not so much to the partner's desire for closeness but to the client's own fear of vulnerability, dependency, and intimacy. These clients should be invited to explore closeness with their partners. However, care must be taken to ensure that they can maintain a sense of personal control during this exploration, lest they feel totally overwhelmed and withdraw.

Preoccupied Attachment Style and Anger

Preoccupation may arise even in normally secure adults in the face of significant distancing that a partner denies ("I don't know why you think I'm having an affair; you're just imagining things") or sometimes as a result of a partner's gradual distancing (the "relationship drift" described by Frank Pittman, 1989) that is either unacknowledged or uncorrected. However, certain individuals are chronically preoccupied, consumed by an internal working model that tells them they are not good enough to keep the person they love. Anger may easily arise with these individuals when the preoccupied partner senses the desire of his or her partner to achieve distance, even for short periods of time. This anger serves as a protest against abandonment but often becomes confused with abandonments or rejections from the family of origin, previous adult relationships, and past interactions with that partner. Anger may also arise when the preoccupied person fails to convince a partner to keep getting closer, since staying at the same emotional distance can be as unsatisfying and threatening as if the partner were actually leaving. Of course, actual rejections and abandonments may be the cause for very angry attacks as the preoccupied person deals with tremendous feelings of rejection while reliving past rejections within the new one. Finally, and paradoxically, a partner's actual attempts at closeness may be angrily rejected as not being good enough since no one act of intimacy can make up for a lifetime of felt rejection.

The treatment focus with preoccupied clients revolves around explaining their strong anger as an often-exaggerated form of protest against separation. Such clients will need help learning how to take in whatever caring, love, and attention is available in the environment while grieving and letting go of past attachment disappointments.

Fearful Attachment Style and Anger

Fearful clients are often angry concerning the theme of distrust: "I know they will betray me. They always do." This distrust may be expressed very actively, perhaps in the form of jealous accusations, but it may also appear in the form of passive aggression, as perfectly expressed by a client of mine who described how he abruptly fled a potentially significant relationship: "We started to get close so one day I just left town without telling her I was going and never talked to her again." In addition, anger may easily be turned against the self because of the fearful person's conviction that protest against relationship injustices are futile. Finally, Dutton notes that some fearful men also experience seething rage about past failures to meet their dependency needs: "Fearful men experience extreme chronic anger as an inevitable byproduct of attachment" (Dutton, 1998, p. 138).

The treatment focus with fearful clients relates their anger to their essential position of distrust. They must learn to challenge their mistaken belief that every potential relationship partner will take advantage of their neediness and vulnerability. Since they also feel relatively helpless about changing their fate in life (to be loveless) it is equally important to emphasize and teach assertiveness skills.

COUPLES COUNSELING FROM AN ATTACHMENT PERSPECTIVE WITH PHYSICALLY VIOLENT COUPLES

Is it ever possible and advisable to undertake couples counseling with partners in which there is an active history of physical violence? The following lists present reasons to be cautious (cons) and reasons to proceed (pros) with couples counseling in this situation:

Cons:

- Couples counseling is inconsistent with the patriarchal domination model of domestic abuse that emphasizes on one hand *individual responsibility* of the male ("No matter what your partner says or does you are fully and solely responsible for your aggression") and *cultural influence* on the other (men beat women because they are explicitly and implicitly encouraged to do so in a society that advocates male supremacy, power, and control).
- Couples counseling might actually increase the risk for violence.
- Some violent individuals may view counseling as an opportunity to convince the therapist that the partner is to blame and try to avoid personal responsibility for their actions.
- Some individuals have severe pathologies (antisocial personality disorder, paranoia, etc.) that might make couples counseling untenable.

- Partners of domestically violent individuals may feel too intimidated to speak truthfully during couples sessions.
- Clients may believe that agreeing to couples counseling means that the therapist believes or promotes the idea that they must stay in the relationship at all costs.

Pros:

- Couples counseling is consistent with systems therapy, communications models, and attachment theory perspectives.
- Both parties may specifically request and desire couples counseling.
- One or both partners may have already worked at the individual level and made significant progress in minimizing their anger and aggressive tendencies.
- The level of violence is fairly infrequent and low level (no or minor injuries).
- Neither partner demonstrates any tendency to leave the relationship even when repeatedly advised to do so.
- Hostile feelings, angry communications, and aggressive behaviors have infiltrated the couple and/or the family system to the point that a mutual effort is necessary to reduce them.
- "Nothing-to-lose" couples, whose interactions have become so dangerous that not attempting couples counseling leaves the survival of one or both partners only to chance, may benefit.

If couples counseling is to be considered seriously when there is a history of domestic violence, two serious objections must be answered: (1) that couples counseling may shift responsibility from the perpetrator of the violence onto the partner, and (2) that couples counseling might increase the risk for violence.

The first objection is related to the strong and appropriate movement in the United States over the last twenty years to protect women from their battering male partners. Mandatory arrest, the creation of numerous anger management groups specifically for male domestic abusers, and a strong emphasis upon women's right to safety in their own homes reflect this deep commitment. Women's rights advocates have noted that all too often the female victims of abuse have been told by church personnel, family members, counselors, and even the courts that they are responsible for the violence against them. "None of this would be happening if you were just a better wife" are words that all too many women still hear today. However, both the male aggressor and the female survivor are now likely to be told almost the diametrically opposite statement: "No matter what the provocation, no matter what the woman's behavior (up to and including her violence, which is characteristically justified as defensive in nature), it is solely and completely the man's responsibility." Certainly this makes sense from the perspective that it is the man's fist that is raised and the man's voice that shouts invective at his partner. This powerful confrontation also helps break through the denial pattern of many batterers who would gladly blame their partners for their problems. Couples counseling, then, is contraindicated from this perspective since the violence that occurs is solely the responsibility of the man.

There is a counterargument though. Systems theory in general, and attachment theory more secifically, posits that a marital relationship is an interactive system in which each person's behavior is highly influenced by that of the other person in an unending series of feedback mechanisms. Marital discord and even domestic violence is not an exception to this process. Indeed, "From an attachment perspective the underlying cause of marital distress is the lack of accessibility and responsiveness of at least one partner and the problematic ways in which the partners deal with their insecurities" (Johnson and Sims, 2000, p. 172) and "an assaulter's abusive episodes can be seen as an adult's version of protest when attachment needs are not satisfied" (Bartholomew, Henderson, and Dutton, 2001, p. 60) by his or her partner. The attachment model implies, furthermore, that these attachment insecurities are unique to each couple and therefore not entirely within the province of the male. A particularly strong argument for this perspective is expressed by Bartholomew et al. (2001): "Contrary to the dominant feminist perspective . . . we believe that relationship abuse is best understood within a dyadic or relationship context."

A reasonable "both/and" approach that utilizes these apparently contradictory theoretical approaches is certainly possible. First, strong emphasis must be placed upon insisting that all perpetrators of domestic aggression take full responsibility for their actions. No "She (or he) made me do it" excuses can be accepted no matter what the specific treatment modality. Second, couples can be seen together to help them work out how they can maximize threat-reducing and safety-enhancing behaviors by both parties. Essentially the goal is to help violent individuals arrive at this thought: "I am fully responsible for everything I say and do, especially my acts of aggression. I must make a commitment to cease being violent no matter what my partner says and does. I will meet in counseling with my partner to help us both learn how to make our relationship as safe, caring, and loving as possible." These statements are applicable for both genders so that female-initiated violence and same-sex aggression can be addressed in addition to male-initiated violence.

I often utilize a simple diagram to help clients understand this double-edged concept. Three interlocking circles represent the relationship, the ones on the sides labeled "me" and "you" (or first names can be used) and the center circle labeled "us." Each person is asked to take complete responsibility for the "me" circle rather than pointing fingers at the other. I try to help clients understand that casting blame is useless in the center circle. Instead, the two partners must learn together to make what goes on in that circle feel mutually safe, respectful, caring, and loving.

The second objection, that couples counseling might actually increase the danger of physical aggression between the partners, must be taken seriously. Certainly learning from a client that he or she was accosted "because of what you told the counselor" or was verbally attacked by someone using the information disclosed in therapy is a terrible, hope-shattering experience for client and therapist. Furthermore, clients conceivably could take a therapist to court for providing couples counseling that goes badly in this manner. For both of these reasons counselors should think very carefully before engaging in couples work with physically abusive or abused persons. The "default option" should be individual counseling for each partner unless and until clear reasons justify couples work.

What might these reasons be? The first reason is the simplest: the couple has asked for this kind of counseling. Each partner, whether abuser, perpetrator, or both, expressly states that he or she desires couples counseling and gives specific reasons for this request. Given that it is made without coercion (and this needs to be checked carefully by discussing the matter in private with each person), it would seem arrogant for the therapist categorically to deny this request. It is more reasonable to consider each request carefully, discussing with the individual or pair the pros and cons of couples counseling before deciding immediate or deferred mutual counseling or a clear decision to avoid that venue.

A second reason for undertaking couples therapy occurs when the aggressor(s) in the relationship has worked diligently at the individual level, taking full responsibility for his or her actions and strongly committing to nonviolence in the relationship. A new round of therapy, with that person's partner, may be quite appropriate so that the client can more fully make amends, gain improved awareness of the partner's needs, etc. Couples counseling in this setting could help restore trust and accelerate reconciliation if the couple has separated.

A third reason for couples work occurs when a couple has a long history of fairly low-level violence (such as pushing and threatening but not closed-hand punching) and neither partner appears to have any real intention of leaving the relationship. Given the low degree of danger, couples counseling may offer these persons a new way to address their issues.

Finally, and most controversially, there are the "little-to-lose" clients. These couples engage in strong unidirectional or mutual violence, to the point where they inflict serious harm such as broken bones, burns, etc. They frequently have a history of police intervention. They also usually have been urged repeatedly by family, friends, attorneys, clergy, criminal justice representatives, and professional counselors to leave the relationship before one or both of them are killed. They stay together, however, perhaps because their unresolved attachment needs make it impossible for them to part. Attempting a couples counseling here is a gamble. Things could go very wrong. However, not attempting couples counseling may be even worse, in effect eschewing utilizing a systems approach that might help save someone's life. Survival odds are a literal concern in this situation: is someone more or less likely to die because of couples therapy or because that kind of therapy was not pursued?

Five guidelines are helpful in directing attachment-focused couples work with violent couples:

1. Couples counseling must be accompanied by a strong commitment on the part of each partner to accept full responsibility for everything that individual says or does.

2. The therapist reserves the right to curtail couples counseling temporarily or permanently if counseling is apparently becoming too dangerous or is ineffective.
3. The first and most important goal is the creation of a place of mutual safety, a safe haven as free as possible from acts of physical and verbal aggression. This safe haven begins in the therapy session but must be extended to real life situations for it to be considered effective. The safe haven may develop gradually as the frequency, intensity, and level of injury of the incidents decrease.
4. As this safe haven develops the couple can better use their relationship as a secure base with which to establish mutual intimacy.
5. Specific attachment problems, such as the fear of abandonment of the preoccupied partner and the fear of intimacy of the dismissive person, should be addressed, challenged, and amended within the framework of the couple's unique relationship.

Differences exist between couples in which violence is primarily unidirectional, when only one partner physically assaults the other, and those in which both partners are regularly violent. With regard to unidirectional aggression, the difficult therapeutic task is to stand firmly against the physical aggression of the attacker while maintaining a stance of empathy for both partners. That means the psychological vulnerability and needs of both partners must be addressed, not just those of the apparent victim. However, the recipient of violence should be offered individual therapy sessions to ensure his or her freedom of speech and safety. That individual should probably receive individual counseling from a different therapist who can act as an advocate when necessary. Meanwhile, the physical aggressor may need extra time and special training in communication and empathy.

With regard to bidirectional domestic violence, one important effort must be to distinguish between a partner's defensive violence and truly mutual aggression; e.g., pushing someone back who has just hit you is defensive violence while striking out against someone for past insults or attacks is part of a mutual aggression pattern. This distinction may be difficult to make, especially when both parties claim that they strike only defensively. The counselor should study each episode of aggression carefully, free from any assumptions. Counselors should get clients to discuss which situations led to one person's aggression, the other partner's aggression, or to simultaneous aggression.

It is also necessary to recognize that the stronger person's aggression is more dangerous than the weaker person's. Practically, that usually means that a male's violence is more dangerous than that of a woman. However, some women are physically quite capable of inflicting serious bodily damage to their partners with their fists and, of course, all individuals can cause lethal damage when armed.

If both partners are angry, any children in the system are also likely to be angry and violent. Family work is addressed in the next chapter. An example from my own practice of working with a violent couple is given in the following case study.

CASE STUDY: COUPLES THERAPY WITH A MUTUALLY VIOLENT COUPLE

Perry, age forty, and Gayle, age thirty-five, have been married for eight years, the first marriage for each person. Both had exceedingly difficult childhoods. Perry is the survivor of incessant and severe physical abuse from his father, a man whom Perry hates and has refused contact with since early adulthood. Gayle's two older brothers abused her sexually, and she was abandoned at age eleven by her alcoholic mother. She traveled from group home to foster home to residential treatment center, always getting pulled out before she could feel secure. While Perry is primarily fearful on attachment measures, Gayle alternates between preoccupation and dismissiveness, from "I can't live without you" to "Who cares?" Perry works as a foreman in a cheese factory and Gayle works part-time in sales at a clothing store. They have no children by choice, saying that they would not want to raise a child because of what they went through as children.

I would give neither of these clients an axis II diagnosis, although Perry clearly has strong borderline personality traits. Neither person suffers from alcoholism or drug addiction. Gayle was treated for depression several years ago but is currently unmedicated and only slightly depressive. Perry can be highly anxious and appears to have experienced panic attacks in the past but has never been treated for anxiety. They each have IQs of approximately 115. Both are artistic and creative, a factor in their favor as they attempt to break through deeply conditioned patterns of mutually assaultive behavior.

Perry and Gayle began pummeling each other during courtship. At first it was mostly Perry doing the hitting, striking the first time when Gayle told him she wanted to spend a weekend with a group of girlfriends. Perry became frustrated because he was already becoming dependent upon Gayle's presence. "I wasn't jealous, just afraid of being alone," he remembered, a theme he would repeat throughout their marriage. He pushed Gayle down and grabbed her wrist to keep her from leaving, then stopped himself and let her up. Gayle was shaken but never considered breaking off the relationship. They courted successfully and married the next year in a civil ceremony attended only by friends.

Perry's aggression gradually worsened. He began having shame-rage episodes (Potter-Efron and Potter-Efron, 1995) in which he reacted suddenly and violently to Gayle's remarks that he considered excessively critical or humiliating. Gayle could indeed be highly critical, able to attack her husband at his weakest points. Sometimes she used her verbal facility defensively to counter his physical superiority, but at other times she seemed to initiate the aggression, striking quickly and decisively in unexpected moments. One time they were having intercourse when she told him, "You are the worst lover I've ever had." This remark greatly wounded Perry, a man with more than average doubts about his masculinity. He reacted angrily and violently, slapping Gayle. From then their sex life felt insecure and dangerous to both of them.

Several years into their marriage (neither could recall exactly when) Gayle began striking Perry. She would punch her hand into his chest, slap his face, pinch his arm, and throw small but heavy objects at him. Interestingly, they seldom both attacked at the same time. They seemingly took turns being physically aggressive but not by conscious agreement and certainly not by mutual choice. Neighbors called the police on two occasions several years apart. Gayle herself called 911 several times a year for temporary help and Perry did the same about once a year. These public accounts of their problems resulted in Perry twice attending court-ordered anger management programs, Gayle going through three rounds of therapy in which she was strongly advised to leave her husband each time, numerous restraining orders and separations, and, inevitably, a return to the marriage. When asked why they kept reconciling, all they could do was shrug and say that they loved each other and wanted to live together despite their problems.

Gayle and Perry contacted me specifically to ask for couples counseling with an anger management specialist. They explained that they had requested such service before but had been turned down repeatedly because of their mutual violence. After interviewing them separately and together, I agreed to meet with them together with the following goals: (1) to help this couple create a place of mutual safety, a shared safe haven in which neither person had to fear attack from the other; (2) to develop a greater mutual capacity for intimacy as they felt safer with each other (this was the "growing edge" of their relationship, made possible with the creation of a relatively secure base between them); (3) to help Perry curtail shame-rage episodes by identifying them within the context of couples work so that he could break the shame-rage connection by staying with his shameful feelings as they occurred; and (4) to help Gayle better understand and curtail her aggressive behavior, in particular words and actions that had the effect of driving her partner away.

During therapy we quickly developed a routine in which each session began with my reminding the couple that the primary goal was to create a place of mutual safety. The first few sessions went well and they reported an almost complete cessation of hostilities that none of us believed would last long. Then came the dreaded bad news: on the way home from the previous therapy session, Perry and Gayle had a physical altercation, resulting in two bruises on Gayle's arm and a three-day separation. Yet here they were. When I suggested that perhaps couples therapy was too dangerous to continue, Perry's response was that he still wanted to continue because even though he struck Gayle he had not hit her in the face as he had been doing recently. Gayle agreed, although she emphasized that she became terrified when he got violent. She noted that she had tried not to attack him verbally even during their confrontation. As for the three-day separation, they said that was commonplace in their relationship.

We decided to continue counseling. Gradually, Perry began recognizing the early signs of an impending shame-rage episode. He would then take a time-out during which he would address his shame issues. One particularly creative idea he had was to draw his shame whenever he felt put down. In effect he externalized his shame into the picture rather than casting it onto Gayle as he had been doing. Meanwhile, Gayle started to recognize that her fear of abandonment fueled her attacks. She needed help in experimenting with opportunities for closeness, at least once in counseling by having her gradually take literal single small steps in Perry's direction. She discovered that her sudden verbal and physical attacks usually occurred when Perry was being most caring and considerate, which actually threatened her more than his physical attacks. This work resulted in Perry becoming less preoccupied as he dealt better with his shame and Gayle becoming both less dismissive and fearful.

This couple is certainly improving. Nevertheless, the reality of treating Perry and Gayle is that they may never become totally violence free. Still, a good chance exists that they will have significantly fewer violent episodes, that they will do less damage to each other when the episodes occur, and that this alleviation of aggression will permit relationship growth so they can experience a richer and deeper intimacy.

SUMMARY

Couples counseling is a difficult and sometimes dangerous task when couples have a history of domestic violence. I have suggested in this chapter that attachment theory offers perspectives and guidelines for couples work. Knowledge of the basic principles of attachment theory, as described in this chapter, and the ability to make connections among the four main adult styles of attachment (secure, dismissive, preoccupied, and fearful) with someone's jealous, aggressive, and violent behavior may help therapists create a place of mutual safety first within the counseling situation and then within the relationship itself.

The next chapter considers the tasks of working with angry children, adolescents, and families.

Chapter 6

Working with Angry Children, Adolescents, and Families

INTRODUCTION

What makes a child or adolescent habitually angry or aggressive? The answer to this question is complex. Apparently, a confluence of risk factors work together, creating a situation in which aggressive behavior is overdetermined and overlearned, and turns children in this direction (Moeller, 2001). These risk factors include biological factors such as a genetic predisposition toward aggression and neurological underarousal that increases risk taking and stimulation seeking; family factors such as attachment difficulties, the presence of parental physical abuse, parental psychological problems including depression, antisocial behavior, and substance abuse; peer relationship difficulties including rejection by peers and affiliation with aggressive/antisocial peers; and such contextual factors as poverty, community violence, stressful life events, and access to weapons (Bloomquist and Schnell, 2002). Aggressive patterns tend to develop early in life and remain constant; children identified as hyperaggressive by age eight are likely to continue that kind of behavior into adulthood (Moeller, 2001). This is not an entirely passive or random experience. Once initially rewarded by aggression, children who develop strong antisocial behavior patterns tend actively to seek out peers and select environments that are conducive to their developing aggressive behaviors. They develop antisocial habits and motivations that take dominance over their prosocial skills and motivations even when they actually have these skills (Moeller, 2001). Since angry feelings, hostile thought patterns, and antisocial behaviors begin young and remain stable into adulthood, beginning treatment for these traits as early as possible makes sense. Such treatment should begin early, include family members if at all possible, and target children's developing thought patterns and overt behaviors (Moeller, 2001).

This chapter is divided into four main sections. The first segment deals with those factors that make it difficult for children and adolescents to contain their angry and aggressive impulses. The second describes selected treatment suggestions when working with angry children and adolescents. The third section provides a discussion of the characteristics of families that promote anger and aggression, however reluctantly. The fourth section looks at how these "angry families" can best be treated from a systems perspective, with the primary goal being that of replacing anger-increasing and aggression-provoking behaviors with more calming, positive, and prosocial interactions.

CHILD AND ADOLESCENT SUSCEPTIBILITY TO ANGER CONTROL PROBLEMS

The human brain can be considered a behavioral inhibitory mechanism (Strauch, 2003), designed at least partially to allow people to contain and control their impulses. Emotional expression is similarly inhibited by the brain. This inhibitory ability centers around the word "no," a word that parents use frequently even during infancy and increasingly thereafter. What begins as an external parental inhibition system ("No, I said don't do that") gradually develops into an internalized mechanism. This allows people both consciously and unconsciously to say in effect to themselves "No, I want to say or do something angry but I better not." Children, however, do not have fully developed internalized inhibitory systems. Nor do they always graciously accept external parental inhibition. Each and every "no" they hear creates stress and the possibility for protest in the child. Protests easily turn into tantrums as children quickly lose control over their reactions to frustration. These tantrums, in turn, are subject to more efforts at socialization as children are taught that they must contain their anger. Gradually, as the brain develops and particularly as the neocortex gains greater control over the limbic system, children and adolescents become more and more adept at controlling and containing their impulses. The expression of anger and the impulse toward aggression are two of the most important areas of escalating containment. However, even in adulthood this ability is never perfectly mastered. Realistically, then, any study of childhood and adolescent anger problems must take into account their relatively limited ability to manage anger. This is especially true for children but also applies to adolescents as they go through a transition period during which they gradually become more able to contain their angry impulses.

Five areas that contribute to the difficulty children and adolescents face in the area of anger management are as follows:

1. Incomplete affect modulation skills
2. Limited conceptualization ability
3. Inflexible and incomplete moral reasoning ability
4. Identity confusion
5. Attachment transition dilemmas

Incomplete Affect Modulation Skills

"Affect modulation" can be defined as the ability to contain physiological and psychological reactivity in the face of emotionally stimulating events. Affect modulation skills are not easily learned since they involve a tuning down of the emotional system at exactly the times when people are most activated by the threat of something bad or the possibility of something good occurring. Nevertheless, affect modulation is a necessary skill that must be mastered in order to thrive in a society, such as the United States, in which intense emotionality is looked upon with suspicion and emotional containment is seen as a sign of maturity (Stearns, 1994). Loss of control is considered in these societies to be shameful and childish, something to be discouraged.

"Flooding" is a key concept that describes what happens to children (Parens, 1987; Green, 1998) and even adults (Gottman, 1999) when they fail to contain their emotions. Physiologically, during flooding the body is overwhelmed by surges of adrenalin, increased heart rate, crying spells, etc. Cognitively, problem-solving skills become effectively impossible. The question "On a scale of one to ten, how serious is this situation?" would be answered with "It's a ten!"

even for situations that appear relatively trivial to adults. Behaviorally, flooded children strike out in rages against the people who are frustrating them at the moment.

Excessive flooding is associated with particularly explosive children (Green, 1998). These children may realize they should contain their emotions but they are simply unable to do so. For example, a nine-year-old boy I counseled for anger problems made this comment: "My teachers tell me I don't have to have a meltdown. They say it's my choice. But I can't stop it. Don't they know I wouldn't melt down if I could stop?"

The parents and caretakers of younger children should be educated about the nature of flooding. In particular, they need to realize that all children will flood from time to time. During those periods parents need to keep their children (and others) physically safe. Discussions of what happened, disciplinary measures, and problem-solving efforts must wait until the child has recovered since he or she will not be able to participate in them during flooding.

Although adolescents have generally far better ability to contain their anger than younger children, their quest for affect containment is also made more difficult in that they undergo many changes to their limbic system during adolescence, especially in their serotonin and dopamine levels, that may make them more emotional in general and in particular far more responsive to stress. Easily overwhelmed by these changes, adolescents may become less responsive to external expectations, demands, and rewards while becoming more susceptible to risk-taking events that increase their internal sense of reward while combating boredom (Steinberg, 2002).

Chronically aggressive children seem to have far more trouble containing their anger than other teens. Moeller (2001) notes that aggressive youths tend to have less empathy and predispositonal guilt but more chronic guilt and shame than less aggressive adolescents and, at the same time, they tend to have higher levels of self-distress and a greater focus on themselves. All of these factors decrease an individual's ability to contain their emotions or to moderate them to match the emotional level of their peers. Furthermore, at least some adolescents appear to have little understanding of their negative emotional states and equally little ability to express those states to others. Kostiuk and Fouts (2002) intently studied four conduct-disordered adolescent girls and described this pattern, adding that these adolescents had few successful strategies for regulating negative affect, were unable to describe an internal state of calmness or contentedness, and were able to reduce their immediate negative feelings only by throwing things, yelling, etc.

The therapeutic goal in this sphere is to help adolescents gain affective containment skills. This should be considered a long-term task that will not proceed in a linear fashion. Adolescent clients will likely need their therapists to appreciate their sense that they simply cannot quit feeling absolutely overwhelmed by onslaughts of emotion. Above all they will need the adults in their lives, including counselors, to stay calm when they cannot do so themselves, thus modeling a state that they cannot yet fully emulate. Basic skills such as taking self-imposed time-outs and relaxation training will also be quite helpful to adolescents as they struggle to control the uncontrollable.

Limited Conceptualization Ability

Children's cognitive capabilities, because of the relatively slow development of the frontal cortex, are quite limited as compared to adults. They think more concretely because of an inability to form abstractions; their sense of morality is preconventional (Kohlberg, in Steinberg, 2002), and their problem-solving ability is severely limited because of their inability to perceive more than one way to do things at a time. These limitations do not completely dissolve during adolescence. However, during the teenage years individuals do generally develop many cognitive skills, such as

1. a greater ability to maintain attention;
2. improved working memory capacity;
3. improved ability to utilize formal operational thinking;
4. increased self-monitoring skills;
5. improved planning, decision making, and goal setting;
6. a better social perspective and ability to understand how others perceive the individual (all above from Steinberg, 2002);
7. improved critical thinking skills (Keating and Sasse, 1996);
8. a greater capacity for empathy (Seiffge-Krenke, 1995); and
9. improved awareness of own limitations (Seiffge-Krenke, 1995).

In general these skills gradually increase throughout adolescence with no single "breakthrough" point.

Nevertheless, typical adolescents have by no means achieved adult levels of cognitive functioning. According to Elkind (Steinberg, 2002), adolescents tend to fail to differentiate between their cognitive interests and those of others. The result is that they create an imaginary audience that allegedly pays strict and continuous attention to the adolescent and a personal fable that makes them unique and special. Three results of this slow pace are that more primitive parts of the adolescent's brain are relatively more dominant, it is more difficult for adolescents to curtail impulsive urges in favor of longer-term benefits, and any effects of trauma on the adolescent brain will have more impact than they might on an adult. Keating and Sasse (1996) add that one half or more of adolescents fail to demonstrate critical thinking skills, which means they are relatively unable to utilize cognitive flexibility, reflective thinking, and executive thinking processes. Finally, Steinberg (2002) notes that adolescents use of their reasoning abilities is often strikingly erratic or self-serving. For example, adolescents might use sophisticated logic to attack ideas they disagree with but accept flimsy evidence to support their positions.

Cognitive development and chronic anger and aggression seem to have an inverse relationship with each other in that the presence of chronic anger and aggression in adolescents predicts that they will have relatively poorly developed cognitive skills as compared with nonaggressive peers their same age. Bloomquist and Schnell (2002) note that adolescents who display antisocial behavior do poorly on measures of executive functioning. They also write that during social interactions aggressive children fail to attend to social interactions, pay too much attention to others' aggressive cues, interpret others' benign behavior as having a hostile intent, generate fewer prosocial and more aggressive solutions to solve interpersonal problems, anticipate fewer consequences for their actions, and expect more positive outcomes from employing aggressive solutions to solve social problems than other children. All of these patterns are likely to continue into adolescence, the result being that relatively aggressive teens perceive the world differently, and in a far more hostile manner, than their peers. In particular, angry adolescents often harbor a "hostile attributional bias" that is triggered by ambiguous situations. This bias often leads angry children and adolescents to conclude wrongly that others harbor hostile intent toward them and therefore deserve to be attacked (Moeller, 2001).

The kind of anger that particularly aggressive youth display is not ephemeral but enduring. Researchers (Cornell, Peterson, and Richards, 1999) in one study, for instance, were able to successfully classify 66 percent of youths studied into high and low aggressiveness based solely on their trait anger scores. Trait anger is often associated with cynicism (Smith et al., 1998), denoted as a stable set of negative personal beliefs held independently from any particular anger-arousing event. A typical cynical thought is that "school is worthless, boring, and nothing is worth learning." Cynicism is a form of hostility, and Smith et al. (1998) found that youths with high hostility scores were twenty-two times more likely to experience multiple forms of school violence than were their less hostile peers.

Counselors will need to be patient as they teach cognitive anger management skills to adolescents. Praise the occasional examples of positive disputations of angry thoughts in the beginning, while emphasizing to teens that they are in the process of developing better skills in this area, rather than focusing on their frequent failures to think like adults. Examples should be kept immediate and concrete. For instance, although few adolescents can master the general concept of angry thought disputation, they may better be able to change one specific "hot thought" in one specific situation (even though they may later fail to use that same "cool thought" in what appears to be an almost identical situation). Chronic hostility and negativity can also be challenged, the earlier the better, although adolescents, having already developed the habit of pessimistic thinking for years, may be quite resistant to reinterpreting their environment and altering their worldview.

In summary, then, children and adolescents in general have more difficulty than adults in utilizing cognitive skills that help modulate anger and aggression, while already angry and aggressive youth are particularly impaired in this process.

Inflexible and Incomplete Moral Reasoning Ability

Moral reasoning is a process that develops slowly over many years, probably well into adulthood. Kohlberg (in Steinberg, 2002) argues that conventional moral reasoning only appears in late childhood or early adolescence while postconventional thinking, in which individuals can assess standard moral rules and decide for themselves upon a far-reaching personal moral code, does not develop until late adolescence or early adulthood (if at all). Furthermore, moral growth may not be a linear process. Eisenberg et al. (in Lerner, 1997) describes middle adolescence (ages fifteen to sixteen) as a time when many teens are so overwhelmed with personal distress reactions that they temporarily regress in their ability to take prosocial action. Adolescents do, however, quickly become aware that most moral standards are the product of subjective moral conventions that are subject to disagreement (Steinberg, 2002). They tend to think of these conventions as arbitrary and not necessarily worthy of their loyalty. Unfortunately, they are better at rejecting the value systems of others than developing their own; Steinberg (2002) reports that most individuals develop value autonomy, the ability to be guided by consistent values based upon abstract reasoning and general principles, around age eighteen to twenty. One result of the combination of this gap between the ability to question the values systems of others before obtaining a personal working value system is a negative approach to morality. For example, many teens are exceptionally adept at pointing out adult hypocrisy and moral failure, noticing even small breeches such as a parent preaching honesty but not putting a quarter in a parking meter, yet at the same time they would gladly bypass that same parking meter without themselves feeling that they are doing anything wrong.

Damon and Gregory (1997) argue that true moral development means more than simply accepting or embracing particular values. Instead, he believes that people gradually come to see themselves as individuals whose set of moral beliefs help provide an ideational core for their sense of identity. In other words they think "I am a moral person" rather than "I am a person with morals." Again, this is probably a gradual developmental process that reaches full bloom only in late adolescence or early adulthood.

Although adolescent prosocial behavior is predicted by the presence of internalized moral standards in childhood (Moeller, 2001), antisocial behavior does not necessarily indicate a simple absence of prosocial values. Instead, antisocial and hyperaggressive youth may embrace a set of unconventional and antisocial values (Hirschi, 1969). Therapists should not only attempt to help their adolescent clients accept and adopt conventional values but they must also be willing to dialogue with them about their loyalty to the actual values they maintain.

Identity Confusion

Erik Erickson (1968) established the concept that the main task of adolescence was the development of a coherent sense of identity. The failure to establish an identity resulted in identity diffusion, essentially an inability to answer the question "Who are you?" in any meaningful manner. Steinberg (2002) writes that the consolidation of a clear sense of identity, including such elements as an actual self, ideal self, and feared self, does not occur until very late adolescence and young adulthood (ages eighteen to twenty-one).

Adolescents face three problems in the establishment of identity. First, they may fail to consolidate a coherent sense of self. Second, adolescents may consolidate a sense of themselves too rapidly, foreclosing the experimentation and exploration process that allows them eventually to craft a personalized and unique sense of self. Third, they may accept a negative identity in which they define themselves as unlikable, troublesome, shameful, etc. One negative identity of particular interest here occurs when adolescents claim the identity of an angry and unhappy person. This identity process goes beyond the "Right now I feel miserable, angry, and irritable—but I'll be okay in a few minutes" feeling commonly experienced and expressed in adolescence. Instead, some teens truly believe that "I am an angry person who will never fit in with others. I'm destined to be unhappy all my life. Nobody will ever understand or care about me."

Interestingly, the development of autonomy, another hallmark of adolescence, is not associated with adolescent rebellion. Instead, those teens most self-governing are those who feel well-connected with their parents, continue to seek them out for advice, feel close to them, and have relatively few conflicts (Steinberg, 2002). Similarly, parents who adapt an authoritative posture toward their children (warm but demanding) are more likely to have children with relatively highly developed internalized moral standards than are parents who are more authoritarian, neglectful, or cold (Baumond in Moeller, 2001).

Self-esteem is one aspect of adolescent identity that fluctuates greatly during early adolescence (ages twelve to fourteen), remains volatile in immediate situations throughout adolescence, but then tends to stabilize over time as adolescents develop a more consistent self-esteem baseline (Steinberg, 2002). Although low self-esteem has been associated with anger and aggression, Moeller (2001) suggests that for many adolescents the anger and aggression itself precipitates the lowered self-esteem when the peers of angry individuals shun them because of their behavior. Moeller also notes that high self-esteem, especially in combination with the presence of grandiosity, narcissism, and dominance, may be associated with aggression, a pattern particularly described in children identified as bullies.

Therapists can best help adolescents deal with their identity issues by regularly discussing with them questions such as "Who are you?" and "Who do you want to be like?" Sometimes it is easier to begin with the negative: "Who don't you want to be like?" especially with young to mid-age adolescents, since they can more readily put their negative perceptions into words than their positive ones. However, if this approach is taken, therapists must remember to move on to the positive realm quickly lest the discussion become mired in negative attacks upon others.

With regard to self-esteem issues, adolescents need encouragement to develop domains in which they can truly earn praise for their competent performance. Blocks to such movement, such as excessive shame, need to be gently challenged but only so that the therapeutic endeavor becomes consistently oriented toward helping teens achieve internal and external validation.

Attachment Transition Dilemmas

The concept of attachment is thoroughly discussed in Chapter 5. More briefly, the nature of a child's bond with his or her primary caregivers is considered to be a critical predictor or how that child will relate to significant others throughout life. Specifically, attachment bonds affect proximity seeking, the development of a safe haven that allows the child a sense of safety, the creation of a secure base from which the child can explore the world, and the degree of anxiety and subsequent protest the child will endure upon separation from key figures (Allen and Land, 1999). Attachment behaviors tend to be consistent, persistent, and predictable. They can be divided into several patterns: secure, insecure-avoidant; insecure-ambivalent/resistant, and insecure-disorganized/disoriented (Bloomquist and Schnell, 2002). Whereas children with a secure attachment style tend to be relatively stable and socially adept, insecure children and adults are more prone to personal problems such as anxiety and depression but especially to relationship difficulties including jealousy and domestic abuse that represent heightened and distorted protests against separation.

Many childhood attachment crises are temporary. One example from my practice centered on an eight-year-old named Frankie whose anger problems developed only after his parents separated and his mother remarried and became pregnant. "Now I don't know where I belong!" he cried during therapy as he explained he was fearful that his mother and stepfather would favor the new baby. Frankie's protests took the form of kicking his mother, getting into fights at school with younger children, and sleep difficulties. Frankie's angry behavior dissipated once these fears were identified and both parents began spending more time with him while somewhat downplaying their excitement about the new member of the family.

Unfortunately, highly traumatized, abused, and neglected children can be so damaged that their attachment difficulties become permanent. Some of these children lose some or virtually all ability to relate to actual and potential attachment figures. These children suffer reactive attachment disorders (Greenberg, 1999) that severely limit their capacity to view others as anything but objects to be manipulated.

Adolescence represents a transition period in which children transfer some of their attachment needs to their peers instead of their parents. Again, secure children are best at this transition since they can more easily balance their needs for autonomy and attachment (Allen and Land, 1999) while harboring more of a "both/and" sense that they can both love their parents and their peers rather than thinking they must make an "either/or" choice between them.

Insecure attachment in adolescents is associated with many individual and relationship difficulties, in part because of their history of not getting their upset feelings assuaged and, consequently, developing a "fight or flight" stance toward life. Adolescent problems linked with insecure attachment include excessive withdrawal and avoidance, dysfunctional amounts of anger, the use of pressuring tactics with peers, hostility, and lack of social skills (Allen and Land, 1999), and with anger, irritability, and noncompliance (Bloomquist and Schnell, 2002). Dismissive adolescents are relatively more likely than secure adolescents to develop externalizing problems such as conduct disorders and drug abuse, while preoccupied adolescents are prone both to these concerns and to internalizing problems such as depression (Allen and Land, 1999).

When working with adolescents who have attachment insecurities, Crittenden (2000) recommends taking a strength approach in which the adolescents are informed that their behavior is intrinsically protective but has now become maladaptive. Crittenden notes that "The failure . . . to modify strategy in the face of changed conditions both causes maladaptation and, at heart, is the maladaptation" (p. 35). Crittenden stresses the need to identify these misfitting survival strategies and transform them in an ongoing manner. Hopefully these adolescents will gradually become better at recognizing strategies that are not working in their current situations, predicting and challenging old relationship errors, and eventually be better able to relate mutually and reciprocally with their peers.

SELECTED TREATMENT SUGGESTIONS WITH ANGRY CHILDREN AND ADOLESCENTS

The treatment of angry young children is a somewhat difficult task in that they may benefit most from play therapy and other specialized counseling skills. The following suggestions are designed for professionals who may see both an angry child and that child's parents. Most adolescents will gain from all the interventions described in Chapter 2. The following ideas are intended to supplement that material.

1. *Children often learn best to handle their anger through play.* Many anger control games are now available. One example is the Conflict Resolution Game (The Center for Applied Psychology, 1995), a board game in which players use anger management techniques as they compete. It is also possible to modify regular games.

For instance, I play the game *Sorry* with families but insist that whoever receives a knock-off card actually apologize about something he or she did to the person they are about to knock off before they can play that card. Beyond specific techniques, though, is the idea that anger management can be fun to learn rather than another boring adult-centered task.

2. *Help children visualize gaining control over their anger.* One analogy I utilize to help children (and their parents) understand the concept of flooding is to compare anger with hot water pouring into a sink. Naturally, the sink of a child is considerably smaller than that of an adult so it overflows much faster. Furthermore, children are less able to turn the hot water off or mix it with cool water. However, they will get better at those skills over time and their sinks will get bigger. Until then, though, they may need their parents' help from time to time in turning off the hot water.

3. *Help parents devise effective and consistent ways to handle tantrums and excessive demands.* Many parents inadvertently reinforce their children's tantrums by first trying to ignore them, then getting mad at them, and then giving in. Instead, parents need to follow a simple guideline: either give in to the child immediately or not at all. Of course, parents need to be flexible and no guideline is meant to be followed with absolute rigidity. Still, it is devastating when families become caught in endless cycles of screaming children, yelling parents, and eventual parental defeat.

4. *Target treatment to fit the adolescent's level of development and intensity of anger problems.* In order to be effective, the treatment of adolescents for anger problems should take into account their level of cognitive, emotional, and moral development. Table 6.1 differentiates between adolescents at three levels of development that are frequently correlated with the frequency and intensity of their anger and aggression difficulties.

Although the basic aspects of anger management apply to all of these adolescents, Level One adolescents will be able to benefit more from relatively abstract, metaphorical, and empathic training than those on Level Two or Three. Level Three adolescents, in particular, will generally do better with more concrete and individualized interventions. For example, although three groups of adolescents certainly need cognitive training, I am more likely to focus the attention of

TABLE 6.1. Three Levels of Anger Problems with Adolescents

Level	Category	Characteristics
One	Relatively high-functioning adolescents	Normal developmental level for age
		Generally stable home situation, although some family conflict probable
		Primarily or exclusively verbal aggression versus physical aggression
		Problems developed only during adolescence as opposed to being apparent in childhood
		Anger only a partial reason for being seen in professional settings as opposed to the primary concern
		Anger a problem but not ruling the lives of these adolescents
Two	Poorly functioning adolescents	Developmentally behind in cognitive areas
		History of impulse control problems in childhood and currently
		History of moderate aggression (e.g., often hits siblings, school altercations, etc.)
		Cynical, suspicious, hostile, negative mood
		May be diagnosed as oppositional defiant
		Anger never far away
Three	Out-of-control adolescents	Seriously aggressive by age eight (destructive attacks, cruelty to animals, etc.)
		Significant cognitive and emotional developmental lags
		Cannot seem to learn from mistakes
		Either in danger of or already institutionalized
		May be diagnosed as conduct disordered
		Anger ruling their lives

Level Three adolescents on one single "hot thought" at a time, helping them change that thought to a "cool thought." Meanwhile, Level One adolescents probably can also understand and utilize a more generalized and abstract form of intervention that teaches them regularly to dispute their anger-provoking thoughts with anger-reducing ones (Potter-Efron, 2001).

5. *Offer hope that the adolescent will gradually improve his or her ability to deal with anger.* Adolescents are in the process of rapidly gaining cognitive skills. Strauch (2003) writes that after a period of rapid neuron growth in early adolescence, a phase labeled "exuberance," adolescents quickly begin a process in which neurons are "pruned" in great numbers. This allows them to develop better control over their emotions and gain considerably improved problem-solving skills. Every effort should be made to point out to adolescents evidence of how they are indeed improving in these skills: "Sondra, you just turned down that anger invitation. Instead of getting furious with your brother you distracted him. I don't think you could have done that six months ago. Do you?" Placing emphasis on the adolescent's improving skills is vital, perhaps especially so with Level Two and Three teenagers who may have abandoned hope that they will ever improve.

6. *Address adolescent oppositionality.* Adolescent oppositionality is part fact and part myth in American society. Certainly many children moving through adolescence increase their autonomy without coming into great conflict with parents and authorities, especially those living with authoritative as opposed to authoritarian or overly permissive parents. However, other adolescents do indeed become more angry and conflict oriented at this time. Furthermore, teenagers most likely to be seen in counseling settings are those with the greatest displays of argumentativeness and defiance of authority.

The challenge in treating adolescent oppositionality is to dialogue with the adolescent without being seen as another adult trying to tell the teenager what to do. Five approaches may help accomplish this purpose:

1. *Avoid power battles:* Since adolescence is a period in which there is a tremendous internal push to develop autonomy, emphasizing the exact opposite during a discussion may easily heighten oppositionality. Although statements such as "I'm right and you're wrong," "Do it my way or else," and "I'm in control here," may be true, each of them increases divisiveness and places adolescents in a position of existential helplessness

and, frequently, impotent rage. If adults do need to step in and take charge, they should do so by giving simple and clear orders in a respectful manner.

2. *Emphasize the adolescent's power, control, and choices:* Angry adolescents often come to the attention of professional counselors during or after a display of impotent rage that centers on the theme of "You can't make me do that!" Unfortunately, they frequently waste their energy on ventilating their anger rather than developing and carrying out a useful course of action that might get them what they want. They need first to realize that "ventilation is not a plan" and then to be asked, "What do you plan to do with your anger?" Since angry adolescents often have difficulty thinking about more than one option at a time, they may need help in developing a list of possible actions that they could take.
3. *Provide face-saving options:* Adam had been suspended for two days from high school because he would not apologize to Mrs. Jensen, his study hall teacher, for swearing at her when she told him to quiet down. Adam then refused to go back even after the suspension was over. He confessed that he wanted to return to school but refused to do so as a matter of honor. However, with help Adam decided he could go to school long enough to talk directly with Mrs. Jensen. He could return to the school for a specific purpose, thus avoiding the humiliation of just coming back in total defeat. Fortunately, the conversation went well and he even said later, "She's okay. I like her now. She's the one teacher I trust."
4. *Listen to the adolescent's sense of outrage:* Teenagers are frequently outraged about situations in which they feel frustrated and disrespected. Furthermore, many adolescents are unable to understand the nuances of adult moral behavior and see adults as hypocritical. The result: the common adolescent complaint "That's not fair!" Counselors and therapists must listen carefully to these protests without taking either the side of the adolescent or that of the parent or authority figure. Professionals also need to guard against making condescending remarks such as "You'll understand all this better when you grow up" or "That's just the way the world is. Get used to it."

5. *Demonstrate respect and interest:* Even though many adolescents are poor at demonstrating respect for their elders, they still desire that behavior from adults. Counselors should remember to display respect at all times, even when the teenager they are speaking with appears disrespectful. In addition to basic respect, counselors should demonstrate a real interest in the adolescent's music, car, etc. By doing so therapists deliver a message that they are interested in the whole human being rather than only the disciplinary problems of that adolescent.

CHARACTERISTICS OF ANGRY FAMILIES

I define an angry family as one in which at least two individuals from two generations regularly display excessive anger and in which anger has become the dominant emotion displayed within family interactions. A simple saying clarifies this concept: "Angry people live in angry families." Of course this statement does not apply universally. Some individuals are uniquely angry within the family unit. However, in these cases anger does not typically dominate the ongoing life of the family unit. For example, a very angry and sulking adolescent may carry on that behavior for months even while the family as a whole has little anger. The situation is perhaps being defined as "Not to worry, he's just going through a stage." Even when one angry and violent person terrifies the others in the family, that dominance may be somewhat limited and not totally overwhelming: "Now kids, Dad's coming home so we have to get real serious. We'll finish the game after he leaves for the bar." I do not label a unit as an angry family when only the couple is engaging in mutual hostilities, if somehow the children are carrying on their lives without excessive anger.

The following list presents many of the patterns of chronically angry families:

1. One or more parents often become angry.
2. One or more children often become angry.
3. Anger drowns out other feelings.
4. Lots of anger and arguing is "normal" (expected).
5. Nobody listens until someone becomes angry.

6. Family members try to solve problems with anger.
7. Family members teach one another to be angry.
8. Negative, critical, and hostile feelings are common.
9. People hit, push, shove, pinch, slap, hold, and threaten one another.
10. Everybody blames one another.
11. Everybody is easily hurt (thin-skinned), hypervigilant, and defensive.

It is helpful when working with angry families to examine these characteristics in detail.

1. *One or more parents often become angry.* "It never fails. Just when things are starting to go well, we have another blowup. Fight, fight, fight, that's all we do around here." Frequently that anger emanates from one or more angry adults who set the tone for the entire family. These parents may have many reasons for being angry: bad jobs, financial stress, health concerns, marriage difficulties, etc. They may themselves have grown up in an angry home since angry people often come from angry families. Whatever the reasons, these angry adults set the tone for the family. They model anger for the children, in effect saying, "Go ahead and get angry. I do."

2. *One or more children often often angry.* Meanwhile, at least one child has become habitually angry, irritable, and actively oppositional. Sibling rivalries abound, more extreme and longer lasting than in less anger-dominated families. Day in and out, children are at one another's throats, often playing off parental divisions to gain advantage while developing mutual hostilities that will endure a lifetime.

3. *Anger drowns out other feelings.* Anger has become the dominant emotion in chronically angry families. Anger takes control of the family like a visitor who came to stay a few days but now refuses to leave. Tension is constant as almost everything that anyone says or does may precipitate a battle. No room is left for "softer" emotions and behaviors such as love, caring, and nurturance. Sadness and fear are banished because they are signs of weakness. Joy, happiness, and contentment also become rare events in chronically angry families and cause for immediate condemnation: "Hey, you, wipe that smile off your face right now. What do you think is so funny? Now get to

work." The choices of family members become limited to two states: they can be angry or neutral.

4. *Lots of anger and arguing is "normal" (expected).* Anger can become as much part of a family's routine as breakfast. Family members come to expect and predict anger. ("Don't tell me you're going to be good at Grandma's. I know better. You're going to get in trouble again like you always do.") Indeed, a day without anyone getting angry would be considered quite unusual. In essence anger has become the "default option" for these families, always turned to "on" unless consciously turned off.

5. *Nobody listens until someone becomes angry.* Furthermore, as family members become habituated to this pattern the frequency and intensity of the anger episodes will likely increase to offset the members' building tolerance toward anger. One adolescent I worked with succinctly described this pattern: "I used to pay attention to Mom when she yelled loud. Now I ignore her until she starts throwing things at me." Mere irritability builds toward verbal anger outbursts that gradually may be replaced by minor physical displays, which themselves are replaced by full-fledged rage episodes.

6. *Family members try to solve problems with anger.* Anger and aggression can be effective ways to get what you want and to deter others from undesired behavior. Learning this reality over time, some members of these chronically angry families intentionally work themselves into rages in order to get what they want. However, the benefits of such behavior tend to be short term and, unfortunately, the use of these bullying tactics forces out normal conflict management skills such as compromise and negotiation. Also, moral development for children in these families may be delayed at the preconventional level when the working model of the unit is "Might makes right." Angry families already have too much anger within them. They need to learn to reward one another for controlling their anger rather than exploding with it.

More generally, the members of angry families seem not to have learned a very important lesson about anger: although anger is an excellent signal that something is wrong, the mere display of anger does not solve any problems. Unfamiliar with studies that demonstrate the ill effects of excessive ventilation, they frequently state that letting off steam is both healthy and useful. What they mean is that sometimes they feel a little better after they explode, although the reality is that often they feel worse because they have lost control and because they have precipitated yet another in a seemingly endless series of family arguments.

7. *Family members teach one another to be angry.* Anger begets anger. Children who watch their parents yell and scream at them and each other learn that getting angry is normal and expected. Furthermore, they notice that nonangry interactions are frequently ignored while angry behavior receives more attention. In addition, parent-child interactions take on a coercive pattern, in which parents display harsh and inconsistent discipline, poor monitoring and supervision, low levels of warmth and nurturance, and high levels of negative verbalizations directed toward the children (Patterson, 1985; Bloomquist and Schnell, 2002). Children in these families then tend to respond with anger, avoidance, and oppositionality. Each person's negative behavior elicits a negative reaction from the other family members. The result is a family mired in negativity.

8. *Negative, critical, and hostile feelings are common.* "Fight, fight, fight. That's all we ever do. I'm so sick of the fighting that I can't wait to go to work." This kind of statement is common in angry families. As this pattern of negative interactions builds, family members give up hope that they will ever be happy together. The family as a whole seems to become depressed and despairing. Family members do not give one another much praise, since praise would break the pattern of almost unremitting negativity. The ultimate result is that everyone over time becomes more defensive, bitter, angry, and hostile.

9. *People hit, push, shove, pinch, slap, hold, and threaten one another.* Although by no means inevitable, physical violence may be a serious problem in chronically angry families. Negative verbal interactions within these families can easily spiral toward violence over time. Grumbling turns into shouting and then shouting converts to threatening, threatening changes into shoving, shoving becomes slapping, and slapping finally yields to hitting. Although not necessarily everyone in the family becomes physically violent, everybody is deeply affected by the aggression. Adults who become violent often feel guilty and not in control of themselves or the family. Nonviolent spouses often feel frightened and helpless. Children can be traumatized when witnessing parental violence or when they themselves be-

come the recipients of harm. They can also learn in this manner that violence is an acceptable form of communication, something they can do either right away or when they grow up and have their own partners and children.

10. *Everybody blames one another.* Members of chronically angry families seldom take responsibility for their own actions. Instead, they blame other family members, essentially playing a game of "It's not my fault." After all, who would want to admit that he or she is contributing to making everyone miserable? People in these families will begin to change only when each person does take personal responsibility for his or her share of the family's anger, resentments, quarrelling, and complaining. Each person will need to make a personal commitment to contain his or her own anger and anger-provoking behaviors before the family as a whole can change.

11. *Everybody is easily hurt (thin-skinned), hypervigilant, and defensive.* Although one might expect family members to become distant and thick-skinned under these circumstances, my experience is that the opposite frequently occurs; instead, family members become exceptionally sensitive to attack. They often become hyper-vigilant, ready to spring to their own defense and all too often misinterpreting as attacks the neutral or even positive remarks of other family members. They may repeat this behavior outside their homes as well, taking a hair-trigger reactivity to threat with them into work, school, dating, and friendship situations. Certain of the inevitability that others will become hostile toward them, these habitually defensive individuals may attack first, thus gaining the reputation of being dangerous, troublesome, and erratic.

WORKING WITH ANGRY FAMILIES

The three goals of anger reduction apply to angry families: to reduce the number of angry episodes, their intensity, and the damage done during these episodes. With this in mind the first effort is to *strongly encourage parents to minimize their use of corporal punishment* as a disciplinary technique. There are many reasons to do so, since research indicates that parental use of corporal punishment is correlated with increased child oppositionality, the delayed development of empathy and an internalized conscience, and reduced self-esteem (McKay et al., 1996). However, many parents believe strongly in the value of, and indeed the necessity for, corporal punishment. Dialogue with these parents about the topics of when, why, and how they use corporal punishment. Hopefully, counselors and parents can at least come to some mutual understanding that protects children from unnecessary parental aggression.

From a systems perspective a single counselor will usually not achieve very much if the main people in the family become or stay totally opposed to the three anger-reduction goals stated previously. For that reason counselors should make every effort to *recruit parents as allies* during the therapeutic process. One way to do so is to share the list of angry family characteristics noted previously so that they can better recognize the pattern and realize that their own family is displaying those behaviors. Another way is to explain to the parents that you need their support order to help their children become less volatile. If parents feel respected and appreciated by the counselor, they may be much more eager to join in the change process than if they believe they are being coerced.

What does it mean practically when at least one parent agrees to be an ally in the name of bringing peace to the family? Although the actual role varies with each parent, in general the parent will remind other family members about this goal, begin modeling the ability to contain his or her own anger, help family members use fair fighting methods, engage the children in more effective problem-solving techniques, and demonstrate a willingness to respect and appreciate each member of the family.

A third point is to *help families learn how they train one another to become and stay angry.* This can be done by going through "Here we go again" repeated family cycles of anger and aggression in which each family member both instigates and reacts to the other members' anger. The goal here is to help each family member make commitments that break the cycle, such as Dad not immediately threatening to spank the children or Mom allowing her son to take a time-out instead of shouting, "You aren't going anywhere. You just sit down and listen to me."

A fourth step in working with angry families is to *dethrone anger,* meaning that anger must no longer be the only or primary emotion expressed within the family. Instead, therapists should encourage family members to notice and share both positive emotions such as happiness and love but also other negative emotions such as shame and sadness. All family members will need encouragement to express these emotions as well as practice in receiving them instead of converting all emotions immediately back into the more familiar terrain of anger.

Also, *help angry families find hope that their lives could improve.* One woman I worked with, a mother of four in an amazingly chaotic and angry family, stated this yearning: "I wish we could just have one night when we could eat dinner without anyone yelling, screaming, cussing, or fighting." That goal was eventually accomplished, becoming evidence that the family was indeed improving.

When setting goals, though, it is wise to *begin with small goals that can lead to immediate success.* Angry individuals are notably impatient; angry families are also impatient and need quick proof that they can change. In most cases it is better to have each person make a commitment to one small change, such as an adolescent agreeing not to use one particularly nasty swear word at the table as opposed to asking that teenager not to swear at all.

Finally, it is critical to *substitute praise for criticism* in habitually angry families. Most members of these families are poor at giving and receiving praise. For instance, one mother I worked with made the following statement when I asked her to praise her daughter: "Missy, I liked it when you did the laundry all by yourself last night *but* you left the clothes in the dryer too long, they got all wrinkly, and now I'll have to do them all over again." Angry family members need to learn how to look for things to praise (activities, accomplishments, effort, appearance, etc.), then how to give praise directly to the person, and finally how to receive that praise without either shrugging it off or converting it into perceived criticism.

CASE STUDY: TREATING AN ANGRY FAMILY

Family members: *Mother:* Bonnie Dillon, age thirty-nine, depressed, anxious, suicide attempts in recent past, bitter, and sarcastic; *Father:* Joe, forty-one, avoidant, quiet, underemployed, strong passive-aggressive tendencies; *Daughter:* Stella, sixteen, the identified patient because of her unpredictable outbursts of rage and defiance of parental authority; *Older son:* Charlie, seventeen, who throws objects and breaks things when he gets angry, which is frequent; *Younger son:* Rickie, five, who still throws "baby tantrums" that include throwing himself on the floor, holding his breath, and screaming loudly for thirty minutes or longer.

Stella's parents brought her to the first session with an attitude typical of the parents of angry children: "Here's our kid. She's angry. Please fix her." They were correctly concerned that Stella was in trouble because of her inability to contain her anger. Indeed, even Stella agreed that her anger was getting out of hand. She was even starting to get angry with her friends and her boyfriend, Harry. But halfway through the first session she asked this question: "Why am I the one who has to come here when everyone in my family gets angry just as much as me?" That led to the discoveries described previously about each person's anger. Indeed, Stella was absolutely correct. Everyone in her family was truly just as angry as she.

At this point the counselor must decide: should I work only with Stella or try to turn this into family therapy? Here the answer seemed fairly obvious, namely, to focus if possible on recruiting the entire family into treatment. Fortunately, Stella's mother quickly acknowledged that the family as a whole had some anger problems. She added that she personally became angry far too often as did her mother and grandmother. She also realized once we discussed the matter that it would be both unfair and unrealistic for Stella to be the only one expected to change. Mom essentially volunteered as the parental change leader despite her long history of depression and suicidal ideation. Meanwhile, Joe, the father, who spent much of the session avoiding eye contact and looking out the window, quietly added that his father had beaten him when he was a child and he hated all the arguing that went on at home. Although Joe could not be expected to take a very active role, his statements indicated that at least he would not resist change.

The three Dillon family members who came to this first session went home with a general agreement to help the family become less angry, accompanied with a handout on fair fighting rules they would attempt to use immediately.

The entire family came to counseling for the next session. Charlie, the seventeen-year-old son, was obviously a very reluctant participant as judged by this statement: "There's nothing wrong with me. I like getting mad. I'm not going to change. And you can shove those fair fighting rules up your ass. I'll leave home first before I'll use them." And that's exactly what happened. Much to his surprise, his parents took a united front and demanded that he use the fair fighting rules and, more important, help reduce the family's angry interactions. Instead, he moved out within three months, explicitly stating that he would never agree to live in such a "stupid" family. However, life on the outside proved more difficult that he anticipated and Charlie moved back home within six months. This time he agreed to the new family lifestyle that had been implemented in his absence. He even seemed to benefit from it as he gradually developed an improved ability to keep his anger in check.

Rickie, the five-year-old, was slowest to change, perhaps because he had the most to lose. His tantrums had gotten him a tremendous amount of attention (and also usually whatever he wanted materially). Instead of giving them up, he temporarily increased their number and intensity. However, his parents had been prepared for this eventuality and were mostly able to ignore Rickie's "hooks" such as whining and crawling after his mother that in the past would have led to a tantrum. When Rickie did throw a tantrum they stayed close enough to ensure his safety but tried not to reward his behavior with attention or by getting angry themselves. After about a month, Rickie's tantrums began to decline in number and intensity. He even said during one session that he was "tired of being a baby" and that he was ready to "grow up."

Stella, the originally identified patient, did not become a perfect child. She continued to make many cynical remarks about the other members of her family. She became sexually involved with her boyfriend and reacted badly when her mother tried to talk with her about at least using contraceptives to avoid an early pregnancy. She certainly experimented with alcohol and drugs, probably to excess. However, Stella did tone down her defiance of her parents and began treating them somewhat more respectfully. She had no desire to leave the home like Charlie and knew her parents would kick her out if necessary if her behavior became too obnoxious.

Bonnie, Stella's mother, did well until overtaken by another severe bout of depression. Even then, though, she still controlled any outward manifestations of her anger. She was beset by inner-directed anger and became suicidal. Her family, fortunately, stayed supportive and did not regress into their previous angry mode. Instead, they were able to offer her empathy and compassion during the two months when her depression was most acute.

Joe, the father, probably benefited the least from family counseling. He continued to be passive aggressive, complaining that nobody appreciated all the work he did around the house even though he could not actually say exactly what it was on which he labored so strenuously. He did become a little more involved, though, when the family did fun things together such as going to the movies. These activities became feasible to undertake as the family anger abated and served as the family's reward for displacing anger from its previous dominance.

SUMMARY

We have discussed five factors that increase the susceptibility of children and adolescents to anger problems: (1) incomplete affect modulation skills; (2) limited conceptualization ability; (3) inflexible and incomplete moral reasoning ability; (4) identity confusion; and (5) attachment difficulties. Selected treatment suggestions for working with children and adolescents were then described. Characteristics of the angry family were presented. Finally, a systems approach to working with angry families was detailed.

Chapter 7

Resentment, Hate, Forgiveness, and Self-Forgiveness

INTRODUCTION

Four interrelated concepts share the focus of this chapter: resentment, hate, forgiveness, and self-forgiveness. Together, these terms represent first the development of and then the resolution for a particularly difficult form of anger. This anger is powerful, intense, and enduring, standing apart from other forms of anger in its tenacity and ability to undermine the quality of a person's life for months, years, and even decades.

Here are definitions for these terms:

Resentment: "A feeling of displeasure or indignation at some act, remark, person, etc., regarded as causing injury or insult" (*Random House Unabridged Dictionary,* Second Edition, 1993, p. 1637). The development of resentment is a process in which anger is stored rather than released.

Hatred: "To dislike intensely or passionately; to feel extreme aversion for or extreme hostility toward another; to detest" (*Random House Unabridged Dictionary,* Second Edition, 1993, p. 876). The development of hatred toward someone represents the end product of the resentment process, a point in which one's anger has metaphorically solidified, the result of which is that the hater develops an intense and unchanging loathing of another.

Forgiveness: "A willingness to abandon one's right to resentment, negative judgment, and indifferent behavior toward one who unjustly injured us, while fostering the undeserved qualities of compassion, generosity, and even love toward him or her" (Enright, Freedman, and Rique, 1998, pp. 46-47). Forgiveness is usually viewed as a slowly developing process in which the accumulated anger and desire for vindication that has built up during the resentment process is gradually released and is sometimes accompanied by a restoration of a sense of compassion toward the offender.

Self-Forgiveness: "A willingness to forego resentment and hatred toward oneself in the face of one's shortcomings and transgressions while fostering feelings of compassion, generosity and love toward oneself" (adapted with alterations from Enright, 1996, p. 108).

Although hostility in general has been a subject of psychological interest for years, secular scientists paid little attention to the development of resentments and especially to the forgiveness process until fairly recently, apparently deciding to leave that area for more religiously focused scholars. Indeed, there is a rich religious tradition in the sphere of forgiveness. Many religions, including Christianity, Judaism, and Islam emphasize the importance of forgiveness (Kassinove and Tafrate, 2002). However, forgiveness research has begun to flourish within the last decade, producing suggestive evidence that forgiving is a positive health factor that probably lessens stress and depressive reactions (Enright and Fitzgibbons, 2000). This combination of religious and secular interest in forgiveness is certainly intellectually exciting and important for clients who too often, as is said in Alcoholics Anonymous meetings, have allowed someone to "have free rent in my brain" and now realize that their lives have been greatly diminished by their inability to let go of their resentments.

This chapter has three main divisions. First, I will describe the process in which people build up resentments. Then I will describe in detail the process of letting go of these resentments through forgiveness work. Finally, I will discuss the little-studied concept of self-forgiveness.

THE DEVELOPMENT OF RESENTMENT AND HATE

Letting go of anger is vital for daily functioning. It is a necessary skill that prevents the continual buildup of negative reactions toward others in the face of the reality that people are inevitably annoying to one another. In many small and occasionally larger ways humans constantly grate on one another's nerves. This is particularly true for intimate partners if only because of the frequency of their interactions. Somehow we must find ways to discharge the bad feelings we have toward each other.

Incidents of anger and aggression usually occur in discrete episodes that follow a predictable sequence. Initially someone becomes aware that something is bothering him or her. This is followed by an assessment phase in which that individual decides whether and how to respond. The next phase is taking action, such as making a verbal protest against perceived unfairness. The message in angry protest is "Stop what you are doing. I don't like it!" The person then gets internal and external feedback about the appropriateness and effectiveness of the chosen behavior. Finally, the individual lets go of the anger so as to be able to go on to a new awareness. Unfortunately, individuals who develop resentments do not progress smoothly through these stages. They have two particular problems. First, they tend to become locked in at the protest stage of an anger episode, in effect sending a message that they will not let go of their anger until they get exactly what they want. Second, they have great difficulty at the last stage, letting go of anger. Unable to let go, these individuals seem to cling to their outrage. The cost of these tendencies is that over time they often become embittered as they are weighed down by the accumulated anger they cannot release. They have developed a spiritual malaise that severely curtails their ability to enjoy their relationships with others. The following paragraphs discuss the common characteristics of the resentment process.

1. *Progressive and expansive over time.* People can begin to form resentments over as small an event as a slightly thoughtless remark. Usually resenters lump one such minor insult with many others ("Well, that's not the first time she was mean to me. Just the other day she . . .) until they conclude that the other person is full of ill will toward them. Thus, the development of a resentment tends to be a progressive and expansive event, gradually evolving from one piece of unfinished business to many unresolved insults. At some point free-flowing anger turns into a more hardened resentment and then

resentment solidifies even further into hate, the absolute conviction that someone, the offender, is evil.

There is one exception to this pattern. Sometimes a previously trusted person does something so terrible that it shatters the worldview (Flanigan, 1992) of the betrayed individual. One example is when a spouse suddenly runs off with the person's best friend. This kind of absolute betrayal is devastating, essentially throwing everything that the offended party has believed about the world into doubt. In these situations people can become almost instantly hateful toward the offender.

2. *A deep sense of being personally wounded.* People who develop resentments are not just complaining about an abstract moral injustice. Instead, they feel deeply personally wounded. Specifically, they complain about three kinds of injuries: commissions, omissions, and shortfalls. *Commissions* occur when people believe someone actively attacks them, such as by stealing their money or being unfaithful. These wounds are relatively easy to identify and are usually what brings clients into treatment. *Omissions* are more difficult to identify because this term refers to situations in which others could have but did not do good, kind, or nice things for the client. An example would be someone who complains about all the times a parent did not come to a ball game or theatrical performance in which the client was participating. Finally, *shortfalls* occur when the offender does "too little, too late." For instance, one of my clients complained that her mother had called her recently to apologize for all the mean things she had told her when she was growing up. "But now I'm a grown woman and the damage has been done. What good does this do me now? After we hung up I just felt even more angry with her." Shortfalls make people painfully aware of how much they have longed for another's love, interest, or caring, and how bitter they have become over the years because they did not receive those gifts to which they feel entitled.

3. *A sense of moral injustice.* Those who carry resentments usually feel morally injured. They believe some fundamental law of social interaction has been breached. The law may seem relatively trivial to others (such as "People should at least be civil to one another") or obviously crucial ("Do not commit adultery") but what matters is that the rule is vital to the offended person's sense of order in the universe. Thus, it is often helpful to have clients describe the specific moral

rule that has been violated by the offender, especially since naming that rule can sometimes point the way toward helping clients eventually release their anger.

4. *Interference with normal life.* Harboring resentments takes time and energy. Individuals who do so often find themselves so caught up in their anger that they do things such as avoiding any function at which the offender might be present, talking repeatedly about the situation, or being unable to develop new relationships. Although clients may recognize this problem, indeed even though that is what brings them to therapy, still they have great difficulty pulling away from their obsessive thoughts and compulsive actions.

5. *Becoming stuck in the past.* Kassinove and Tafrate (2002) note that two important unforgiving responses of clients are rehearsing past aversive events and harboring grudges. Together these two cognitive patterns ensure that resenters stay mired in the past. It is as if they took a picture of the offender at the moment of attack, had that picture developed immediately, and have ever since carried it with them so that they could look at it at least once or twice a day. The picture never changes, of course, because it is just a single snapshot. Nor does their reaction to that image change: they essentially retraumatize themselves every time they look at it. They remain stuck at the moment of injury, locked in endless protest. Indeed, one common saying about forgiveness is that "forgiving means accepting the fact that the past can never be changed." Many resenters have difficulty doing just that.

6. *Regressive splitting pattern.* One of the most notable aspects of the resentment process as it develops is that resenters begin to see the offender as totally bad or evil and themselves as completely innocent victims of the offender's malevolence. This can be seen at the individual level, for example, when a recently divorced person claims that his or her former mate is totally worthless, or at the national level where entire nations or religions become viewed as demonic. This splitting process serves as a reminder that children only gradually learn that their "good Mommy" and "bad Mommy" are actually the very same person. Certainly some adults, most particularly those with borderline personality disorders, tend to split frequently, so that they vacillate between idealizing and then vilifying their partners. However, even nonborderline adults have a tendency toward splitting when stressed. Unfortunately, splitting in the face of an offense by a

significant other can magnify a negative spiral in which the splitter views more and more of the other person's behavior as bad, wrong, and despicable and thus becomes ever more resentful.

Dozier (2002) notes that this splitting reflects a relatively primitive "us-them" dualism centered in the survival-oriented limbic system of the brain. He describes a primitive brain system centered on the amygdala that almost instantly divides external stimuli into threatening and nonthreatening status. Hate develops when a person or group of individuals becomes associated with threat at that level and when that person or group becomes further infused with a sense of danger emanating from higher cortical areas. For more on the limbic involvement with anger and aggression see Chapter 9.

7. *Vengeful fantasies.* Resenters easily harbor fantasies of vengeance once splitting has occurred and the offender has been reduced to a subhuman state of wickedness. People can spend endless hours thinking about getting back at their offenders, their malevolence almost always rationalized by the idea that justice will be served and an injustice expunged only by severely punishing the wrongdoers. All too often resenters act out their fantasies as well, having an affair "just to get even," spreading rumors about the offenders, verbally or physically attacking and occasionally killing their adversaries, etc. Furthermore, some resenters seem to believe that settling the score is a necessary condition for getting on with their lives.

8. *Active search for allies.* Resenters, in their splitting process, tend to reduce the world around them to those who are for them and those who are not. The proof of being for them is that someone must agree they are innocent and that the offender is totally bad. This presents great difficulty to those caught in the middle such as the children of a divorced couple, one or both of whom demand that the children love one and hate the other. These children may be "brainwashed" by the parent by being told terrible and often exaggerated stories about the other parent. Children caught in this situation soon learn that they must at least appear to agree totally with the resenting parent in his or her presence, loudly renouncing the other parent. Some of these children absorb the resenter's belief system completely and renounce the other parent while others attempt, usually in a somewhat hidden manner, to remain connected and loving with the disdained parent.

9. *Tendency to expand, generalize, endure, and intensify.* Resenters may start off hating just one person only to expand gradually the num-

ber of parties on their "s— list" as they think about all the people who are like the offender in certain ways (same manner of speaking, same gender, same hair color, etc.) or who fail to fully ally with them. The result of this expanding circle of anger is increased distrust of others, more frequent pessimistic and depressed cognitions, increased bitterness and spiritual malaise, and behavioral withdrawal. In addition, strong resentments do not necessarily fade over time. Amazingly, some grow even stronger. Indeed, some of my clients report that they are angrier and more full of hate toward the offender at the time they are seeing me than when the offense occurred years earlier. All this time has been filled with endless repetitions of their victimization scenes, images that have gradually become more extreme as the resenter erases any sense of personal responsibility for his or her injuries and attributes the cause of the hostility entirely to the offender.

FORGIVENESS AS ONE WAY TO DIMINISH RESENTMENT AND HATE

Therapists must utilize their complete repertoire of interventions with resenting clients. Cognitive therapy that challenges distorted beliefs is definitely valuable. Family of origin work may help clients discover the core wounds they have endured that are then projected onto more current relationships. Behavioral therapy that focuses on ending negative and vengeful actions reduces the risk of violence. In addition, any approach that helps resenters live more fully in the present is beneficial. However, encouraging the possibility of forgiveness is the one approach that stands out as particularly powerful and effective in the area of hate reduction. To understand why, consider four possible goals when working with clients who want to become less resentful.

Therapists can offer at least four conceivable goals to clients who want to reduce the amount of time and energy they spend resenting others.

1. Find ways to *let go* of the offense and the offender so that the client can lead a more normal life focused upon the present instead of the past. The aim here is not to work through the issues that have caused the resentment but simply to help clients get on

with their lives. Clients who accept this goal usually state that they are sick and tired of carrying their resentments around with them. They want and need encouragement to socialize and have fun. They may still become upset when they think about the offending party, but success is measured by their report that they are thinking about that person less and less frequently.

2. Achieve a state of *emotional indifference* toward the offender, as indicated by someone saying, "I don't have any real emotional response anymore when I hear that person's name. I used to get so upset but now I don't care." This state of indifference is usually associated with the ability of the client to achieve a good life despite past wounds, particularly in the areas in which the most damage occurred. ("My uncle stole my inheritance but I more than made up for that loss within a few years; I don't need that money so I don't think about that much anymore.")
3. Initiate *physical restoration or reconciliation* of a damaged or broken relationship. This development usually demands a restoration of trust between the parties, something most difficult to achieve when a serious betrayal has occurred within a relationship.
4. Achieve a state of *compassion* toward someone who has been hated. This last goal demands an end to the splitting process in that the offender is recognized once again as a human being who can be respected and loved.

This transformative process normally requires energy, commitment, and hard work over an extended period. Forgiveness is the name for this process.

Forgiveness is a complicated process with many components. A look at six different definitions of forgiveness is illustrative:

- "Letting go of hurt and bitterness" (Berecz, 2001, p. 260).
- "To let go of resentment and release the offender from possible retaliation" (Freedman, 1999, p. 39).
- "One possible response to a deep, long-lasting injury . . . a voluntary choice or decision by the injured party to forego anger, revenge or justice in response to the injurious act" (Kaminer et al., 2000, p. 345).

- "A motivational transformation whereby people in close relationships become less motivated to retaliate . . . and more motivated to initiate constructive responses . . . as a function of their ability to experience both cognitive and affective empathy for the offender" (McCullough, Worthington, and Rachal, 1997, p. 322).
- "Allowing someone back into your heart" (Karen, 2001, p. 21).
- "A willingness to abandon one's right to resentment, negative judgment, and indifferent behavior toward one who unjustly injured us, while fostering the undeserved qualities of compassion, generosity, and even love toward him or her" (Enright, Freedman, and Rique, 1998, pp. 46-47).

Berecz's short definition of forgiveness, to let go of hurt and bitterness, basically defines the end product of forgiveness especially with its emphasis on ending the bitter feelings that accompany resentments. Then Freedman adds an important notion, that of making a commitment to cease acts of vengeance directed against the offender. This decision is absolutely necessary since every retaliatory act only perpetuates the resenter's anger. Kaminer then adds another vital idea, that forgiveness must be a voluntary choice. In other words, a therapist cannot insist that clients forgive someone. Instead, the therapist should advance the possibility of forgiveness as a possibly beneficial pathway for the client if and when that client chooses to walk in that direction.

McCullough's definition of forgiveness leads people past the simple renunciation of negative feelings toward the offender and toward a restoration of compassion. Empathy is the tool McCullough utilizes in order for this process to develop, a tool described in more detail later in this chapter. Compassion is achieved when people allow the offended party back into their hearts, as noted by Robert Karen. Finally, the definition suggested by Enright, Freedman, and Rique summarizes the entire forgiveness process while indicating that no offender can ever earn the right to be forgiven. In that sense forgiveness is always a freely given gift to an offender, a gift offered by the resenter without expectation, obligation, or demand.

Forgiveness is often confused with other concepts; therefore clients may find helpful a list that indicates what forgiveness is (described previously) and what it is not. Forgiveness is *not*

- *Reconciliation* (although it can lead to reconciliation). Although some authors suggest that reconciliation is indeed part of the forgiveness process (Smedes, 1984; Hargrave, 1994; Coleman, 1998), I believe there is a fundamental difference between these two functions. Forgiveness, to me, is an internal process that centers around individuals rediscovering a sense of compassion for the offenders. Reconcilation, on the other hand, is an active social process in which contact is renewed and some positive relationship redeveloped between the offended party and the offender. The key for effective reconciliation, then, would be a renewal of trust in the offender, whereas forgiveness involves a renewal of caring.
- *Forgetting*. Although "forgive and forget" is a popular saying, this concept probably is responsible for a great deal of the confusion that surrounds the concept of forgiveness as well as many people's reluctance to undertake the process. Simply forgetting an offense would allow people to set themselves up for being hurt again in the same manner. Real forgiveness does not necessitate forgetting the offense. Rather, forgiveness is better stated to be a way of remembering without bitterness and hatred.
- *Excusing, pardoning, or minimizing an injustice*. People who have been harmed may choose these actions as ways to end hostilities. However, they are by no means a necessary or expected part of forgiveness. Furthermore, these choices may actually conflict with forgiveness if offered too quickly or if they allow the offender to deny responsibility for his or her behavior. The message of forgiveness is "I care for you despite what you've done to me," not "It doesn't matter what you did to me because I care for you."
- *A loss or sign of weakness*. Some clients confuse forgiveness with submission. They mistakenly believe that forgiving means giving in to the offender. The truth is that forgiveness is a sign of strength and positive self-esteem. People need courage to confront their wounds. It is perfectly reasonable simultaneously to forgive another while making a powerful internal commitment

not to allow oneself to be used or abused again by that same person. If anything, forgiveness evens the balance of power between the two parties as the wounded person renounces the role of victim.

One situation in which forgiveness would be a sign of weakness, however, is when someone forgives another because of extreme pressure from that person ("I said I'm sorry so now you have to forgive me") or others such as friends, family, or clergy. These acts of forgiveness will usually prove false in the long run since they were made to appease others rather than from a sense of internal conviction.

- *Letting go.* As noted previously, this phrase more implies choosing not to think or feel about what happened rather than working through the hurt and pain of a difficult experience. Forgiveness does help facilitate getting on with life, but more by experiencing the event rather than just letting it go.
- *Just a decision.* Forgiveness work usually takes time and energy. Indeed, it can be a lengthy process, stretching into months or years. The decision most people make is to begin this process. In other words, "I want to forgive you" precedes "I forgive you." For that matter, forgiveness is not just a thought or a feeling. Forgiveness also involves altering one's behavior by declining to undertake acts of hostility toward the offender and possibly treating that person more kindly.

Possible Benefits from Forgiveness

Clearly, the forgiving process is frequently fairly long and difficult. Nevertheless, people make this effort because they realize that they will reap many benefits if they can forgive their offenders:

- Healing and resolving pain from an old wound
- Releasing long held anger that interferes with daily functioning and emotional well-being
- Expressing anger appropriately rather than merely complaining or aggressing inappropriately against the offender ("One cannot forgive if one cannot express and recognize their anger" [Freedman, 1999, p. 46])

- Expressing anger appropriately rather than misdirecting it against others or oneself
- Suffering less depression, hopelessness, cynicism, suspiciousness, anxiety
- Gaining an improved ability to live in the present instead of the past
- Setting the stage for reconciliation and restoration of relationships if the other party is available and responsible
- Achieving a sense of personal empowerment while freeing oneself from playing the role of a victim
- Increasing psychological maturity: moving from a relatively primitive splitting process to a more integrated sense of self and others
- Developing greater moral integrity: more specifically, gaining the ability to undertake a "supererogatory" moral task (one that is not absolutely compulsory but a positive moral choice) (Enright and Fitzgibbons, 2000)

Certainly not all clients consciously think about all these possible benefits of forgiving, but most realize that in hanging onto old resentments something has gone wrong in their lives. They sense that they can improve their lives through forgiving their offenders. Forgiveness is not a gift simply and only to oneself. It is also a gift to the offending person in that forgiveness opens the possibility for reconciliation. This double-sided aspect of forgiveness reveals "the paradox of forgiveness. . . . When we give to others the gift of mercy and compassion, we ourselves are healed" (Enright, Freedman, and Rique, 1998, p. 54).

Conditions That Improve the Likelihood of Successful Forgiving of an Offender

Forgiveness is always possible no matter the severity of a wound. Mothers have forgiven the murderers of their children (Jaeger, 1998), spouses their partners who have betrayed them, adult children their parents who physically or sexually abused them. Nevertheless, certain conditions improve the likelihood for successful forgiveness to occur. One such condition is that the wounding event is over and not being repeated. Who, for instance, would ask a wife to forgive a wayward husband for his womanizing while that man clearly intends to continue that behavior unabated? Forgiveness can definitely be utilized with relatively fresh wounds (although some clients should be warned against fleeing from their anger by too hastily forgiving an offender before fully dealing with the wounding event and its immediate sequelae), but clients should have a realistic sense of physical and emotional security before attempting to do so.

It also greatly helps when the offender expresses sincere remorse repeatedly (Fitness, 2001) and when the offender makes persistent constructive efforts to repair the relationship. For instance, one of my clients decided to confront an elderly relative who had sexually abused him years before. Expecting denial, minimization, and justification from the relative, my client was astonished when that man fully acknowledged his wrongdoing, repeatedly spoke of his great remorse for having damaged my client, and begged him for forgiveness. The offender had gone through treatment years before for his unacceptable sexual proclivities but had been unable to locate my client to make amends. My client was still reluctant to trust his abuser but over time was able both to forgive and reconnect with this man.

In addition, recent research in the area of shame and guilt (Tangney and Dearing, 2002; Potter-Efron, 2002) appears to predict that forgiveness will be most successfully accomplished when both the wrongdoer and the injured party experience relatively little shame and the wrongdoer feels more guilt than shame. This is probable because guilt feelings tend to push people toward restorative actions that heal relationships whereas shame leads toward interpersonal withdrawal.

Two Critical Processes in Forgiveness: Empathy and Reframing

As forgiveness has been studied more extensively, two cognitive processes, empathy and reframing, have emerged as seeming necessary in order to achieve the desired result.

Empathy certainly plays a central role in this effort (McCullough, Worthington, and Rachal, 1997). Ciaramicoli (2000) suggests two definitions for empathy: "the capacity to understand and respond to the unique experiences of another" (p. 3) and "the bridge spanning the chasm that separates us from each other" (p. 12). His focus is on the need of individuals, especially in this concern wounded parties, to abandon their egocentric position in order to be able to better see and understand their offenders (Emmons, 2000).

McCullough, Worthington, and Rachal (1997) note two kinds of empathy, cognitive and emotional. Cognitive empathy could be defined as "attempting to fully understand the thoughts and reasoning of another" while emotional empathy would then be "attempting to fully comprehend the emotional experience of another." Both processes involve an active, searching, reaching out toward the other (Berecz, 2001) and a reaching inward to make connections between one's own experience and the possible experience of another (Berecz, 2001). This latter effort inevitably involves projection in that empathizers recall experiences from their own lives that might come close to matching the experiences of another and recollect their thoughts and feelings during those times. However, no two people can have exactly the same total experience, so even the best empathic connections are doomed to be only an approximation of the other's thoughts and feelings. Still, forgiveness is greatly aided through empathy because the forgiver, temporarily at least, makes a concerted effort to withdraw from a narcissistic focus on oneself in order to connect with the offender both emotionally and intellectually. Forgiveness is enhanced when the forgiver can better understand the other's interest and viewpoint (Hargrave, 1994) in this manner.

Empathy demands that the forgiver become curious about and take interest in the offender as a human being. In this regard Ciaramicoli (2000) suggests several key questions that the forgiver could ask the offender (either face to face or in imaginative dialogue):

> Who are you?
> What do you think?
> What do you feel? What means the most to you?
> What can I learn from you and about you?

I would add:

> How are we alike?
> How are we different?
> What would it feel like to be you?

I would also suggest two more useful empathy-increasing questions: Have you ever needed another's forgiveness for something you said or did? What was that like? These questions might help lessen the good/bad split that underlies hating another person.

Reframing is another related process that also enhances clients' ability to forgive. Reframing has been defined as "to rethink a situation and see it with a fresh perspective" (Enright and Fitzgibbons, 2000, p. 79) and as "seeing the wrongdoer in context" (North, 1998, p. 24). More specifically, North (1998) suggests that reframing involves understanding the pressures the offender was under at the time of the offense, appreciating the person's personality as a result of his or her developmental history, and separating the wrongdoer from the wrong committed.

Enright and Fitzgibbons (2000) suggest that people wanting to forgive ask these questions:

> What was it like for the offender growing up?
> What was it like for the offender at the time of the offense?
> Can you see him or her as a member of the human community?
> Is he or she a child of God?
> What was your relationship like other than in the context of the specific offense?
> How may you have contributed to the offender's questionable behavior?

This last question must be asked cautiously if at all. For example, it might be inadvisable to ask it of a person struggling to escape overwhelming feelings of maladaptive guilt (Potter-Efron, 2002) about participating in incest as a child. However, the question might be very relevant in situations, such as a particularly nasty divorce, in which both parties became mean-spirited and vindictive toward each other.

One client I worked with made use of many of these empathy and reframing questions as part of his effort to forgive his father. Melvin, a forty-year-old roofer and recovering drug addict, asked for help figuring out how to relate to his actively alcoholic father, a man who had brutalized him in the past and once had literally thrown Melvin in a dumpster because "You are garbage so you belong in the garbage can." Melvin maintained a fragile relationship with his father but often felt hatred toward him as he remembered past abuses. Furthermore, his father still became verbally abusive after he had been drinking, coming over to Melvin's house to berate Melvin and all his siblings for being ungrateful to their poor old dad. Still, Melvin wanted some relationship with his father "because after all he is the only father I'll ever have." I asked him the previous series of questions over a period of two or three sessions. Here are some of Melvin's responses.

Empathy questions:

Who is he? "A sad old man who hates the world."

What does he think? "That everybody hates him—and he's right. I'm the only one left in the family who even talks with him anymore."

What does he feel? "Bitter. Abandoned."

What means the most to him? "His booze. That's all he has left."

What can you learn from him? "Never to go back to my drugs or I'll end up like him."

How are you alike? "We're both addicts. We're both full of hate."

How are you different? "I want to quit feeling that way; he doesn't."

What would it feel like to be him? "Terrible. He's miserable. He's so unhappy."

Have you ever needed another person's forgiveness? "Yeah, my wife's for all the drinking and drugging I used to do."

Reframing questions:

What was it like for your father growing up? "His dad was an alcoholic too. They were dirt poor."

What was it like for your dad that day he threw you in the dumpster? "He was drunk. He'd just lost his job. He was probably depressed too."

Can you see him as a child of God? Can you see him as a member of the human community? "I'm trying."

How may you have contributed to the offender's questionable behavior? [Not asked.]

What was your relationship like other than when he was abusing you? "Sometimes we had a real good time together. We were fishing buddies down at the lake near our home and we'd spend hours there just fishing, not talking much, just being there with each other."

Melvin's animosity toward his father gradually abated as he was able to see that man as a human being rather than a monster. His honest response to the question about whether he could see his father as a child of God or a member of the human community—"I'm trying"—was especially poignant. Since forgiveness is usually a slowly developing state of consciousness, many clients can get there only by trying, failing, and trying again until they finally do achieve a true sense of forgiveness.

Stages and Processes of Forgiveness

Many writers on forgiveness suggest that forgiveness takes place slowly with the forgiver gradually passing through several stages. However, each person's experience is different. Also, few people travel through these stages in a linear fashion. Instead, many individuals travel rather unpredictably from one to another, back and forth, often revisiting many times various stations on the path of forgiveness. As might be expected, the names for the stages vary by author. Furthermore, some models emphasize not only forgiveness but also reconciliation while others concentrate only upon forgiveness per se.

Here are some of the stage models suggested in the literature:

Berecz (2001):

I. Rapport	I. Rapport
II. Reframe	II. Reframe
III. Reconcile *or*	III. Release

The value of this framework is in its flexibility. Berecz allows for two possible end products of the forgiveness process. Reconciliation can occur under certain circumstances, which I associate with the redevelopment of trust. On other occasions the forgiver releases the offender from further antagonism and in doing so releases himself or herself from hate.

Enright and Fitzgibbons (2000); Enright (2001):

I. *Uncovering:* Gain insight into how injustice and injury have compromised life.
II. *Decision:* Understand the nature of forgiveness and commit to forgiving.
III. *Work:* Gain cognitive understanding of the offender and begin to view offense in a new light that helps produce a positive change in affect toward the offender.
IV. *Deepening:* Find increased meaning in the suffering, feel more connected with others, display less negative affect and a renewed purpose in life.

This is a very detailed stage model that is further subdivided into twenty phases. Each phase is described carefully and clients are given information as to how to understand and utilize each.

Smedes (1984):

I. Hurt
II. Hate
III. Heal
IV. Coming together

This reconciliation model is gently presented in Smede's small and easily comprehended book intended for the general public.

Hargrave (1994):

I. *Exonerating phase:* The goal here is to salvage a relationship through insight and understanding.
II. *Forgiving phase:* The goal here is to reconcile by giving the offender an opportunity to make compensatory efforts and with overt acts of forgiveness.

This is another reconciliation model that focuses on the appropriate acts of contrition made by the offending person.

Coleman (1998):

I. Identifying the injury
II. Confronting the other to confirm the reality of the injury
III. Dialogue to make sense of the suffering
IV. Forgiveness as a leap of faith and willingness to trust
V. Letting go of the wound

The fourth stage includes both a leap of faith and a willingness to trust the offender. Therapists must be careful here to help clients delay these actions until some evidence indicates that taking them is safe.

Flanigan (1992):

I. Naming the injury
II. Claiming the injury
III. Blaming the injurer
IV. Balancing the scales
V. Choosing to forgive
VI. Emergence of a new self

Flanigan's model was developed by questioning survivors of exceptionally painful betrayers. These survivors initially believed that the offenses they had endured were unforgivable. Nevertheless, many of them did manage to forgive their offenders through stages that they described retroactively.

Although Enright's model is probably the best researched of those presented, the names and details of forgiveness stages probably will continue to be elaborated and clarified over the next several years. Any of the ones presented here could be helpful for clients who need some direction.

Exercises/Helpful Ideas for Clients As They Experience the Forgiveness Process

Clients often need help as they attempt to go through the forgiveness process, in part because no absolutely clear path inevitably takes one there. Here are some suggestions that may be useful to offer.

1. *Make lists of the ways in which carrying one's resentments harms the client.* Forgiving is not entirely self-centered in that acts of forgiveness re-create bridges between people and may lead to reconciliation. Still, the primary beneficiary of forgiving is the forgiver since that person will be freed from his or her obsessive thinking about the offender and related compulsive behaviors. Thus it may be useful to make lists both of the ways that continuing to carry a resentment hurts the client as well as of possible gains that would occur as the client forgives the offender.

2. *Make a daily commitment to forgiveness.* "Today I will try to forgive . . ." Achieving a state of forgiveness takes time, during which

people often vacillate between wanting to keep hating and truly wanting to forgive their offenders. For this reason the saying "trying is dying" does not apply. Instead, clients should be encouraged to try to forgive (Enright, 2001) and rewarded for that effort even when the results are less than completely successful.

3. *Read about forgiveness.* Many excellent books are available for the general public that describe and encourage forgiveness from either a secular or religious perspective. Clients should be encouraged to read as much as they can on this topic since each volume is likely to handle the topic slightly differently.

4. *Journaling.* It is useful for some clients to keep a daily journal in which they can complete specific forgiveness assignments (Enright, 2001) as well as have a place in which to write about their desire to forgive along with the difficulties in so doing. This journal should not be used a general diary and should be utilized only for forgiveness materials.

5. *Forgiveness rituals.* Rituals are valuable with many clients because they serve as a way to let go of the symbols of old wounds. Each ritual must be individually tailored to the needs and style of the client. Caution should be used in these rituals, however, not to increase the splitting process, for instance by burning every picture one has of the offender. Rather, a client would be better encouraged to put those pictures away for a while (to be replaced with pictures of what or whom?) until the client feels ready to allow positive feelings about the offender back into his or her thoughts.

6. *Letter writing.* No-send letters shared in therapy but not usually mailed to the offender can be very rewarding. Early in therapy these letters could describe the wounding that the client suffered because of the offender's behavior. Later, they might either offer or withhold forgiveness. These letters might include such phrases as

> "I am not ready to forgive you yet because . . ."
> "I am beginning to think I can forgive you because . . ."
> "I can let go of you now."
> "I have begun feeling compassion toward you."
> "I forgive you."

7. *Prayer, positive visualizations, and gift giving.* The common theme of these three actions is the need for clients to move from a totally negative perception of the offender toward a more positive per-

ception of that person as a normal human being for whom the client can feel positive regard despite the injuries that the individual has caused. Praying for the offender is often useful for religiously oriented clients, especially those who have split so strongly that they have come to believe the offender is in league with the devil.

Patricia Potter-Efron developed a visualization (Potter-Efron and Potter-Efron, 1991b) in which clients first visualize something good happening to themselves, such as getting hugs from all their children, and then imagine something just that wonderful happening to the person they are trying to forgive. This task helps clients feel compassion toward the offender and also helps them realize the difference between simply pitying the offender as opposed to truly wishing the person peace and joy.

Prayers and visualizations may be followed by the concrete action of giving the wrongdoer the gifts of a smile, a small present, or a few kind words. One way to approach this is to have clients develop an "as if" list (Potter-Efron and Potter-Efron, 1991b) of positive things they could do with or for each person. Then they are free to do some or all of these things over time, with no insistence that any specific behavior must ever be done. This process both allows clients to stay in control of their behavior and encourages them to change what they do over time.

8. *Develop metaphors or analogies for the forgiving process.* Clients may gain a more clear sense of mission when they develop a metaphor that vividly describes a forgiving process. One person might utilize a scene in which he or she loads one's resentments onto a train and sends the train far away to dump the stuff (and then returns to be used again as needed). Another person might envision a cleansing scene such as bathing under a waterfall of forgiveness.

9. *Discuss the difference between a wrongdoer's apparent intent and the impact of his or her actions.* An offender, temporarily angry at his wife, shoves her out of his path as he leaves the room. Yes, he wanted at that moment to harm her, but he certainly did not realize shoving her that way would cause her to twist her back and leave her with a permanent injury. Should she hold him responsible for only his intent (to harm her a little) or the impact of his action (permanent damage)? What should her forgiveness work center on? The answer is probably both, since both intent and impact are meaningful con-

cepts both legally and morally. However, the two concepts should be separated in the client's mind and work, especially since injured parties may erroneously assume that the wrongdoer intended all aspects of the harm done to them, while the wrongdoer may confuse lack of intent to harm another with lack of damage to that party (Ferch, 1998).

10. *Discuss times the wrongdoer needed forgiveness from others.* As noted previously, this thought process helps clients lessen their tendency toward splitting that turns them into helpless victims and their offenders into manifestations of evil.

11. *Utilize empathy and reframing questions.* These questions, described previously in this chapter, are useful to lessen splitting and to increase feelings of compassion, respect, and love toward the offender.

12. *Role-play having the client speak to or with the wrongdoer: empty chair or two-chair dialogue.* Two exercises long associated with Gestalt therapy can be useful with clients seeking to work through some of their feelings toward an offender. The first simply involves imagining that the offender is sitting in front of the client in an empty chair (or one in which the client has placed a picture of the offender). This monologue would begin with a phrase such as "Here's what I want to say to you, so listen carefully . . ." and the client might express any mixture of anger, rage, sadness, compassion, and love. The second exercise involves the client moving between two chairs and role-playing the imagined responses of the offender to his or her comments. This process might be particularly useful when the offender is deceased or physically unavailable.

SELF-FORGIVENESS

Self-forgiveness seems to be a forgotten child in the literature when compared with forgiveness. Little has been written or researched about this subject. Self-forgiveness scales do not correlate well with forgiveness of others scales, so the two appear to be conceptually distinct. This makes sense in that self-forgiveness becomes necessary when people have directed their anger inwardly against themselves while forgiveness of others is called for when people desire to quit wanting to punish a transgressor (Mauger et al., 1992; Coates, 1997).

Several authors (Flanigan, 1996; Reed, 1999) in this area specify that self-forgiveness becomes relevant only when the individual feels guilty about having caused harm to others. These authors distinguish between self-forgiveness and self-acceptance, where self-acceptance addresses the failure to live up to one's standards. This shifts attention from shame toward guilt and from vague complaints about oneself to specific transgressions. Thus, Enright (1996) defines self-forgiveness as "a willingness to abandon self-resentment in the face of one's own objective acknowledged wrong, while fostering compassion, generosity and love toward oneself" (p. 116) and Coyle (1999) describes self-forgiveness as "the cessation of self-punishment and self-condemnation and the merciful acceptance of the self as a valuable human being in spite of one's vulnerability to sin or hurtful acts" (p. 6).

However, I suggest four situations produce self-resentment and self-hate and therefore could provide a need for self-forgiveness:

1. *Someone has caused harm to others* via *a transgression*. For example, a man stole money from a good friend or beat his children; or a recovering alcoholic mother believes she ruined the lives of her children because of the abuse she inflicted upon them while intoxicated.
2. *Someone has caused harm to himself or herself* via *a transgression*. For example, while driving home drunk a person crashed a car and became partially paralyzed.
3. *Someone has caused harm to others* via *his or her shortcomings*. For example, the soldier in the film *Saving Private Ryan* becomes paralyzed with fear and cannot bring ammunition to his comrades; the recovering alcoholic mother believes she ruined her children through neglect.
4. *Someone has caused harm to himself or herself* via *his or her shortcomings*: For example, the butler in *The Remains of the Day* never finds a way to approach the woman he loves; a man blames "taking her for granted" for the loss of his marriage.

These situations combine guilt (1 and 2), which emphasizes transgression, or shame (3 and 4), which focuses upon a person's failure to act or shortcomings (Potter-Efron, 2002) with damage done to others (1 and 3) or to oneself (2 and 4). If indeed all four of these situations produce self-hatred, then Enright's (1996) definition of self-forgiveness needs to be expanded to "a willingness to forego resentment and hatred toward oneself in the face of one's shortcomings and transgressions, while fostering feelings of compassion, generosity and love toward oneself."

Self-forgiveness appears to be needed when someone's inappropriate actions ("Never in a million years did I believe I would do something like that, but I did—and then I did it again!") or failures to act ("All I had to do was speak up but I was too cowardly to do so") attack the core of one's moral self-concept. This produces a state of self-hatred, self-condemnation, and self-punishment that continues until the person can restore his or her sense of being a worthwhile human being (Horton, 1999; Flanigan, 1996), thus alleviating both the shame and guilt that occur when the individual scrutinizes his or moral identity.

Keys to Reparative Work in the Area of Self-Forgiveness

Although authors vary on the exact process, all agree that self-forgiveness is difficult, takes a long time, and goes through various stages. For instance, Flanigan (1996) describes these stages: confront self; hold self responsible; confess flaws; transformation. Enright's (1996) four stages parallel his work on forgiving others: uncovering; making a decision to self-forgive; work; outcome.

Some specific approaches therapists can utilize to encourage their clients to become more self-forgiving include the following:

1. Help clients become as clear as possible about exactly what they have done or not done that caused severe problems in their lives. This step includes noticing how they have defended against taking responsibility for their behavior by denial, shifting blame, etc.
2. While doing so, help clients guard against excessive attacks on the self perpetrated by others who are falsely blaming the client or by the client exaggerating his or her blameworthiness in a particular situation (e.g., the adult who feels responsible for being sexually abused as a child).
3. Determine the core personal value or values that clients have violated by their actions or inactions ("I never thought I would . . ."). Help them fully express remorse about these violations while

recognizing that the remorse indicates they do hold those values even though they were once ignored or broken.

4. Determine how this violation has damaged their sense of self as a moral and good human being. This often means helping clients go from "I'd never do that" to "Yes, I did it and I have to accept that fact about myself."
5. Discuss how they have punished themselves and continue to punish themselves because of their failures and transgressions. Discuss and dispute with clients their belief that "I'm such an awful person that I deserve continuing punishment. I don't deserve forgiveness from myself or others."
6. Encourage clients to make amends if possible when the moral violations or failures have harmed others. However, clients should be cautioned not to expect to be forgiven by those they have harmed when they make amends to them. On the other hand, clients do need to be encouraged to accept forgiveness if offered and to try to take in the other person's compassion.
7. Explain that clients should make a serious commitment to changing their behaviors and thoughts so as to minimize the likelihood of repeating the transgression or shortcoming. This step helps the clients go through self-acceptance into self-forgiveness.
8. Assist clients to reconcile with the self as a person who has recommitted to his or her major values even while recognizing his or her limitations, greediness, meanness of spirit, and capacity for wrongdoing. This is a transformative process in that the client feels compassion for oneself not for being an unflawed human being or even in spite of being flawed but for being a whole human being.

CASE STUDY: A LESSON IN FORGIVENESS

Molly is a thirty-five-year-old woman of average intelligence but with specific learning disabilities that make change difficult though not impossible. She has an excellent vocabulary and a willingness to work. Molly has come regularly to counseling for years and once attended my anger management group. Nevertheless, she has great difficulty letting go of old resentments, often bringing up old wounds, defending herself against past insults, and obsessing about how others have mistreated her, even reinitiating contact in order to try (usually unsuccessfully) to resolve arguments. Molly struggles with feelings of shame associated with her difficulties in holding jobs and receiving disability payments.

Molly had rented a room for several years in the home of a woman named Betty, with whom she initially got along well. Gradually their relationship deteriorated, however, because of a series of small disagreements, possible misunderstandings, and Molly's difficulties in understanding Betty's positions. Several months ago Betty decided she wanted Molly to move out. She called in a mutual friend named Pamela to help her deliver the news. According to Molly the two of them were very insulting to her, blaming her for the failure of the relationship, and refusing to reconsider their decision. Molly was reduced to tears. She called her boyfriend, James, who drove over and took her out of the situation. James helped her make new living arrangements that have proven quite satisfactory and Molly is actually happier than she was while residing with Betty. However, Molly continues to dwell on the hostile way that Betty and Pamela treated her that day.

Having worked with Molly for years on other resentments she had developed and then could not release, I knew that Molly could easily spend the next several years obsessing about her unfair treatment, finding reasons to maintain contact with Betty and Pamela and destroying the quality of her life. Furthermore, Molly became generally bitter and angry when harboring resentments. James was already growing tired of listening to her repetitive complaints. Molly could easily lose this relationship (and develop still another resentment) unless she could find a way to release her anger toward Betty and Pamela.

I mentioned to Molly that forgiving is one way to get through this kind of situation. Her response was "It will be a long time before I could do that" and she declined the implicit invitation to work in that area. However, during the next two weeks she brought in material on forgiving she had "happened to run into" in two different books (one religious and one secular). When I invited her again to work in this area she accepted.

Molly has accepted and completed a number of tasks that are helping her forgive Betty and Pamela. Here are a few assignments she has accepted:

1. To complete Robert Enright's Forgiveness Inventory (1994), which divides forgiveness into six areas: positive cognitions, feelings, and actions; and negative cognitions, feelings, and actions
2. To find items from the questionnaire that she can begin to change from negative to positive
3. To wake up each morning and make a commitment to try to forgive Betty and Pamela
4. To visualize herself making prosocial contact with Betty
5. To recognize that she is a strong person who has the ability to absorb the pain of this attack against her, much like a tree that grows around a wound and becomes stronger than it was before the injury

6. To answer the following questions:
   - What causes Betty a lot of emotional pain? ("Her daughter's mental problems.")
   - What has Betty ever done for you instead of hurting you? ("She gave me shelter when I had no place to live.")
   - Can you think of Betty as a normal person, both good and bad, not just as a bad person or evil woman? ("Not yet, but I have begun praying for her.")
7. To write a no-send letter to Betty in which she tears up Betty's debt to her

Molly's no-send letter is generally quite appropriate and useful. However, Molly's last response in the letter demonstrates the ambivalence that clients often have toward forgiving those who have offended them "I forgive you and ask nothing in return. I will no longer expect you to call me, come over, contact me, or even apologize to me *because you showed how much of a coward you really are*." The last phrase indicates that Molly cannot quite yet bring herself to end the psychological splitting process and see Betty as a normal human being.

What value has all of this been for Molly? First, she now spends far less time obsessing about what happened. Second, she realizes that she has some control over her feelings and therefore she does not need to adapt a helpless victim stance with regard to this incident. Third, Molly and James are still together and she has applied her forgiveness learning to their relationship, cutting off the development of resentments by letting go of perceived insults more quickly. Fourth, she views herself as a better person for having undertaken this task, an especially difficult one for someone with her normally inflexible personality structure. Hopefully, Molly will continue to utilize this new ability to get through life with greater flexibility and happiness.

SUMMARY

People seem to have an amazing capacity to remember and retain images about negative occurrences in their lives. Perhaps that helps them survive by keying them to all the potential dangers in the world. Normally this process is balanced by people's capacity to notice the goodness in the same individuals who have harmed them. However, this balance is not automatically achieved. The failure to find this balance results in the development of enduring and accumulating hostility toward the other person that eventuates in the development of firm resentments and hatred toward the offenders. In addition, some persons develop this same tendency to accumulate resentments toward themselves, resulting in self-hatred. Forgiveness and self-forgiveness are the two processes that help individuals restore the balance between good and evil in their lives.

Self-forgiveness often becomes a goal during therapy because clients have turned their anger inwardly against themselves. The topic of anger turned inward is the subject of the next chapter.

Chapter 8

Anger Turned Inward

INTRODUCTION

The topic of anger turned inward is a relatively neglected area in today's anger management field. That was not always the situation, however. In the 1980s, for instance, popular books such as Harriet Lerner's *The Dance of Anger* (1985) emphasized the need for people, and in particular women, to accept the reality of their anger and to use it appropriately instead of "stuffing" it. Gestalt therapy (Polster and Polster, 1973), with its emphasis on ventilating one's emotions, was exceptionally popular then as well and also served to give clients permission to express their anger. However, the emphasis in anger management changed gradually from helping overly inhibited clients get angry to helping overly demonstrative clients contain their anger. A related effort to curtail domestic abuse added to this tendency. Although clients are certainly still encouraged to express their feelings (in moderation) and to take assertive actions when appropriate, the concern with anger turned inward has become so subordinate in most anger management programs that it is not even covered in the agenda.

My definition of anger turned inward is global, referring to "any conscious or unconscious process in which an individual directs anger toward the self." Thus, anger turned inward (as I am using it) includes but is not limited to suppressed anger. I define anger *suppression* as "a conscious effort not to express felt anger behaviorally or verbally." Anger turned inward may be a conscious effort, as just noted, or an unconscious one, in which case the proper term is anger *repression:* "an unconscious blocking of angry sensations from the consciousness of the angered individual so that he or she is unaware of being angry." Finally, individuals may consciously direct their anger against themselves in situations in which others would express their anger outwardly, sometimes in relatively minor ways such as accepting blame for something gone wrong instead of accusing others but sometimes in such pathological forms as banging one's head into a wall rather than allowing oneself to feel or express rage against another person.

Please note that my usage of "anger turned inward" is more inclusive than Spielberger's (2001) concept of "Anger-In" as measured in the State-Trait Anger Expression Inventory-2 previously discussed. Spielberger defines Anger-In as the frequency that anger is suppressed after anger has been experienced and focuses exclusively on consciously suppressed anger. He also gauges "Anger Expression Control-In" with a scale measuring the frequency that an individual tries to lessen the *intensity* of felt anger by calming down or cooling off, another exclusively conscious effect.

Three main topics are discussed in this chapter: (1) identifying patterns of behavior that indicate the presence of anger turned inward as well as the reasons why clients might develop this pattern; (2) general therapeutic approaches to treating excessive anger turned inward; and (3) self-damaging patterns of behavior that represent a combination of anger and shame turned against the self and their treatment.

IDENTIFYING ANGER-TURNED-INWARD PATTERNS OF BEHAVIOR

It is certainly appropriate for people occasionally to suppress anger or even to redirect it toward themselves. However, some individuals seem to have lost a sense of choice in this matter; they automatically redirect anger toward themselves that could legitimately be expressed outwardly. These persons could benefit from treatment for anger turned inward with the stated goal of helping them achieve a better balance between the two poles of turning anger in and out.

I have developed an "Anger Turned Inward Quiz" that helps identify clients who might need counseling in this area (see Appendix A). This instrument has not been scientifically normed, however, so it should be utilized in an advisory fashion only. Nevertheless, it is helpful both to gather information and to educate and motivate clients.

The quiz is based on the following questions:

Items are scored on a scale of 1 to 5:
1 = That's not what I do at all.
2 = I do that only once in a great while.
3 = I do that fairly often.
4 = I do that a lot.
5 = I do that all the time.
What is your total score?_________

1. I feel really angry with someone but don't say anything.
2. I don't show my anger because I don't want to hurt someone's feelings.
3. I'm afraid others will be angry with me if they see I'm angry with them.
4. I indirectly let people know I'm angry by pouting, sulking, going silent, etc.
5. I tell myself I shouldn't become angry even when most people would get angry about something someone has done or said.
6. I "stuff" my anger and then get headaches, a stiff neck, stomachaches, etc.
7. I handle conflict more by giving in or avoiding problems than by negotiating, being assertive, or clearly stating what I want.
8. I feel very responsible for others even when I'm angry with them.
9. I put on a good front by smiling and looking happy even when I'm upset.
10. I don't generally share any of my feelings, including anger.
11. I feel guilty or shameful whenever I become angry, no matter how justified my anger might be.
12. I become so angry with myself that I call myself ugly names or even physically attack myself (scratching, head banging, burning, suicide attempts, etc.).

It is useful to discuss with clients any single item that they have scored at least a "3" on. Also, I suggest that a score of 36 points (an average of 3 points per item) is indicative of some anger turned inward issues while a score of 48 points (an average of 4 points per item) is indicative of a definite tendency toward excessively turning anger onto the self.

Tendencies of Individuals with Anger Turned Inward

As can be seen from the quiz, clients with strong tendencies toward turning their anger inward have many identifiable patterns of behavior. These patterns frequently emanate from a central prohibition against directly expressing anger against others. However, therapists should be cautious about overinterpreting all acts of anger turned inward as signs of suppressed anger against others in the light of Spielberger's (1999) findings that Anger-In and Anger-Out are relatively uncorrelated. Some individuals can be high on both Anger-In and Anger-Out while others may be low on both variables. It might be better to keep two concepts in mind and apply them as appropriate: "I am angry at myself *instead* of letting myself be angry with you" and "I am angry with myself *as well as* being angry at you."

Treatment for individuals who are high on both Anger-In and Anger-Out will be discussed later in this chapter. Still, the average client I see with excessive tendencies toward turning anger inward better fits the "either/or" model than the "both/and" one in that they preferentially turn anger against themselves rather than toward others. The remainder of this discussion describes patterns of thought and action common with these individuals.

Many of these clients have essentially renounced their anger. They believe that good people do not and should not get angry very often if at all. Thus, they regret and attempt to suppress any negative feelings they have toward others. If they cannot do that all the time, and they need to admit to themselves that they are really upset about something, they can at least make a commitment not to let others know that they are angry. Thus, many of these persons become habitual anger and conflict avoiders, tending to handle conflict more through avoidance and accommodation than through negotiation, compromise, or collaboration. Compromise and collaboration cannot be pursued because people must address and promote their desires, raising the possibility for anger and aggression.

Over time, though, some "anger stuffers" recognize that they are far more angry than they want anybody to realize. Still, they rigorously attempt to maintain and display a "public self" even within their families that is very different from their own sense of self. They loyally play the role of happy, never angry people but know that is not their real self. Some of these clients come to therapy smiling and laughing even while seething with undisclosed fury against the world. They feel rageful inside but refuse to disclose their feelings to anyone, least of all those who have offended them.

Others who direct their anger inwardly allow hints of their dissatisfaction to leak out, announcing their anger through pouting and sulking (Forgays et al., 1998) or occasionally allowing their stifled anger out in sudden and unpredictable "stuff and blow" episodes. These individuals suddenly become extremely and disproportionately irate over seemingly small problems. Their thoughts on these occasions usually approximate the idea that "I couldn't take it anymore" when they finally blow up. Unfortunately, such dramatic ventilations seldom prove useful because they do not lead to effective problem solving. Indeed, these persons are likely to conclude only that they made a mistake by getting mad and in this way reinforce their tendency to direct their anger inwardly.

Passive-aggressive resistance to authority, in which anger is displayed more through inertia than direct protest, may be another indicator of anger turned inward. Although some passive-aggressive persons do not consciously recognize their anger, others know full well that they are upset with people but cannot give themselves permission to say so directly. Instead, they continually frustrate their partners, family, work associates, and anyone else whom they believe wants to have power over them.

Since clients whose anger is primarily directed inwardly are poor communicators who have difficulty directly addressing their grievances, they tend to hold grudges. Letting go of old insults, much less truly forgiving the offender, is hard when people cannot even acknowledge to others, and sometimes themselves, how truly angry they are.

All of these patterns are destructive to an individual's health. Suppressed anger has been linked with proneness toward anxiety, depression, somatic complaints, and heart disease (Martin et al., 1999; Begley, 1994; Lisspers, Nygren, and Soderman, 1998). Begley (1994) notes that people who turn their anger inward often feel very responsible for others even though they are angry with them. This combination of high anger turned inward and high responsibility for others is particularly associated with anxiety, depression, and somatic complaints. This combination of thoughts translates to "I'm angry with you right now but if I expressed my anger I would hurt you so I can't do that because I also feel responsible for you. That means I must keep my anger at you to myself." Alcohol or drug abuse may also develop as individuals utilize these substances either to help them contain their anger or to become disinhibited enough to express anger at others (Tivis, Parsons, and Nixon, 1998).

Finally, Martin et al. (1999) mention that many people who do not disclose anger are generally emotionally inexpressive. These individuals do not experience and/or do not express other emotions as well as anger. Thus, such persons will need therapeutic help to express the entire range of their emotions, not just anger, during counseling.

Reasons Why Anger May Be Turned Inward

Several possible reasons promote the tendency to direct one's anger inwardly. The more these justifications are endorsed by a particular individual, the stronger is the belief that anger should or must be turned inward.

- *Appropriate response to personal mistake or transgression.* Getting angry with oneself may be perfectly reasonable in certain circumstances, especially when someone has done something that has caused harm either to themselves or others. This response may lead to reparative efforts in the same way that anger against others may lead to altered social interactions. The appropriate therapeutic question here is, "How can you use your current anger at yourself to make things better?"
- *Fear of harming others.* As just noted, one reason people direct their anger inward is a strong sense that they are responsible for the feelings of others. Not wanting to hurt anyone, even when angry, they choose instead to keep quiet even at the cost of their own emotional, mental, and physical well-being. Although counselors promote the expression of anger as necessary and even beneficial in relationships, some individuals believe that expressing anger is almost inevitably harmful, causing immediate or long-term damage to the target of the anger. Turning anger onto oneself then deflects the damage onto oneself, a decision that would be viewed as a better moral and practical choice.

- *Compliance with learned moral training.* Closely related to the previous point, some people learn in childhood that they *should* direct their anger toward themselves instead of others in ambiguously frustrating situations. Thus, suppressing one's anger is morally superior to lashing out with it. The painful and unacceptable cost of expressing one's anger here is guilt. On the other hand these individuals may feel a certain pride in turning their anger inward, a sense that they are behaving in a socially valued and morally correct manner.
- *Disavowal of protest.* Anger turned inward may be linked with early childhood socialization in many ways. Beyond simply being discouraged from getting angry or from expressing emotions in general, some families specifically reject the right of children to object to perceived injustices. As Robert Karen (2001) writes, "One of the most devastating things we experienced [as children] was the rejection of our protests—they were dismissed as wrong, irrational, illogical, rude, insulting, disloyal, ungrateful, and so on" (p. 89). When children are taught that they should never protest they may instead suppress their anger or even attack themselves whenever they sense an angry impulse in order to quash that impulse before it is exposed.
- *Safe target.* Sometimes protests may be more than just discouraged. They may instead be severely punished through physical attack, loss of love, and verbal aggression. In these situations it may be too dangerous for children to direct their anger at someone else even when that other person is the cause of their anger. They may attack themselves as a far safer target.
- *Relationship maintenance.* Expressing anger can be immediately disruptive to the smooth flow of relationships. Normal routines become disrupted when someone's anger "rocks the boat," causing disruption and "wasting" time and energy. Needs, vulnerabilities, wants, and desires become exposed when anger is expressed, sometimes bringing with them the threat of impending chaos. Given these risks, some individuals decide that turning their anger inward is better than risking the potential loss of a relationship.
- *Intro-punitive response to personal mistake or transgression.* This response occurs when individuals believe they should pun-

ish themselves after making a mistake or transgression. Intropunitive attacks are not reparative because the nature of the problem is not addressed. Instead, the individual makes a personal attack upon the self in reaction to the mistake or transgression. The reasoning process is somewhat primitive: "I did something bad so I must hurt myself." Sometimes this pattern has developed in situations of extreme external threat, as with parental physical abuse. In effect the child develops a habit of punishing himself or herself before the parent does so, at least partly to maintain a limited sense of control over a life-threatening situation.

- *Shameful sense of self.* Deeply shamed individuals may have powerfully internalized an abiding sense of badness, worthlessness, incompetence, etc. that leads to chronic, continuing self-condemnation. Turning their anger onto themselves is a way of endorsing their internal sense of defectiveness. Instead of "I did something bad so I must hurt myself" as in the previous example, they think "I am bad inside so I must punish myself."

THERAPEUTIC CONCEPTS, GUIDELINES, INTERVENTIONS, AND EXERCISES FOR TREATING ANGER TURNED INWARD

General Therapeutic Concepts and Guidelines

Many opportunities are available for therapeutic intervention with clients who primarily direct their anger inwardly. Several of these possibilities are described next.

1. *Help clients recognize the signs and signals that they are getting angry.* Clients may not be fully aware of how often they direct their anger inward. This is especially true for individuals who have thoroughly habituated this pattern to the point that they automatically direct anger onto the self, and for people whose strong and rigid moral stance against anger forces hostile feelings into unconsciousness. Consequently, clients may need to become more aware of the signs they are becoming angry and/or directing their anger at themselves. Some of these signs include relatively direct physical cues such as making fists or aggres-

sively scratching themselves; suggestive somatic symptoms such as headaches or fatigue; thought patterns that predict or precede "stuff and blow" episodes in that clients suddenly lose control of their anger; behavioral cues, such as avoiding others or diving harder into work, that occur when clients are nearing the limits of their ability to contain their anger; emotional symptoms such as increased depression or anxiety that might be related to the existence of suppressed anger; and existential or spiritual symptoms including hopelessness and despair. Of course the mere appearance of these behaviors is not positive evidence for anger turned inward. Patterns of behavior and cognition need to be established that repeatedly correlate these events with inwardly focused anger.

2. *Help clients recognize indirect expressions of anger.* Some clients who primarily direct their anger inwardly, especially those who very consciously suppress their angry feelings toward others, may discover, with help, that their anger "leaks out" in relatively subtle fashion. Typically, they frequently make slightly cynical, suspicious, or negative remarks (for instance, "Oh, really; I would never have thought of that" in the face of someone's obvious statement). Passive aggression is a second indirect pattern in which anger is expressed through inaction rather than defiant oppositionality. Examples of typical passive-aggressive behaviors include excessive forgetting to do things important to others, delaying, silence, making false promises just to "get others off my back," and excessive incompetence in areas that are particularly frustrating to significant others. A third tendency is to project anger onto others so that the clients believe they are the victims of hostility rather the perpetrator of that feeling.
3. *Discuss positive and negative aspects of turning anger inward.* Anger turned inward has its rewards and these must be discussed with clients in order to discover which of these advantages is most relevant to them. Practical advantages include lessening the risk of harming others with one's anger, avoiding retaliation, and avoiding perhaps unnecessary conflicts. In addition, cognitive and conceptual advantages include the sense that turning one's anger inward is morally appropriate or consistent

with the client's self-concept. However, there are also significant negative aspects when people primarily direct their anger onto themselves. These include such practical disadvantages as nonresolution of conflictual issues because legitimate concerns are not addressed, needs not being met because they are not expressed, the eventual resultant buildup of resentments, loss of self-esteem, and the health risks mentioned previously. Equally significant may be the client's invalidation of his or her emotions ("No, I'm not angry") and excessive guilt at the mere thought of expressing anger ("It's not OK to feel angry"). Finally, individuals with chronic patterns of internalized anger, especially when combined with excessive shame, may develop self-damaging patterns of behavior that will be described later in this chapter.

Selected Specific Therapeutic Interventions and Exercises

The following discussions and exercises are useful because they help clients recognize the extent to which they utilize anger turned inward and also the consequences of doing so.

First, have clients describe in detail how, when, where, and with whom they turn their anger inward, including their justifications for doing so. The "Anger Turned Inward Quiz" is quite useful in developing this dialogue, as is this series of questions:

1. Is the anger turned inward best described as anger that (a) the client has completely not perceived, or (b) the client knows about but minimizes its intensity, or (c) the client is aware of but doesn't want to express outwardly?
2. How intense or powerful is this anger?
3. How *important* is it to the client to contain this anger?
4. How *difficult* is it for the client to contain this anger?
5. What does the client think might happen if he or she were to express anger outwardly more often?
6. What are the gains and costs to the client when he or she suppresses or turns the anger onto himself or herself?

7. What forms does the anger turned inward take (self-neglect, self-blame, self-sabotage, self-attack, or self-destruction)? *Note:* This material is presented later in this chapter.
8. To what extent does the client want to (a) stop being as angry with himself or herself and/or (b) redirect the anger toward external targets?

With regard to this last question, the counselor generally should act as a neutral party who helps clients decide when to continue turning anger in and when to change its direction. However, on occasion it may be appropriate to become an advocate for turning anger away from the self and toward others, for example, in situations in which the client is clearly being misused or abused by others. Here the therapist can become a voice for action by giving clients permission and encouragement to express anger directly to others.

Motivation to redirect anger externally may be insufficient, though, if clients have not developed the requisite skills. Therefore counselors may need to teach specific skills such as making "I" statements, saying "no" to unreasonable or excessive requests, asserting oneself, using conflict management techniques, and negotiating, all of which serve to help build both the client's competence and confidence. Role-playing expressing and receiving anger with clients also improves their ability to direct their anger outwardly. These role-plays can be graded by beginning with the therapist acting the part of someone quite willing to be confronted ("Jackie, I'm really glad you told me that my coming home late bothers you; I didn't know that at all.") and evolving into people who are initially defensive ("What are you talking about? I'm not coming home late.") or outright aggressive ("Who the hell are you to tell me what to do? I'll come home whenever I want!").

Another useful intervention is questions designed to help clients recognize their choices. Four of these questions are "If you weren't angry at yourself right now, with whom would you be angry?" "If your anger had a voice, what would it be saying to you?" "What is the message in your anger that you need to act upon?" "If your anger at yourself is appropriate, then what do you need to do to become less angry at yourself?"

Finally, a Gestalt therapy two-chair dialogue in which clients alternate between the part of themselves that directs anger onto the self and the part of themselves that would prefer directing it externally can be quite effective in helping individuals to validate both aspects of themselves so that they can more effectively select the best action to take in the varied situations they face.

What If Clients Exhibit Both *Anger Turned Inward and Outward?*

Many clients are habitually and chronically angry at others as well as themselves. Their anger directed inwardly, though, may be missed in traditional anger management group programs that by necessity focus upon anger and aggression against others. One result may be that clients confuse "stuffing" their anger, i.e., redirecting it inwardly, with learning how to express their external anger appropriately. Furthermore, untreated inner-directed anger may actually sabotage clients' efforts to contain their externally directed anger since they still have not fundamentally altered their relationship with their anger. If anger remains the dominant emotion in someone's life, that individual is unlikely to be able to maintain a commitment to nonaggression.

Once clients are recognized to be high on both directions of anger, the problem should be addressed primarily as an excess of anger rather than a directional issue. Clients need to be encouraged to make a commitment to lessening the totality of their anger. That means setting goals of becoming angry both at the self and others less frequently and decreasing the intensity of both anger experiences. The alternative is to experience and express anger in moderation in both spheres.

Therapists can help their clients discover what circumstances are most likely to trigger turning anger inward, outward, or in both directions. For example, a client may regularly turn anger inward with a spouse but direct it outwardly toward children (or vice versa). Clients who can learn to identify their key trigger thoughts in response to anger invitations from the environment may discover that some issues trigger internal attack ("I did it again; I'm worthless.") while others trigger external aggression ("Nobody can say that to me!"). Another related therapeutic task is to find out how the messages clients give themselves when turning their anger upon themselves are similar or different to the messages they give others when their anger is directed outward.

Should one direction of anger be treated first? My preference is to allow the client to set initial priorities on which anger direction to treat but continually to address both issues and their relation to each other. However, externally directed anger containment may need to be the initial focus if the client is extremely hostile or violent. If so, the client still needs to receive treatment for both directions of anger.

Clients who are high in both anger directions will need help developing a compassionate attitude toward themselves, significant others, and the world. Love, caring, empathy, and kindness must find more room in the clients' mental universe. Otherwise, they will continue to be besieged with angry thoughts, feelings, and behaviors.

SELF-DAMAGING PATTERNS AND THEIR TREATMENT

The combination of excessive levels of anger turned inward and shame may result in a variety of self-damaging behaviors. Excessive shame often leads clients to think they are no good, not good enough, and unlovable. They believe they do not belong anywhere, and, in the extreme, that they should not exist (Potter-Efron and Potter-Efron, 1989). Meanwhile, the simultaneous presence of high levels of anger turned inward may result in a tendency toward self-punishment. Combined, shame and anger turned inward predicts a variety of self-damaging attitudes and behaviors, as illustrated in Figure 8.1. The behaviors at the base of the pyramid are the most common but least damaging while those at the top are least common but most destructive.

Self-Neglect

Shame most commonly drives people to withdraw from whatever causes their shame (Tangney and Dearing, 2002; Potter-Efron, 2002). When that source is the self, then shamed individuals may flee from self-awareness and self-attentiveness. The result is self-neglect, defined as "disinterest in and inability to attend to oneself." Although

FIGURE 8.1. Pyramid of Self-Damaging Thoughts and Behaviors

not essential to the pattern of self-neglect, these individuals are also likely to fail to recognize and express their external anger, especially if those individuals also feel shameful enough to believe they are not good or good enough to merit attention, and if they believe they are less valuable in general than others. Given that combination of elements, anger at others may be redirected toward oneself in the relatively passive form of self-neglect.

One of the characteristics of self-neglect is that individuals may appear to be disinterested in themselves while being highly focused on the welfare of others. Clients may justify this pattern of self-neglect on moral grounds, arguing that they are taking care of others while neglecting themselves because that is the morally correct thing to do. Their message is "Let me take care of you because that is the right thing to do" but the underlying theme is "Let me take care of you because I myself am not worthy of care." Nagged by this mostly unconscious conviction, self-neglecting persons often fail to notice or attend to their basic wants and needs, such as making doctor appointments, getting exercise, and sleeping. Furthermore, they will have difficulty and feel excessively guilty saying "no" to others even when angry about those people's expectations or demands. These individuals have difficulty either listening to their anger as it signals a problem ("Something's wrong here!") or to utilize the energy that accompanies anger in order to change their environment.

One cost of self-neglect is that individuals who are unable to attend to their own needs and are overresponsive to others may periodically collapse when overwhelmed by their responsibilities. Even then, though, they will be reluctant to receive help from others, and they will make every effort to restore the equilibrium as quickly as possible.

The treatment for self-neglect must address both helping clients gain better awareness of their anger and challenging the internalized shame that keeps them from addressing their needs. In particular they must become much more comfortable saying "no" to others and "yes" to themselves, a pattern diametrically opposed to their self-neglecting tendencies. That means discovering and listening to their inner self-nurturing voice, but to do so they first must become more curious about and interested in themselves as human beings worthy of attention.

Self-neglecting persons must be challenged to question the absolute moral correctness of giving priority to others instead of themselves. "Who told you that?" is often a good starting place for this challenge, especially if they received strong family of origin messages to take care of others first, last, and always. Naturally the idea is not to turn such individuals into totally hedonistic, self-centered egotists but to help them balance their care for others with self-care. Doing so will help prevent the periodic collapsing burnout pattern described previously.

Self-Sabotage

Self-sabotage is the second self-damaging combination of anger turned inward and shame. Self-sabotage is essentially passive aggression turned inward. Here anger against the self is displayed through a variety of failure patterns. For example, clients often demonstrate an inability to finish projects even when they say they personally desire to do so, they do not get around to making personally important phone calls, etc. Driven by a combination of shame and anger turned inward, these clients fail at least partially in order to exact punishment against their inadequate selves.

Passive aggression against others represents a quiet rebellion against authority, control, and being told what to do. Similarly, self-sabotage may represent the client's perpetual rebellion against internalized demands. The client says "You can't make me" not to others but to an internalized voice that demands achievement and success. The result, unfortunately, is the creation of an abiding negative routine in which clients seemingly destroy almost every opportunity they have for personal happiness.

The treatment for self-sabotage involves helping clients challenge their internalized "I don't deserve to succeed" messages. These messages must first be identified, then linked with shame and anger turned inward, and then challenged through standard cognitive therapy approaches such as disputation. Therapists should also discover and challenge the personal failure patterns and rituals of such clients because people usually fail repeatedly in the same manner. For instance, one of my clients developed a highly predictable pattern of carrying through with great success on a number of projects just until the very last step, such as turning in the final paper for a college class. Then he simply stopped working, as if he were paralyzed by the threat of accomplishment. Identifying this pattern helped this client begin to break this routine. In this case it was helpful to treat the ongoing failures of this client like a phobia, setting small goals so he could take small steps toward success.

Self-Blame

The presence of shame and anger turned inward might need to be inferred in self-neglect and self-sabotage, but that is hardly the case with self-blame. Here clients are more than ready consciously to attack themselves, almost as if they lived by the slogan "When in doubt it must be my fault." Shame-bound (Kaufman, 1996), the working model of these persons is that they are to blame for everything that goes wrong because they possess an irrational sense of responsibility for all problems. Metaphorically, these clients seem to possess an internalized scolder and flaw seeker, a part of themselves that continually scans the environment looking for things they have done wrong. Quick to blame themselves, their anger turned inward takes the form of blistering verbal accusations: "Dummy, why did you do that?" "What's wrong with you anyhow?" "How could you think anybody would ever love you?"

Treatment for self-blaming begins with helping clients challenge the idea that they are always to blame for everything that goes badly ("Who told you that?"). They need to recognize the connections between their self-blaming reproach and the existence of internalized shame. That in turn might allow them to quit taking excessive responsibility for others and to exchange their negative scanning pattern for more neutral or positive scanning patterns. Eventually they may learn to see themselves in a more positive light so that they can give themselves praise as well as criticism as befits the actual situation.

It may also be useful with self-blaming clients to have them describe and externalize their internalized scolder and flaw seeker, perhaps by writing their imagined critic a letter to be read and discussed in therapy or by engaging in a two-chair dialogue in which clients alternate speaking on behalf of the critic ("I'm only telling the truth; you are really a pitiful excuse for a human being") and the part of themselves that wants to accept the self ("Leave me alone; I'm a good person and I'm tired of feeling ashamed of myself all the time").

Self-Attack

The fourth form of self-damaging behavior occurs as clients increase their verbal aggression and add physical aggression to their attack against the self. By now the anger turned inward has become rageful. It is as if these individuals possessed an internalized punisher. This intro-punitive agent, often primitive in thought, sometimes literally demands blood, triggering episodes of self-mutilation in which the primary message becomes "I am bad. I deserve pain. I must suffer. I must hurt myself to demonstrate my badness to everyone." This behavior may signal others not to attack since the self-attacker is already at work, especially with those individuals who have been badly verbally, physically, or sexually abused as children.

Interpersonally, some clients mired in self-attack may tend to attract punishing partners. These abusive partners externalize the client's internal attack; in response to their internalized statement "I am a bad person who deserves punishment" their partner responds with "Yes you are and I will be the one who hurts you." However, this interpretation must be used very cautiously around clients who are in abusive relationships. No matter what the internal cognitive state of the recipients of abuse may be, abusive partners must not be given an excuse to perpetuate their actions.

Treatment for self-attacking clients begins with helping them commit to lessening the frequency and intensity of self-attack episodes, in particular self-mutilation events. However, before they can do this, some clients may need to describe the characteristics of their internalized punisher, including sensed age, gender, most common thoughts, etc. Gathering this information helps clients contest the need to be punished and sometimes, when the internalized punisher is found to be an introjected form of a punishing parent or other significant figure, clients can then begin to externalize and reject the internalized figure. In other situations, those in which clients are diverting rage against others onto themselves, they must learn to listen for the underlying message in their physical aggression against themselves. For instance, a client who engages in butting his head into a wall may really want to smash through an adversary or, less obviously, that client might be almost desperately wanting someone important to step in and stop his or her suffering. Finally, but critically, self-attacking persons must learn to select nonpunitive friends, employers, and partners. Self-attackers can thrive only in the presence of others who fully appreciate their goodness and who refuse to join in with the person's internalized punisher.

Self-Destruction

Self-destruction is the most extreme combination of anger turned inward and shame. The internalized shame message is "I should not be" (Potter-Efron and Potter-Efron, 1989), a message that strongly promotes suicidal ideation. In addition, clients develop a powerful splitting process that places their selves into an "all bad" (evil) category while practically everyone else is good. The result is a sense of hopelessness and despair that serves to prevent these individuals from taking in praise, comfort, or love. These persons seem to be haunted by the presence of "internalized annihilators" that produce a sense of inevitable doom within themselves. They think it makes no sense to live when life is only bad.

The long-term treatment for self-destructiveness lies in helping clients convert their "I should not be" messages to messages that simply state "I am." This usually represents a long and difficult journey because clients must learn to bypass their shame and internalized anger, to quit trying either to prove they should or should not exist, and instead learn how to view themselves without judgment, approval, or disapproval. Some of these persons could benefit by learning about the concept of splitting and how their particular splitting process makes them appear totally bad and evil to themselves. Therapists will certainly need to help self-destructive clients voice and gently challenge their despair, being careful to check for the presence of a major depressive condition in the process. Those clients closest to suicide will need to remember and take in the love of others even when in despair and to acknowledge how others would be affected by their death. It may also be useful to help these clients get in touch with their inner self-preserver, the part that wants to survive and that brings them to therapy.

CASE STUDY: THE LADY WHO QUIT SMILING

Jenni Calloway, forty-five, came to counseling after a strange, out-of-character incident that left her shocked and confused. This woman describes herself as generally quiet, unassuming, conflict avoidant, and over-responsible for others, the kind of woman who can always be counted on to bake a cake for the church fund drive even if she baked three for the one just last month.

Jenni wears a constant smile even while discussing distressing events. She explains that when she was growing up her mother always told her that people only like you when you smile. Lately, though, life has been hard for Jenni. Her husband, Paul, has suffered a serious back injury that put him out of work and he is quickly developing an addiction to pain medications. Her oldest daughter, Sue, accused Jenni of being selfish because she asked to have Christmas at Sue's house instead of her own due to Paul's condition. Furthermore, people at work have been taking advantage of Jenni by dumping unpleasant duties on her.

Jennie admits that she "stuffs" her anger a lot: "I'm like that old saying about a pressure cooker that keeps gaining pressure until it blows up." But she never had exploded until the week before she came to counseling. Then, in a single day she swore at one of her work colleagues, told Paul to "get off that stinking couch and do something with your life" and blasted her daughter over the phone. Shaken, she signed up for therapy. True to form, she told the counselor that her goal was to get back to being someone who could smile again.

Jenni scored fifty-two points on the Anger Turned Inward Quiz, indicative of a high level of anger turned inward. Five-point items included: "I 'stuff' my anger and then get headaches, a stiff neck, stomachaches, etc.," "I put on a good front by smiling and looking happy even when I'm upset," "I feel guilty or shameful whenever I become angry, no matter how justified my anger might be," and "I feel very responsible for others even when I'm angry with them." Guilt emerged as her dominant emotion, since she was usually either feeling guilty about her alleged transgressions (especially "selfishness") or desperately trying to please others so as to avoid guilt. Excessive guilt prevented Jenni from setting appropriate boundaries with others because saying "no" to anyone, however unreasonable their request, made her feel terrible. As for the anger she felt toward those who demanded so much from her, Jenni turned it inward by telling herself that it was her fault that she could not gracefully accept their demands.

The combination of internalized anger and excessive guilt always makes treatment difficult and slow. The first step was to help Jenni recognize what she was doing with her anger and its relationship to her maladaptive guilt. Some family-of-origin work regarding the family myths and belief systems that supported Jenni's continual smiling was necessary. However, the bulk of work was present oriented with emphasis on her right and ability to make choices, say "no," and set boundaries. Jenni read books on assertiveness and practiced confronting her work colleagues during role-plays in the office. She eventually decided exactly what single specific action to contest: a co-worker's habit of dropping off work on Jenni's desk as that woman headed out the door. Jenni stopped that person, told her to take that work back, and handled her inevitable guilt by reminding herself she was doing the right thing even though it felt bad. After her success at work Jenni spoke with her husband and daughter about how she was changing. She told them she was not going to smile quite as much as they were used to. She also stated that she might even get angry from time to time. Fortunately, her family supported her efforts once they realized that a more assertive Jenni might also be a more truly loving Jenni.

Jenni still feels guilty frequently, but now she uses that guilt in a new way. "Whenever I start to feel guilty I ask myself what I am angry about. When I figure that out I ask myself what I want to do about it. And then, if I can, I talk directly to whomever I need to about it." In other words, Jenni has learned to direct her anger outwardly instead of constantly turning it upon herself.

SUMMARY

The theme of anger turned inward is complex. It involves anger suppression, anger repression, and angry attacks upon the self. The general therapy for excessive anger turned inward, though, is relatively easy to describe: help clients to (1) recognize the patterns of anger turned inward they have developed; (2) change those patterns by becoming better able to balance anger turned inward with outwardly expressed anger; and (3) convert the behaviors and cognitions consistent with internalized shame into ones associated with self-worth and self-respect.

Chapter 9

The Emotional Brain: Anger, Fear, and Therapy

INTRODUCTION

As in many other areas of psychotherapy, a developing convergence exists between the art of therapy and scientific research. In particular, the tremendous surge of interest in what has been labeled "emotional intelligence" has allowed many different researchers and theorists (e.g., Schore, 1994; Panksepp, 1998; Cozolino, 2002) to consider how emotions are processed in the brain. Part of this chapter will describe one small portion of that research, namely, how stress and trauma can reconfigure the brain for survival at the cost of higher level functioning.

A great many researchers have become interested over the last decade in the questions of how and why the brain processes emotion. Some relevant questions include:

1. What specific electrical circuitry and chemical exchanges are involved in processing each emotion?
2. Are emotions primarily conscious or unconscious phenomena?
3. What is the purpose of emotions?
4. What is known specifically about how the brain creates the sensations that become labeled as "anger"?
5. What happens within the brain when trauma affects the development of the brain's emotional processes?
6. How can our current understanding of emotional brain processes inform therapeutic endeavor?

These questions will be discussed in this chapter.

WHAT ARE EMOTIONS? WHY DO WE HAVE THEM?

The words "affect," "mood," "emotion," and "feeling" are so interwoven in both common and scientific discussion that it is difficult to distinguish meaningfully between them. In general, the word "affect" is used to refer to specific body sensation states, while "emotion" refers to a more complex state that has multiple components that are activated in response to some real or imagined object, person, or situation (Kring, 2001). LeDoux (1996, 2002) emphasizes that emotional processes are primarily unconscious or preconscious as the brain responds to certain situations by activating a cascade of physiological processes. Damasio (2000, 2003) distinguishes between three classes of emotions: background emotions that reflect a person's general sense of well-being or discomfort of being; primary emotions such as anger and fear that are hard-wired in the brain for rapid response; and social emotions such as shame, guilt, and pride that regulate more sophisticated interpersonal processes. Although Damasio appears to agree with LeDoux that emotions are primarily preconscious, he adds that their full impact is realized only when they are sensed consciously, at which point he designates them as "feelings."

However defined, the more interesting question is this: What is the overall value of emotions to human beings? The answer is that the brain regions implicated in emotions have developed, mostly from brain structures originally utilized to detect smell (Ratey, 2001), to help individuals quickly and effectively respond to significant situations, especially those situations that could threaten survival. Thus, emotions can be conceived as a chain of loosely connected brain pathways and behavioral sequences that are activated whenever physical or social survival is potentially threatened. Plutchik (2001) describes two of these sequences in which an external stimulus event creates physiological arousal that in turn triggers overt behavior. With fear, the sequence goes from

1. the immediate perception (not necessarily conscious) of a threat, to
2. an inferred cognition of danger, to
3. a physiological feeling state of fear, to
4. escape behavior, so as to
5. restore safety.

With anger the sequence becomes

1. an awareness of an obstacle that
2. creates an inferred cognition of there being an enemy,
3. which produces the physiological state of anger,
4. which in turn leads to attack behavior with the goal of destroying the obstacle.

Before continuing, let me add a note of caution. Very little is known about how the brain functions at this time since only recently has it been possible to gather systematic information about it from living individuals. Furthermore, the brain is a very complex organ, composed of approximately one hundred billion neurons, each of which might make as many as ten thousand connections with other neurons (Ratey, 2001). Also, the brain's development is never complete. One reason is that parts of the brain continue to develop well past childhood, including, for instance, cells in the hippocampus that contribute to impulse inhibition (Cozolino, 2002). Another equally significant fact is that new brain circuitry is continuously created as new pathways are developed as the result of new learning and experiences. Excellent reviews of brain structures and mechanisms are presented in the works of Cozolino (2002), Ratey (2001), LeDoux (2002), Lane and Nadel (2000), and other writers. More specifically, Niehoff (1998) describes many aspects of the biology of violence in her book (also see Volavka, 2002), while LeDoux (1996) and Cozolino (2002) describe the effects of trauma on the brain particularly clearly and Damasio (2003) describes the three previously mentioned subsets of emotions: background, primary, and social emotions.

Emotions are particularly difficult to study because they are "the result of multiple brain and body functions that are distributed over the whole person" rather than being localized within one part of the brain or body (Ratey, 2001, p. 223). Also, there is no single brain center for aggression (Volavka, 2002), so malfunctions in any part of the brain, including the limbic area and the neocortex, may result in poor emotional regulation. Nevertheless, certain locations in the brain are regularly associated with emotional functioning. These include the amygdala and its nearby extensions (Aggleton and Young, 2000), which allow for immediate reactions to potential threat, and the hippocampus (LeDoux, 1996), which is particularly important in the formation and retrieval of both verbal and emotional memories (Teicher, 2002).

More specifically, several discrete areas of the brain have been linked in a circuit that produces affective aggression and probably the related feeling of anger. Panksepp (1998) links the amygdala, hypothalamus, and periaqueductal grey (PAG) areas of the brain to what he labels the RAGE response. According to Panksepp, these three areas are hierarchical in that the amygdala's ability to respond to anger-provoking stimuli depends upon the well functioning of the hypothalamus, which in turn depends upon the well functioning of the PAG. Thus, a lesion in the PAG would affect the entire system, whereas a lesion in the amygdala would have a lesser effect. As such, the PAG is central to the anger experience: "Probably the most important area for the actual integration of the overall anger response is in the PAG" (Panksepp, 1998, p. 198).

Panksepp notes that affective aggression is one of three basic kinds of animal aggression; the other two are predatory and inter-male aggression. Only affective aggression, however, is linked with what would normally be considered an angry state of being. Panksepp states one cause for this kind of aggression: "anything that restricts our freedom will be viewed as an irritant deserving our anger, contempt and revolutionary intent" (Panksepp, 1998, p. 189). He notes that restricting access to desired resources is another trigger for affective aggression.

The previous description refers to normal mammalian displays of anger and aggression. As such, anger and aggression are not necessarily problematic, even in the increasingly complex societies human beings create. They serve the function of activating the system against threat and toward sought-after but blocked resources. Furthermore, the relatively primitive circuitry described previously is highly mediated in humans through higher cognitive processes centered within the prefrontal cortex of the brain. It takes a highly functioning brain to mediate all the mutually interactive systems that eventuate in a particular response. However, many kinds of damage, including that caused by stress and trauma, can strongly affect the functioning of the brain in these areas.

THE STRESSED AND TRAUMATIZED BRAIN: FEAR AND ANGER

Many possible links exist between physical aggression and brain dysfunctions. For example, violent offenders often show diminished prefrontal cortex brain activity (Ratey, 2001; Niehoff, 1998), implying that they may not understand moral concepts and are less able to inhibit subcortical areas associated with aggression. A definite link occurs between diminished serotonin levels and aggression (Niehoff, 1998); individuals with low serotonin levels are more likely to experience "knee-jerk" overreactions, becoming edgy and bad tempered. In addition, clients with attention deficit disorder and others who display signs of brainwave underactivity may become impulsively aggressive because of their need for brain stimulation (Volavka, 2002).

One especially interesting line of brain research focuses upon how the brain can be reconfigured by stress and trauma to become an organ that is selectively attuned to survival instead of thriving. Many clients who have been diagnosed with depression, impulsive anger, post-traumatic stress disorder and other anxiety disorders, or antisocial personalities share signs of suffering from impaired stress response mechanisms.

The amygdala and hippocampus have been particularly well studied with regard to the long-term effects of trauma upon their interactions. Figure 9.1 illustrates how, over time, the natural balance between these two components of the brain can be disrupted, causing permanent alterations to an individual's perception of the world.

The stressed and traumatized brain has been studied extensively, in particular by Joseph LeDoux (1996). LeDoux suggests that post-traumatic stress disorder and related phobic problems are best understood by a "sensitization" model in which continuing stress produces quicker and more intense reactions over time. LeDoux's main hypothesis is that long-term stress can cause permanent changes in brain structure as the brain becomes wired for survival rather than thriving.

One set of changes that occurs in the face of continuing or traumatizing threat is in the balance between activating and calming signals within the brain itself. The brain normally develops and main-

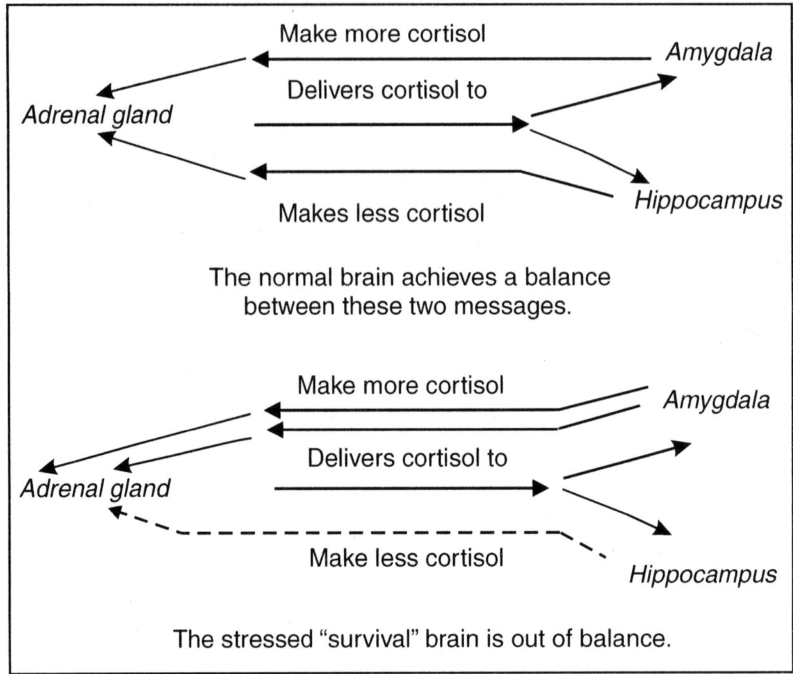

FIGURE 9.1. How the Stressed Brain Becomes Survival Oriented Over Time

tains a balance between *excitatory/activating processes* (triggered by the chemical glutamate) and *inhibitory/sedating processes* (triggered by the chemical GABA). However, this delicate balance can be permanently altered by extreme or ongoing stress because stress triggers the release of the hormone *cortisol* from the adrenal gland. Cortisol increases the intensity of fear reactions. Excessive amounts of cortisol particularly reprogram one area of the brain—the *hippocampus*—that is responsible for much of conscious (declarative) memory function, the labeling of emotionally threatening events, and for signaling the adrenal gland to quit releasing cortisone. Therefore, the more stress damages the hippocampus, the more a vicious spiral ensues; the messages to quit making cortisol are reduced because of the damage, more cortisol is produced, which causes more damage to the hippocampus, which then sends even fewer messages to the adrenal gland to quit making cortisol, etc.

Meanwhile, another nearby part of the brain, the *amygdala,* is an activator that tells the adrenal gland to keep releasing cortisone. The amygdala is concerned with creating the emotional content of memories. Over time stress causes the amygdala to become smaller and hypersensitive to threatening situations. The result is that the brain goes into a state of hypervigilance, as if serious threats were imminent. The body responds with continual flight or fight reactions, frequently to cues that others would consider minimally threatening or nonthreatening.

The combination of a damaged hippocampus (as much as 16 percent smaller than average for traumatized persons) (Teicher, 2002) and overreactive amygdala, in effect, doubly prepares the stressed individual to live in a dangerous world. The brain has essentially been reconfigured for *survival* in a constantly threatening world. However, the individual with this kind of brain will function inefficiently in a safer world.

Stress also appears to damage the *corpus collosum* (Teicher, 2002), the part of the brain that connects the two hemispheres, making it difficult for traumatized or highly stressed individuals to integrate logic with emotional information that would help them respond appropriately to possible threatening cues.

The amygdala is the main destination of Joseph LeDoux's label, the "low road" brain communication system. Here danger cues go directly from the thalamus to the amygdala, producing an instantaneous "freeze" reaction, followed by very rapid flight-or-fight behavior. The quality of information, however, is poor (Look out! There's a snake shape!).

Also, a "high road" runs from the thalamus through the visual cortex and then to the amygdala. This takes longer but provides more detailed information (Relax! It's a stick, not a snake.) and integrates more information from past experience. Stress, abuse, and trauma tend over time to do more damage to the high-road process than the low road. The result is that individuals are more likely to be flooded with vaguely understood, confusing, but very threatening sensations.

Emotional memories are difficult to eradicate. One reason for this problem is that far more neuronal pathways link the amygdala to the cortex than link the cortex to the amygdala (Johnson, 2003). As a result, traumatic emotional memories are persistent, easily triggered, and can actually build in intensity over time. Also, the brain gives priority to the amygdala during threatening situations. Furthermore, situations are increasingly defined as threatening during cumulative experiences of trauma. The more often situations are perceived as threatening, then the more control the amygdala will assume over day-to-day life.

THE ANGER AND AGGRESSION CONNECTION WITH THE STRESSED BRAIN

Handling anger well presents difficult challenges to individuals even when their brains are functioning at maximum efficiency. Many clients who need help with anger management have far less than optimized brain function. Some have obvious damage due to falls or fights; others may have sweeping limitations caused by low general intelligence; and, since many angry people grew up in violent homes in which they witnessed and/or were subject to physical, verbal, and emotional abuse, they may have developed the same survival-oriented brain structures described previously with excessively fearful clients.

The pathways regulating fear and aggression are very similar: "Research has uncovered surprising congruencies between the neurobiological mechanisms underlying stress disorders and those underlying aggression" (Niehoff, 1998, p. 50). Fear and anger share common pathways, as one would expect from the long-recognized "flight or fight" reactions people have in the face of danger. Anger, especially when experienced by the individual as defensive in nature, is, like fear, a core reaction to threat (LeDoux, 1996). Defensive aggression thus becomes one strategy to handle fear-invoking situations. Fear and anger then may become interlocked: "When [interpersonal] interchange has become hostile . . . the struggle to balance response and demand strains the physical boundaries of the nervous system and the dynamic interplay . . . degenerates into a vicious cycle, spiraling toward violence and rotating compulsively back toward fear" (Niehoff, 1998, p. 52).

Some interpersonal violence can be described from this model as a developmental process between individual and environment that has created lasting, perhaps irreversible, neurobiological effects upon the violent person's brain.

Trauma resets the brain to favor defensive behavior. Specifically, stress may produce a condition labeled "limbic irritability" (Teicher, 2002), which in turn produces symptoms of aggression, exasperation, and anxiety. In addition, smaller amygdala size is associated with depression, irritability, and hostility (Teicher, 2002).

Many anger management clients were raised and may continue to live in physically and emotionally threatening environments. They may well need to have available a quick response mode to these threats that takes the form of defensive verbal or even physical aggression. This aggression is adaptive, but only if the individual's ability to assess threat is accurate. However, as noted previously, the survival-oriented brain tends to misinterpret situations in the direction of perceived threat, becoming less and less accurate at assessing both whether a particular situation is threatening and the degree of threat involved. These persons develop maladaptive patterns of anger and aggression: they become angry with the wrong people, for the wrong reasons, at too elevated levels of intensity, at the wrong times, and in the wrong places. Their frequently misguided sense of threat produces misguided incidents of aggression as they respond automatically but inaccurately to unsubstantiated and misinterpreted dangers.

This slide away from good reality perception can be progressive (Niehoff, 1998). Each angry reaction leads to false alarms to the stress system (increased norepinephrine; epinephrine, and cortisol; increased blood pressure, etc.) that further erode the ability of the brain to accurately assess risk. Eventually many survival-oriented individuals feel persistent hypertension, relentless suspicion, and a need for ceaseless vigilance. Their brains and bodies have been placed in a permanent defensive mode that can be relaxed only with great difficulty.

THERAPY FOR ANGRY AND AGGRESSIVE BEHAVIOR

What can be done, from a neurological perspective, to help excessively angry clients, in particular those who function with the survival-oriented brain patterns described previously? Niehoff (1998, p. 264) writes that "The key to tempering violent behavior is adjusting the calculation of threat so that the intensity of the response matches the true demands of the situation." This may be done partly through therapy and partly with medications. Although no single medication is effective with every excessively angry person, many medications offer at least partial relief of angry affect and cognitions and of aggressive behavior. Minor tranquilizers (the benzodiazepines) and antipsychotics (e.g., Geodon, Abilify) may be particularly useful to counter acute anger episodes whereas beta-blockers (e.g., propranolol), anti-convulsants (e.g., Tegretol, Depakote), anxiolytics (e.g., BuSpar), mood alterers (e.g., lithium), and SSRI antidepressants (e.g., Prozac) are all utilized to lessen angry outbursts (Blumenreich, 1993; Panksepp, 1998). Psychostimulants may also be utilized, in particular with clients who have been diagnosed with attention deficit disorder (Blumenreich, 1993).

Therapeutically, angry and aggressive behavior may best be altered through programs that provide safety, promote attachment to others, and encourage the development of cognitive strategies that help the clients contain their initial protective and defensive reactions to perceived threat. In addition, certain medications help clients become less impulsively aggressive by increasing the "reflective delay" (Niehoff, 1998) between stimulus and response. These include antidepressants, anticonvulsants, antimanic drugs, and opiate blockers that prevent craving. The basic goal of both therapy and medications is to help free the brain of defensively aggressive persons from survival mode so that they can live better in (and help create) a safer world.

More generally, Cozolino (2002) indicates that one major goal is to help clients integrate all their neural networks and, in particular, to integrate the affect and cognition systems. Since many clients have had to sacrifice their long-term well-being for the purpose of immediate survival in the face of stress and trauma, therapy should be used to reconnect circuits that have been disconnected. By doing so clients will eventually gain far greater cognitive control over their behaviors as they lessen their tendencies to dissociate action and experience from conscious awareness. Cozolino describes several approaches that help clients develop these integrated neural networks, such as by simultaneously alternating the activation of the emotional and cognitive neural networks, creating "safe emergencies" that allow clients to master moderate amounts of stress, and cocreating new narratives that redefine the client's past and present experiences. These kinds of therapeutic endeavors eventually might raise the client's ability to tolerate and regulate affect, especially anger and fear. Cozolino cites the therapeutic approach labeled Eye Movement Desensitization and Reprocessing (EMDR) (Shapiro, 1995) as one specific technique that appears to help integrate neural circuitry in the manner described previously. EMDR is rather mysterious in that nobody is sure how it works, but apparently the rapid activation of stimulation of alternate sides of the face and body, and hence alternate brain hemispheres, creates opportunities for traumatized individuals to cease automatic dissociative reactions to memories or associations with the trauma.

However, special techniques may not always be necessary when seeking to integrate neural circuitry with habitually angry clients. Taking a time-out, for instance, helps clients do exactly that by cutting off the intensity of their emotional response before it short-circuits a client's cognitive abilities. This simple technique, when practiced appropriately, helps clients learn how to proceed from "think or feel" to "think and feel," especially when followed by the question, "Now what are you planning to do with your anger?" in other words, "How are you planning to use your anger to help you take action that is socially productive?" Anger management counselors must keep in mind the goal of helping their clients learn how to think and feel simultaneously rather than solely promoting the mindless ventilation of feelings or the creation of thought processes that are ungrounded in feeling.

CASE STUDY: A DISSOCIATIVE CLIENT LEARNS TO STAY CONSCIOUS WHEN ANGRY

Jane, age thirty-eight, is a survivor of severe child abuse. Like most host personalities in a dissociative system, Jane is generally quiet, depressed, and so absolutely terrified of conflict that she frequently dissociates at the first glimmer of internal anger. She then "goes into the black" while an alter named "The Bull" appears. The Bull is a rager who sometimes physically assaults those people who have bothered Jane but usually only swears vehemently at them. The Bull lives in a perpetual "fight-or-flight" world.

Jane has been in therapy for several years. During that time she has worked diligently on the goal of staying conscious more often, even in emotionally challenging situations. Recently she reported an episode in which she certainly would have dissociated in the past. Her nineteen-year-old daughter, Trina, had come home drunk the night before and Jane attempted to talk with her the next morning. Trina was still hungover, though, and screamed at her mother to go away. In fact, Trina ordered her mother to dissociate by calling out the name of one of her other alters, a child named Cutesy who would let Trina do anything she wanted. However, Jane did not dissociate this time. Instead, she got angry enough with Trina to tell her she would have to quit drinking or move out. After the argument Jane started to shake with fear and hid in the bathroom for an hour. Still, she was proud of herself: "That's the first time I remember not going away when my daughter yelled at me. I stayed up front and handled it myself."

SUMMARY

This chapter's discussion of how certain brain functions affect the client's experience of anger and aggression points to the future of anger management therapy. As understanding increases, therapists will likely be able to offer to their excessively angry clients an increased repertory of both interpersonal and medical interventions. As anger management treatment becomes more sophisticated, therapists will be able to move from "one-size-fits-all" treatment programs to more individualized treatment modalities. The result, hopefully, will be that the world becomes a safer and better place both for these angry individuals and for all those who live with and among them.

Appendix A

Anger Assessment Forms

This appendix contains: (1) an Intake Questionnaire designed to help counselors quickly gather a wide range of relevant information from clients who might need help in the area of anger management; (2) a Treatment Planning Form that helps counselors plan efficient and effective treatment; (3) an Anger Styles Questionnaire that helps counselors identify ten different possible anger concerns; and (4) the Anger Turned Inward Quiz, which focuses attention on that relatively ignored area of anger management. The first three instruments are discussed in Chapter 2, and the latter is discussed in Chapter 8.

The Intake Questionnaire will take between thirty minutes and two hours to complete in face-to-face interaction with clients, depending upon how informative the client is and also upon how much the counselor uses this instrument to begin treatment, as well as to gather information. The questionnaire may also be sent home with clients or given to them in advance to be filled out and then reviewed in session.

The Treatment Planning Form primarily allows counselors to set priorities with their clients. The goal is to answer questions such as: How much energy should be devoted to the prevention of anger as opposed to its containment and problem resolution? How much emphasis should be placed on behavioral change versus cognitive, spiritual, and affective treatment? Given the decreasing number of sessions most clients can have in treatment, this form may help counselors determine how best to utilize their limited time.

The Anger Styles Questionnaire, a thirty-item quiz modified from its original form (Potter-Efron and Potter-Efron, 1995), identifies ten ways that people handle situations in which they might get angry. For instance, one person might react to someone forgetting to meet him or her for lunch with sudden anger, and another person might try to begin to develop a long-term resentment. I have found this tool to be quite useful in that it helps people identify their primary habits of anger response, habits I label "anger styles."

Finally, the Anger Turned Inward Questionnaire is designed to help clients determine how frequently they turn their anger on to themselves. Each item in the questionnaire corresponds to statements found in the research literature about the nature and costs of this process.

Please note that neither of these last two quizzes has been scientifically researched. They do have face validity, however, in that clients report that they accurately describe how they feel and act when they become angry. They have proved very useful in clinical work, steering clients toward a greater understanding of their anger patterns.

ANGER/AGGRESSION INTAKE QUESTIONNAIRE

I. PLEASE TELL ME ABOUT ANY CONCERNS YOU OR OTHERS HAVE ABOUT YOUR ANGER.

II. DESCRIBE YOUR *MOST RECENT* EVENT INVOLVING YOUR ANGER OR AGGRESSION.

A. When did this occur?
B. With whom?
C. How did it start?
D. While this was going on what did you
1. think?
2. feel?
3. say?
4. do?
E. How did it end?
F. Were alcohol or drugs used by anyone involved?
G. Were physical violence, force, threats, etc., used?
H. What effects (immediate or long term) did this event have on you?
I. What effects (immediate or long term) did this event have on others?

III. NOW PLEASE TELL ME ABOUT THE *WORST* INCIDENT YOU'VE EVER HAD INVOLVING YOUR ANGER OR AGGRESSIVENESS.

A. When did this occur?
B. With whom?
C. How did it start?

D. While this was going on what did you
1. think?
2. feel?
3. say?
4. do?
E. How did it end?
F. Were alcohol or drugs used by anyone involved?
G. Were physical violence, force, threats, etc., used?
H. What effects (immediate or long term) did this event have on you?
I. What effects (immediate or long term) did this event have on others?

IV. FREQUENCY OF PROBLEMS.

A. How often have you had trouble with your anger?

	Never	**Once or twice**	**Weekly**	**Several times/ week**	**Daily**	**More than once/day**
1. This month?						
2. Over the past six months?						
3. Previously as an adult?						
4. When you were a teenager?						
5. When you were a child?						

6. Would you say that lately you become angry
____ more often than a year ago?
____ less often than a year ago?
____ about the same as a year ago?
7. Would you say that lately when you become angry you have
____ more control than previously over what you say and do?
____ less control?
____ about the same amount of control as before?
8. Would you say thay lately when you get angry you do
____ more damage than before?
____ less damage?

____ about the same amount of damage?
____ not believe your anger/aggression is damaging?

9. When upset are you more likely to become angry at
   ____ others?
   ____ yourself?
   ____ both yourself and others?

B. With whom do you become angry and how often do you become angry with them?

	Daily	**Several times/week**	**Occasionally**
Partner/boyfriend/girlfriend			
Parents/stepparents			
Your children/stepchildren			
Other relatives			
Employers/co-workers/employees			
Teachers			
Friends			
Strangers			
Others (whom?):			

V. IMMEDIATE STRESSORS.

A. What occurred in your life now or in the past several months that has caused you stress, concern, or anxiety?

Financial troubles:
Relationship problems:
Health concerns:
Job or school difficulties:
Legal issues:
Emotional problems:
Concern about someone else:

Religious or spiritual crisis:
Other (specify):

B. How have these troubles affected your mood or behavior?

VI. ANGER HISTORY.

A. Family of origin.

1. Describe what the following people did or do with their anger, especially when you were growing up.
a. Your father/stepfather:
b. Your mother/stepmother:
c. Your brothers and sisters:
d. Other relatives:
2. Is there any family history of bad temper, assaults, homicides, or suicides?
3. Were you spanked as a child? What do you think about that?
4. Were you physically or sexually assaulted? If so, how do you think that has affected you, especially in terms of anger?
5. In general, what did you learn about anger from your family?

B. Friendship groups, culture, religious training, etc.

1. Describe how your attitudes toward anger and aggression have been affected by messages you received from members of the following groups.
a. Your gender:
b. The opposite gender:
c. Your nationality:
d. Your race:
e. Your religion:

f. Social groups or gangs to which you belonged:
g. Other people or groups:

VII. POSSIBLE MEDICAL AND/OR PSYCHOLOGICAL FACTORS.

A. Do you have any current problems or past history of problems with the following?
____ Alcohol or drug abuse
____ Antisocial personality disorder
____ Anxiety disorders
____ Attention deficit disorder (with or without hyperactivity?)
____ Bipolar disorder
____ Borderline personality disorder
____ Brain injury, concussions, seizures
____ Chronic illness
____ Dementia
____ Depression
____ Diabetes or hypoglycemia
____ Disabling injury
____ Paranoia
____ Post-traumatic stress disorder
____ Premenstrual syndrome
____ Schizophrenia
____ Other major illness or condition (specify): ______________

B. Are you currently taking any medications? If yes, what?

VIII. LEGAL HISTORY RELATING TO ANGER AND AGGRESSION.

A. Any current problems with the law?
B. Are you on probation or parole?

C. Are you coming here as part of a criminal diversion program?
D. Any past anger- or aggression-related legal difficulties?
E. Any brushes with the law because of your anger or aggression that did not result in charges being filed?
F. If yes to any of these questions, please give details:

IX. USE OF ALCOHOL/DRUGS.

Substance	Current or recent use	Past use	Frequency
Alcohol			
Amphetamines			
Barbiturates			
Cocaine			
Inhalants			
Marijuana			
Prescribed medications			
Opiates			
Other (designer drugs, etc., specify):			
Drug combinations? (specify):			

X. WHAT CONNECTIONS COULD EXIST BETWEEN YOUR USE OF THESE SUBSTANCES AND YOUR ANGER OR AGGRESSION?

A. When I use ______________ I often become more angry than usual.
B. When I use ______________ I can become violent.
C. When I use ______________ I get argumentative.
D. When I use ______________ I become controlling or demanding.
E. When I use ______________ I have poor judgment.
F. When I use ______________ I get jealous or paranoid.
G. I only get in trouble with my anger when I use ______________ .
H. Others tell me I get angrier or more violent when I use ____________.
I. Mixing ____________ and ____________ makes me more aggressive.

J. I often use _______________ to try to cool down.
K. Another connection between my using and my anger is ________ _______________ .
L. _____ I don't see any connection between my use of alcohol or drugs and my anger or aggression.

XI. HOW HAVE YOU ATTEMPTED TO CONTROL YOUR ANGER?

_____ I never have.

_____ I talk to myself. What do you usually say that helps you cool down?

_____ I leave the scene. Where do you go? What do you do?

_____ I talk with people. With whom?

_____ I go to a self-help group such as AA.

_____ I do something physical. What do you do?

_____ I do something else. What do you do?

XII. WHAT DO YOU THINK IS THE FIRST THING YOU NEED TO DO TO HELP YOU CONTROL YOUR ANGER OR AGGRESSION?

XIII. WHAT ELSE DO YOU NEED TO DO?

XIV. HOW HOPEFUL ARE YOU THAT YOU CAN BECOME LESS ANGRY OR AGGRESSIVE?

XV. CAN YOU TELL ME ANYTHING ELSE THAT MIGHT HELP ME UNDERSTAND YOUR CONCERNS ABOUT ANGER AND AGGRESSION?

ANGER STYLES QUESTIONNAIRE

Directions: Please answer the following thirty Yes/No questions by circling the most correct answer based on the ways you generally handle your anger. There are no correct or incorrect answers. If you think that the best answer would be "Sometimes" then still try to select a best "yes" or "no" answer, and add the letter "S" to your response.

1.	I try never to become angry.	Yes	No
2.	I get really nervous when others become angry.	Yes	No
3.	I feel I am doing something bad when I become angry.	Yes	No
4.	I often tell people I'll do what they want but then frequently forget.	Yes	No
5.	I frequently say things like "Yeah, but . . ." and "I'll do it later."	Yes	No
6.	People tell me I must be angry but I'm not certain why they say that.	Yes	No
7.	I frequently become jealous, even when there is no reason.	Yes	No
8.	I don't trust people very much.	Yes	No
9.	Sometimes I feel as if people are out to get me.	Yes	No
10.	My anger comes on really fast.	Yes	No
11.	I act before I think when I become angry.	Yes	No
12.	My anger goes away quickly.	Yes	No
13.	I become angry when people criticize me.	Yes	No
14.	People say I'm easily hurt and oversensitive.	Yes	No
15.	I become angry easily when I feel bad about myself.	Yes	No
16.	I become angry in order to get what I want.	Yes	No
17.	I try to fighten others with my anger.	Yes	No
18.	I sometimes pretend to be very angry when I really am not.	Yes	No
19.	Sometimes I become angry just for the excitement or action.	Yes	No
20.	I like the strong feelings that come with my anger.	Yes	No
21.	Sometimes when I'm bored I start arguments or pick fights.	Yes	No

22. I seem to become angry all the time.	Yes	No
23. My anger feels like a bad habit I can't break.	Yes	No
24. I get mad without thinking— it just happens.	Yes	No
25. I become very angry when I defend my beliefs and opinions.	Yes	No
26. I often feel outraged about what other people say and do.	Yes	No
27. I always know I'm right in an argument.	Yes	No
28. I hang onto my anger for a long time.	Yes	No
29. I have a hard time forgiving people.	Yes	No
30. I hate many people for what they've done to me.	Yes	No

TREATMENT PLANNING FORM

1. Prioritize these three anger goals with regard to the client's immediate need to develop skills in these areas:
   ____ Prevention
   ____ Containment
   ____ Problem resolution

Name one specific skill in top area to develop:____________________

2. Prioritize these four treatment areas with regard to the client's immediate need to develop skills in these areas:
   ____ Behavior
   ____ Thoughts
   ____ Feelings
   ____ Spirit

Name one specific skill in top area to develop: ____________________

3. Prioritize people/life spheres on which to concentrate attention:
   ____ Partner
   ____ Child or children
   ____ Parents
   ____ Siblings
   ____ Work
   ____ Teachers
   ____ Friends
   ____ Driving
   ____ Legal figures
   ____ Strangers
   ____ Others (specify):____________________

4. Indicate any complicating factors that must also be addressed to help the client manage his or her anger:
   ____ Alcohol or drug use
   ____ Depression, anxiety, etc. (specify): ____________________
   ____ Immediate stressors (specify): ____________________
   ____ Anger/aggression in other family members
   ____ Legal concerns
   ____ Other (specify): ____________________

5. Based on the STAXI-2, identify which of these problems needs attention (at least 65 percent on test scale):
   ____ Immediate anger (State anger)
   ____ Trait anger: Angry temperament

____ Trait anger: Angry reaction
____ Anger-expression out
____ Anger-expression in
____ Anger-control out
____ Anger-control in
____ Total anger (Anger-Expression Index)

6. Which of the following anger styles needs to be addressed (indicated by the client checking at least two of three items in designated section of questionnaire):
   ____ Avoidance
   ____ Sneaky
   ____ Paranoia
   ____ Sudden
   ____ Shame-based
   ____ Deliberate
   ____ Addictive
   ____ Habitual
   ____ Moral
   ____ Resentment

7. What else needs to be addressed? ______________________________

ANGER TURNED INWARD QUIZ

Here is a quick checklist to determine how often and how much you turn your anger inward. Please score each item from 1-5 points, for which

1 = That's not what I do at all
2 = I do that only once in a great while
3 = I do that fairly often
4 = I do that a lot
5 = I do that all the time

1. _____ I feel really angry with someone but don't say anything.
2. _____ I don't show my anger because I don't want to hurt someone's feelings.
3. _____ I'm afraid others will be angry with me if they see I'm angry with them.
4. _____ I indirectly let people know I'm angry by pouting, sulking, going silent, etc.
5. _____ I tell myself I shouldn't become angry even when most people would be angry about something someone has done or said.
6. _____ I "stuff" my anger and then get headaches, a stiff neck, stomachaches, etc.
7. _____ I handle conflict more by giving in or avoiding problems than by negotiating, being assertive, or clearly stating what I want.
8. _____ I feel very responsible for others even when I'm angry with them.
9. _____ I put on a good front by smiling and looking happy even when I'm upset.
10. _____ I don't generally share any of my feelings, including anger.
11. _____ I feel guilty or shameful whenever I become angry, no matter how justified my anger might be.
12. _____ I become so angry with myself that I call myself ugly names or even physically attack myself (scratching, head banging, burning, suicide attempts, etc.).

What is your total score? _____

Appendix B

Anger Management Reading Assignments

I described three different anger management group treatment formats in Chapter 4. Here I add suggested reading assignments. The assignments are taken from my workbook (Potter-Efron, 2002), which is a required text for the participants. Many excellent workbooks are available in the field. I present my own here simply because I am most familiar with these assignments and I have found that clients will actually use them.

TWELVE-WEEK ANGER MANAGEMENT PROGRAM FOR MINIMALLY OR MODERATELY PHYSICALLY AGGRESSIVE INDIVIDUALS

Session One: How Anger Messes Up Your Life. Discuss how anger has caused problems in each person's life. Address such issues as health, family-of-origin conflicts, current family problems, work and school difficulties, finances, legal involvements, spiritual concerns, damage to friendships, and mood and personality changes.

Required assignments for Session Two: "Choices" and "Who Has Been Driving the Bus of Your Life?," pp. 6-8 and 32-34.

Session Two: Three Goals of Anger Management and Four Ways You Can Change. The three goals are prevention, containment, and resolution. The four ways are changes in behavior, thoughts, feelings, and spirit. Use the "Choices" exercise to introduce the concept of "anger invitations" and the "Who . . ." exercise to increase motivation.

Required assignment for Session Three: "Know Your Hot Thoughts," pp. 18-19.

Session Three: Prevention Techniques. Discuss the concept of prevention. Utilize the "hot thoughts" exercise to help participants gain a sense of control over their anger regardless of the words or actions of others.

Required assignment for Session Four: "Time Out," pp. 70-71.

Session Four: Controlling Your Emotions. Discuss the concept of containment (control). Present the time-out exercise as absolutely necessary for anger containment when nearing loss of control.

Required assignments for Session Five: "I Statements" and "Fair Fighting," pp. 99-103.

Session Five: Problem Solving. Discuss the concept of problem resolution as a skill that can be improved over time. Keep discussions concrete through the use of I statements and individualized fair fighting reminders.

Required assignments for Session Six: "The Substitution Principle" and "Do Something Different," pp. 9-10 and 53-55.

Session Six: Changing What You Do. Here the emphasis shifts from stopping undesired behavior to beginning prosocial actions and thinking.

Required assignments for Session Seven: "Disputations and Anger Control" and "Understanding the Other Person's Feelings," pp. 64-65 and 120-122.

Session Seven: Changing How You Think. This session revisits cognitive therapy but from a more general perspective. Instead of addressing one hot thought at a time, the goal is to explain the general process of cognitive disputation. The concept of empathy is also introduced.

Required assignments for Session Eight: "Staying Calm—Relaxation" and "Notice Your Other Feelings," pp. 30-31 and 70-71.

Session Eight: Changing Your Feelings. Participants learn to relax with an in-session relaxation session and they also are encouraged to explore their neglected other feelings.

Required assignments for Session Nine: "Challenging Your Angry Spirit" and "Why Am I So Critical of Others?," pp. 36-37 and 83-85.

Session Nine: Changing Your Spirit. Chronically angry people live chronically unhappy lives. This session offers participants a chance to confront their own negativity.

Required assignment for Session Ten: "Forgiving Those Who Have Harmed You," pp. 134-139.

Session Ten: Forgiveness. Forgiveness should be presented as a positive but not required possibility. Participants must realize that forgiveness takes time and effort.

Required assignment for Session Eleven: "Self-Hate: The Saboteur of Anger Management," pp. 42-43.

Session Eleven: Anger Turned Inward. The themes of anger suppression and self-attack are discussed to help participants recognize that "stuffing" one's anger or attacking oneself are not positive anger management goals.

Required assignment for Session Twelve: "The Final Line: Doing More Good Than Harm," pp. 144-145.

Session Twelve: Where Do You Go From Here? A recapitulation session with emphasis on keeping one's personal commitments to managing anger.

TWELVE-WEEK ANGER MANAGEMENT PROGRAM FOR SEVERELY PHYSICALLY AGGRESSIVE INDIVIDUALS

Session One: How Anger Messes Up Your Life.

Required assignments for Session Two: "I Know Exactly How to Hurt Them But I Won't" and "Shouting Won't Make You Feel Better," pp. 51-52 and 73-74.

Session Two: Climbing Down the Anger and Violence Ladder. Use the ladder from *Angry All The Time* to continue last week's discussion and to help participants make a commitment to nonaggression.

Required assignments for Session Three: "Accepting Reality" and "Keeping Things in Perspective," pp. 38-39 and 115-116.

Session Three: Accepting Reality. This session deals with the egocentric world of many violent persons who mistakenly believe that others are there to serve them.

Session Four: Prevention Techniques. Reading: "Know Your Hot Thoughts," pp. 18-19.

Session Five: Controlling Your Emotions and Noticing Other Feelings. Readings: "Time-Out" and "Know Your Other Feelings," pp. 48-50 and 70-71. Note: This session combines parts of Sessions Four and Eight from the first listed program.

Session Six: Problem Solving. Readings: "I Statements" and "Fair Fighting," pp. 99-103.

Session Seven: Changing What You Do. Readings: "The Substitution Principle" and "Do Something Different," pp. 9-10 and 53-55.

Session Eight: Changing How You Think. Readings: "Disputations and Anger Control" and "Understanding the Other Person's Feelings," pp. 64-65 and 120-122.

Session Nine: Changing Your Spirit. Readings: "Challenging your Angry Spirit" and "Why Am I So Critical of Others?", pp. 36-37 and 83-85.

Required assignments for Session Ten: "Breaking the Shame—Rage Connection" and "Don't Jump to Conclusions (Don't Get Paranoid)," pp. 75-78 and 60-61.

Session Ten: Shame-Rage and Paranoia. These two topics are particularly critical in lessening the risk for violence. Shame-rage occurs when people defend against shame by attacking the alleged shamer; paranoia represents a thought distortion that turns people into enemies.

Required assignments for Session Eleven: "Understand the Other Person's Feelings" and "Non-Defensive Conflict: Looking for the Grain of Truth in the Other Person's Viewpoint," pp. 120-122 and 110-112.

Session Eleven: Understanding Others Better. Basic empathy training that can be utilized even during conflict.

Session Twelve: Where Do You Go From Here? Reading: "The Final Line: Doing More Good Than Harm," pp. 144-145.

TWELVE-WEEK ANGER MANAGEMENT PROGRAM FOR MEN WHO COMMIT ACTS OF PHYSICAL DOMESTIC ABUSE

Session One: What Is Domestic Abuse? Why Do Men Hit Their Partners? My definition of domestic abuse (adult partners) is: "an act of physical aggression (hitting, pushing, shoving, slapping, pinching, etc.) and/or threats to aggress committed by one person against their relationship partner (boyfriend, girlfriend, spouse)." A domestic abuser (batterer) engages in *repeated* acts of domestic abuse. A serial domestic abuser repeatedly has engaged in these behaviors with two or more relationship partners. Possible reasons for male domestic abuse include traditional male beliefs about domination, poor communication skills, and personal insecurity.

Session Two: Climbing Down the Ladder of Domestic Abuse. Readings: "I Know Exactly How to Hurt Them But I Won't" and "Shouting Won't Make You Feel Better," pp. 51-52 and 73-74. *Note:* this is essentially the same session as described previously but with all examples drawn from domestic violence situations.

Session Three: Accepting Reality. Readings: "Accepting Reality" and "Keeping Things in Perspective," pp. 38-39 and 115-116.

Session Four: Prevention Techniques. Reading: "Know Your Hot Thoughts," pp. 18-19.

Session Five: Controlling Your Emotions and Noticing Other Feelings. Reading: "Time Out" and "Know Your Other Feelings," pp. 48-50 and 70-71.

Session Six: Problem Solving. Readings: "I Statements" and "Fair Fighting," pp. 99-103.

Session Seven: Changing What You Do. Readings: "The Substitution Principle" and "Do Something Different," pp. 9-10 and 53-55.

Session Eight: Changing How You Think. Readings: "Disputations and Anger Control" and "Understanding the Other Person's Feelings," pp. 64-65 and 120-122.

Session Nine: Changing Your Spirit. Readings: Challenging your Angry Spirit" and "Why Am I So Critical of Others?" pp. 36-37 and 83-85.

Session Ten: Shame-Rage, Paranoia, and Jealousy. Readings: "Breaking the Shame-Rage Connection" and "Don't Jump to Conclusions (Don't Get Paranoid)," pp. 75-78 and 60-61. Note the added emphasis on the topic of jealousy, a particularly necessary aspect of domestic violence treatment.

Session Eleven: Better Understanding Your Partner and Children. Readings: "Understand the Other Person's Feelings" and "Non-Defensive Conflict: Looking for the Grain of Truth in the Other Person's Viewpoint," pp. 120-122 and 110-112. Note the extra emphasis on parenting, an attempt to help participants generalize their learning from partner to the entire family unit.

Session Twelve: Where Do We Go From Here?

Note: Twelve sessions may be too few with this population. A sixteen-week program could include two sessions on behavior change, two on cognitive change, two on existential/spiritual change, and one on alternative responses to the shame-rage reaction.

Appendix C

Covariances of Anger/Aggression with Substance Abuse

TABLE C.1. Covariances of Substance Abuse and the Behavioral States of Aggression and Violence.

Drug Name or Category	Intoxication	Intoxication Delirium	Withdrawal	Withdrawal Delirium	Idiosyncratic/ Paradoxical Response	Substance-Induced Dementia	Chronic Substance-Induced Paranoia	Drug-Procuring Violence
Alcohol	c		c	occ	occ	occ	occ	occ
Other sedatives/ hypnotics	occ		c	c	occ			
GHB (Gamma hydroxybutyrate)*	c	occ	c		occ			
Phencyclidine (PCP)	c	c					c	occ
Ketamine ("Special K")*	c	c					c	occ
Cocaine	c						occ	occ
Other stimulants	c						c	occ
Ectasy (MDMA)*	occ	occ					occ	occ
Dextrometh-orphan (DM)*	occ	occ			occ			
Hallucinogens					occ			
Cannabis		occ			occ			
Inhalants		occ				occ		

Source: © 1990-2004 M.M. Miller, MD, R. Potter-Efron, PhD

*often referred to as club drugs; c = common trait; occ = occasional trait

TABLE C.2. Covariance of Substance Abuse and the Emotional/Psychological States Associated with Irritability and Anger.

Substance	Production of Irritable "Short-Fused" State	Introduction of Acute Paranoid Thoughts and Behavior	Exacerbation of Underlying Paranoid State	Disinhibition of Intrinsic Anger	Unmasking of Irritability/ Anger[a]
Alcohol or sedative intoxication (includes GHB)	2+ to 3+	1+	0 to 2+	3+	0
Alcohol or sedative withdrawal	3+ to 4+	1= to 2+	1+ to 2+	0	0 to 2+
Stimulant intoxication (includes cocaine and Ectasy)[b]	3+ to 4+	3+ to 4+	3+ to 4+	0	0
Stimulant withdrawal (includes caffeine and Ectasy)	0	0	0	0	0
Opiate intoxication	0	0	0	0	0
Opiate withdrawal	3+	0	0 to 1+	0	0 to 1+
Hallucinogen intoxication	0 to 1+	0 to 1+	1+ to 3+	1+	0
Cannabis intoxication	0 to 1+	2+ to 4+	2+ to 4+	1+	0
Cannabis withdrawal	1+ to 2+	0	0	0	1+ to 3+
Phencyclidine (PCP) intoxication (including ketamine and dextromethorphan	2+ to 4+	2+ to 4+	4+	0	0

Source: Designed, revised, and expanded by Michael M. Miller, MD, Meriter Hospital, Madison, WI © 2004

Note: The numbers above are for comparative purposes, with 0 indicating no known association and 4+ indicating a very strong association between a particular substance-induced state (during intoxication or withdrawal) and the presence of irritability or anger.

[a]Irritability/anger that had been masked by chronic drug use.

[b]Includes caffeine in large doses.

References

Aggleton, J. and Young, A. (2000). The Enigma of the Amygdala: On Its Contribution to Human Emotion. In R. Lane and L. Nadel (Eds.), *Cognitive Neuroscience of Emotion* (pp. 106-128). New York: Oxford University Press.

Alberti, R. and Emmons, M. (2001). *Your Perfect Right* (Eighth Edition). Atascadero, CA: Impact Publishers.

Alcoholics Anonymous (1976). *Big Book.* New York: A. A. World Service.

Allen, J. and Land, D. (1999). Attachment in Adolescence. In J. Cassidy and P. Shaver (Eds.), *Handbook of Attachment* (pp. 319-335). New York: Guilford.

American Psychiatric Association (2000). *Diagnostic and Statistical Manual of Mental Disorders,* Fourth Edition. Washington, DC: American Psychiatric Association.

Anderson, J. (1997). *Social Work with Groups: A Process Model.* New York: Longman.

Bartholomew, K., Henderson, A., and Dutton, D. (2001). Insecure Attachment and Insecure Intimate Relationships. In C. Clulow (Ed.), *Adult Attachment and Couple Psychotherapy* (pp. 43-62). London: Brunner-Rutledge.

Beck, A. (1976). *Cognitive Therapy and the Emotional Disorders.* New York: International Universities Press.

Beck, A. (1999). *Prisoners of Hate: The Cognitive Basis of Anger, Hostility and Violence.* New York: HarperCollins.

Begley, T. (1994). Expressed and Suppressed Anger As Predictors of Health Complaints. *Journal of Organizational Behavior* 15(6), 503-516.

Berecz, J. (2001). All That Glitters Is Not Gold: Bad Forgiving in Counseling and Preaching. *Pastoral Psychology* 49(4), 253-275.

Berman, W., Marcus, L., and Berman, E. (1994). Attachment in Marital Relations. In M. Sperling and W. Berman (Eds.), *Attachment in Adults* (pp. 204-231). New York: Guilford Press.

Berman, W. and Sperling, M. (1994). The Structure and Function of Adult Attachment. In M. Sperling and W. Berman (Eds.), *Attachment in Adults* (pp. 1-30). New York: Guilford Press.

Bloomquist, M. and Schnell, S. (2002). *Helping Children with Aggression and Conduct Problems.* New York: Guilford Press.

Blumenreich, P. (1993). Pharmacotherapy of Violence. In P. Blumenreich and S. Lewis (Eds.), *Managing the Violent Patient* (pp. 53-78). New York: Brunner/Mazel.

Bowlby, J. (1969). *Attachment and Loss:* Volume One. *Attachment.* New York: Basic Books.

Bowlby, J. (1973). *Attachment and Loss:* Volume Two. *Separation: Anxiety and Anger.* New York: Basic Books.

Bowlby, J. (1980). *Attachment and Loss*: Volume Three. *Loss: Sadness and Depression.* New York: Basic Books.

Brennan, K., Clark, C., and Shaver, P. (1998). Self-Report Measurements of Adult Attachment: An Integrative Overview. In J. Simson and W. S. Rholes (Eds.), *Attachment Theory and Close Relationships* (pp. 46-76). New York: Guilford Press.

Bushman, B., Baumeister, R., and Stack, A. (1999). Catharsis, Aggression and Persuasive Influence: Self-Fulfilling or Self-Defeating Prophecies? *Journal of Personality and Social Psychology* 76, 367-376.

Buss, A. and Durkee, A. (1957). An Inventory for Assessing Different Kinds of Hostility. *Journal of Counseling Psychology* 63, 452-459.

Buss, D., Larsen, R., Westen, D., and Semmelroth, J. (2001). Sex Differences in Jealousy: Evolution, Physiology and Psychology. In W. G. Parrott (Ed.), *Emotions in Social Psychology* (pp. 143-149) Bristol, PA: Taylor and Francis.

Ciaramicoli, A. (2000). *The Power of Empathy.* New York: Dutton.

Clulow, C. (2001). Insecure Attachment and Abusive Intimate Relationships. In C. Clulow (Ed.), *Adult Attachment and Couple Psychotherapy* (pp. 85-104). London: Brunner-Rutledge.

Coates, D. (1997). The Correlations of Forgiveness of Self, Forgiveness of Others, and Hostility, Depression, Anxiety, Self-Esteem, Life Adaptation, and Religiosity Among Female Victims of Domestic Abuse. *Dissertation Abstracts International* 58 (5-B), 2667.

Coleman, P. (1998). The Process of Forgiveness in Marriage and the Family. In R. Enright and J. North (Eds.), *Exploring Forgiveness* (pp. 75-94). Madison, WI: University of Wisconsin Press.

Conflict Resolution Game (1995). King of Prussia, PA: The Center for Applied Psychology, Inc.

Cornell, D., Peterson, C. S., and Richards, H. (1999). Anger As a Predictor of Aggression Among Incarcerated Adolescents. *Journal of Consulting and Clinical Psychology* 71(1), 108-115.

Cowan, P. and Cowan, C. (2001). Attachment Theory and the Therapeutic Frame. In C. Clulow (Ed.), *Adult Attachment and Couple Psychotherapy* (pp. 62-82). London: Brunner-Rutledge.

Coyle, C. (1999). Self-Forgiveness: Dangerous Myth? *The World of Forgiveness* 2(3), 6-8.

Cozolino, L. (2002). *The Neuroscience of Psychotherapy.* New York: W. W. Norton.

Crittenden, P. (2002) Transformacions en las Relaciones de Apego an la Adolescencia: Adaptacion Frente a Necrsidad de Psicoterapia. (Transformations in Attachment Relationships in Adolescence: Adaptation Versus Need for Psychotherapy). *Revista de Psicoterpia* 12, 33-62 (English translation available at www.patcrittenden.com>).

Damasio, A. (2000). A Second Chance for Emotions. In R. Lane and L. Nadel (Eds.), *Cognitive Neuroscience of Emotion* (pp. 12-23). New York: Oxford University Press.

Damasio, A. (2003). *Looking for Spinoza: Joy, Sorrow, and the Feeling Brain.* Orlando, FL: Harcourt, Inc.

Damon, W. and Gregory, A. (1997). The Youth Charter: Towards the Formation of Adolescent Moral Identity. *Journal of Moral Education* 26(2), 117-130.

Deffenbacher, J. (2003). Anger Disorders. In E. F. Coccaro (Ed.), *Aggression, Psychiatric Assessment and Treatment* (pp. 89-111). New York: Marcel Dekker.

Deffenbacher, J. and Stark, R. (1992). Relaxation and Cognitive-Relaxation Treatments of General Anger. *Journal of Counseling Psychology* 39, 158-167.

Diamond, D. and Blatt, S. (1994). Internal Working Models and the Representational World in Attachment and Psychoanalytic Theories. In M. Sperling and W. Berman (Eds.), *Attachment in Adults* (pp. 72-97). New York: Guilford Press.

Dozier, M. and Tyrell, C. (1998). The Role of Attachment in Therapeutic Relationships. In J. Simson and W. S. Rholes (Eds.), *Attachment Theory and Close Relationships* (pp. 221-248). New York: Guilford Press.

Dozier, R. (2002). *Why We Hate: Understanding, Curbing and Eliminating Hate in Ourselves and the World.* Chicago: Contemporary Books.

Dutton, D. (1998). *The Abusive Personality.* New York: Guilford Press.

Dutton, D., van Winkel, C., and Landolt, M. (1997). Jealousy, Intimate Abusiveness, and Intrusiveness. *Journal of Family Violence* 11(4), 411-423.

Eckhardt, C. and Deffenbacher, J. (1995). Diagnosis of Anger Disorders. In H. Kassinove (Ed.), *Anger Disorders* (pp. 27-48). Washington, DC: Taylor and Francis.

Ellis, A. (1962). *Reason and Emotion in Psychotherapy.* New York: Lyle Stuart.

Ellis, A. and Harper, R. (1975). *A New Guide to Rational Living.* Hollywood, CA: Wilshire Books.

Ellis, A. and Tafrate, R. (1997). *How to Control Your Anger Before It Controls You.* Secaucus, NJ: Carol Publishing.

Emmons, R. (2000). Personality and Forgiveness. In M. McCullough, K. Pargament, and C. Thoresen (Eds.), *Forgiveness: Theory, Research and Practice* (pp. 156-175). New York: Guilford Press.

Enright, R. (1994). *The Enright Forgiveness Inventory.* Madison, WI: International Forgiveness Institute.

Enright, R. (1996). Counseling Within the Forgiveness Triad: On Forgiving, Receiving Forgiveness and Self-Forgiveness. *Counseling and Values* 40, 107-126.

Enright, R. (2001). *Forgiveness Is a Choice.* Washington, DC: American Psychological Association.

Enright, R. and Fitzgibbons, R. (2000). *Helping Clients Forgive.* Washington, DC: American Psychological Association.

Enright, R., Freedman, S., and Rique, J. (1998). The Psychology of Interpersonal Forgiveness. In R. Enright and J. North (Eds.), *Exploring Forgiveness* (pp. 46-62). Madison, WI: University of Wisconsin Press.

Erickson, Eric (1968). *Identity: Youth and Crisis.* New York: W. W. Norton.

Evans, D., Hearn, M., and Saklofske, D. (1973). Anger, Arousal and Systematic Desensitiz ation. *Psychological Reports* 32, 625-626.

Ferch, S. (1998). Intentional Forgiving As a Counseling Intervention. *Journal of Counseling and Development* 76, 261-270.

Fitness, J. (2001). Betrayal, Rejection, Revenge and Forgiveness. In M. Leary (Ed.), *Interpersonal Rejection* (pp. 73-101). New York: Oxford University Press.

Flanigan, B. (1992). *Forgiving the Unforgivable.* New York: Macmillan.

Flanigan, B. (1996). *Forgiving Yourself.* New York: Macmillan.

Forgays, D., Spielberger, C., Ottaway, S., and Forgays, D. (1998). Factor Structure of the State-Trait Anger Expression Inventory for Middle-Aged Men and Women. *Psychological Assessment* 5(2), 141-155.

Fraley, R.C., Davis, K., and Shaver, P. (1998). Dismissing-Avoidance and the Defensive Organization of Emotion, Cognition and Behavior. In J. Simson and W.S. Rholes (Eds.), *Attachment Theory and Close Relationships* (pp. 249-279). New York: Guilford Press.

Freedman, S. (1999). A Voice of Forgiveness: One Incest Survivor's Experience Forgiving Her Father. *Journal of Family Psychotherapy*, 10(4), 37-60.

George, C., Kaplan, N. and Main, M. (1996). *Adult Attachment Interview Protocol* (Third Edition) Unpublished manuscript, University of California at Berkeley.

Gottman, J. (1999). *The Seven Principles for Making Marriage Work.* New York: Crown.

Green, R. (1998). *The Explosive Child.* New York: HarperCollins.

Green, R. (1999). *MMPI-2: An Interpretive Manual,* Second Edition. New York: Allyn and Bacon.

Greenberg, M. (1999). Attachment and Psychopathology in Childhood. In J. Cassidy and P. Shaver (Eds.), *Handbook of Attachment* (pp. 469-496). New York: Guilford Press.

Groetsch, M. (1996). *The Battering Syndrome.* Brookfield, WI: CPI Publishing.

Hargrave, T. (1994). *Families and Forgiveness.* New York: Brunner/Mazel.

Hauck, P. (1974). *Overcoming Frustration and Anger.* Philadelphia: Westminster.

Hirschi, T. (1969). *Causes of Delinquency.* Berkeley: University of California Press.

Holmes, J. (1996). *Attachment, Intimacy, Autonomy.* Northvale, NJ: Jason Aronson, Inc.

Holmes, J. (2001). Foreword. In C. Clulow (Ed.), *Adult Attachment and Couple Therapy* (pp. xii-xx). London: Brunner- Rutledge.

Holtzworth-Munroe, A., Marshall, A., Meehan, J., and Rehman, U. (2003). Physical Aggression. In D. Snyder and M. Whisman (Eds.), *Treating Difficult Couples* (pp. 201-230). New York: Guilford Press.

Horton, C. (1999). Self-Forgiveness: A Reflection. *The World of Forgiveness* 2(3), 16-19.

Jacobsen, N. and Gottman, J. (1998). *When Men Batter Women.* New York: Simon and Schuster.

Jaeger, M. (1998). The Power and Reality of Forgiveness: Forgiving the Murderer of One's Child. In R. Enright and J. North (Eds.), *Exploring Forgiveness* (pp. 9-14). Madison, WI: University of Wisconsin Press.

Johnson, S. (2003). Negative Emotions. *Discover* March, 31-39.

Johnson, S. and Sims, A. (2000). Attachment Theory: A Map for Couples Counseling. In T. Levy (Ed.), *Handbook of Attachment Interventions* (pp. 169-191). San Diego: Academic Press.

Kaminer, D., Stein, D., Mbanga, I., and Zungu-Dirwayi, N. (2000). Forgiveness: Toward an Integration of Theoretical Models. *Psychiatry* 63(4), 344-357.

Karen, R. (1994). *Becoming Attached.* New York: Oxford University Press.

Karen, R. (2001). *The Forgiving Self.* New York: Doubleday.

Kassinove, H. and Tafrate, R. (2002). *Anger Management.* Atascadero, CA: Impact Publishers, Inc.

Kaufman, G. (1996). *The Psychology of Shame,* Second Edition. New York: Springer.

Keating, D. and Sasse, D. (1996). Cognitive Socialization in Adolescence: Critical Period for a Critical Habit of Mind. In G. Adams, R. Montemayer, and T. Gullotta (Eds.), *Psychosocial Development During Adolescence* (pp. 232-255). London: Sage Publications.

Klohnen, E. and John, O. (1998). Working Models of Attachment: A Theory-Based Prototype Approach. In J. Simson and W. S. Rholes (Eds.), *Attachment Theory and Close Relationships* (pp. 115-142). New York: Guilford Press.

Knobloch, L., Solomon, D., and Cruz, M. (2001). The Role of Relationship Development and Attachment in the Experience of Romantic Jealousy. *Personal Relationships* 8, 205-224.

Kostiuk, L. and Fouts, G. (2002). Understanding of Emotions and Emotion Regulation in Adolescent Females with Conduct Problems: A Qualitative Analysis. *The Qualitative Report* 7(1), 1-14.

Kring, A. (2001). Emotion and Psychopathology. In T. Mayne and G. Bonanno (Eds.), *Emotions: Current Issues and Future Directions* (pp. 337-360). New York: Guilford Press.

Kuhn, T. (1996). *The Structure of Scientific Revolutions,* Third Edition. Chicago: University of Chicago Press.

Lane, R. and Nadel, L. (Eds.) (2000). *Cognitive Neuroscience of Emotion.* New York: Oxford University Press.

Lazarus, R. (1991). *Emotion and Adaptation.* New York: Oxford.

Leary, M., Koch, E., and Hechenbleikner, N. (2001). Emotional Responses to Interpersonal Rejection. In M. Leary (Ed.), *Interpersonal Rejection.* New York: Oxford University Press.

LeDoux, J. (1996). *The Emotional Brain.* New York: Touchstone.

LeDoux, J. (2002). *Synaptic Self.* New York: Viking.

Lerner, H. (1985). *The Dance of Anger.* New York: Quill.

Levy, T. and Orlans, M. (2000). Attachment Disorder As an Antecedent to Violence and Antisocial Patterns in Children. In T. Levy (Ed.), *Handbook of Attachment Interventions* (pp. 1-25). San Diego: Academic Press

Lisspers, J., Nygren, A., and Soderman, E. (1998). Psychological Patterns in Patients with Coronary Heart Disease, Chronic Pain and Respiratory Disorder. *Scandinavian Journal of Caring Sciences* 12(1), 25-31.

Martin, R., Wan, C., David, J., Wegner, E., Olson, B., and Watson, D. (1999). Style of Anger Expression: Relation to Expressivity, Personality and Health. *Personality and Social Psychology Bulletin* 25(10), 1196-1207.

Mauger, P., Perry, J., Freeman, T., and Grove, D. (1992). The Measurement of Forgiveness: Preliminary Research. *Journal of Psychology and Christianity* 11, 170-180.

McCullough, M., Worthington, E., and Rachal, K. C. (1997). Interpersonal Forgiving in Close Relationships. *Journal of Personality and Social Psychology* 73(2), 321-336.

McKay, M., Davis, M., Paleg, K., and Landis, D. (1996). *When Anger Hurts Your Children.* Oakland, CA: New Harbinger Publications.

Mikulincer, M. and Florian, V. (1998). The Relationship Between Adult Attachment Styles and Emotional and Cognitive Reactions to Stressful Events. In J. Simson and W. S. Rholes (Eds.), *Attachment Theory and Close Relationships* (pp. 143-165). New York: Guilford Press.

Moeller, T. (2001). *Youth, Aggression and Violence.* London: Lawrence Erlbaum Associates.

Neidig, P. and Freidman, D. (1984). *Spouse Abuse: A Treatment Program for Couples.* Champaign, IL: Research Press.

Niehoff, D. (1998). *The Biology of Violence.* New York: Free Press.

North, J. (1998). The "Ideal" of Forgiveness: A Philosopher's Exploration. In R. Enright and J. North (Eds.), *Exploring Forgiveness* (pp. 15-34). Madison, WI: University of Wisconsin Press.

Novaco, R. (1975). *Anger Control: The Development and Evaluation of an Experimental Treatment.* Lexington, MA: D.C. Heath.

Panksepp, J. (1998). *Affective Neuroscience: The Foundations of Human and Animal Emotions.* New York: Oxford University Press.

Parens, H. (1987). *Aggression in Our Children.* Northvale, NJ: Jason Aronson.

Parrot, W.G. (2001). The Emotional Experiences of Envy and Jealousy. In W. G. Parrott (Ed.), *Emotions in Social Psychology* (pp. 306-320). Bristol, PA: Taylor and Francis.

Patterson, G. (1995). A Microsoual Analysis of Anger and Irritable Behavior. In M. Chesney and R. Rosenman (Eds.), *Anger and Hostility in Cardiovascular and Behavioral Disorders* (pp. 83-100). New York: Hemisphere Publishing.

Pittman, F. (1989). *Private Lies.* New York: W. W. Norton.

Plutchik, R. (2001). The Nature of Emotions. *American Scientist* 89(July-August), 344-350.

Polster, E. and Polster, M. (1973). *Gestalt Therapy Integrated.* New York: Vintage.

Potter-Efron, P. and Potter-Efron, R. (1999). *The Secret Message of Shame.* Oakland, CA: New Harbinger Publications.

Potter-Efron, R. (1994). *Angry All the Time: An Emergency Guide to Anger Control.* Oakland, CA: New Harbinger Publications.

Potter-Efron, R. (2001). *Stop the Anger Now: A Workbook for the Prevention, Containment and Resolution of Anger.* Oakland, CA: New Harbinger Publications.

Potter-Efron, R. (2002). *Shame, Guilt and Alcoholism,* Second Edition. Binghamton, NY: The Haworth Press.

Potter-Efron, R. (2004). *Angry All The Time: An Emergency Guide to Anger Control,* Second Edition. Oakland, CA: New Harbinger Publications.

Potter-Efron, R. and Potter-Efron, P. (1989). *Letting Go of Shame.* Center City, MN: Hazelden.

Potter-Efron, R. and Potter-Efron, P. (1991a). *Anger, Alcoholism and Addiction.* New York: W. W. Norton.

Potter-Efron, R. and Potter-Efron, P. (1991b). *Ending Our Resentments.* Center City, MN: Hazelden Publications.

Potter-Efron, R. and Potter-Efron, P. (1995). *Letting Go of Anger: The Ten Most Common Anger Styles and What to Do About Them.* Oakland, CA: New Harbinger Publications.

Random House Unabridged Dictionary (Second Edition) (1993). New York: Random House.

Ratey, J. (2001). *A User's Guide to the Brain.* New York: Vintage Books.

Reed, G. (1999). What Is Self-Forgiveness? *The World of Forgiveness* 2(3), 20-22.

Rholes, W.S., Simpson, J., and Stevens, J. (1998). Attachment Orientations, Social Support, and Conflict Resolution in Close Relationships. In J. Simson and W. S. Rholes (Eds.), *Attachment Theory and Close Relationships* (pp. 166-188). New York: Guilford Press.

Roberts, N. and Noller, P. (1998). The Associations Between Adult Attachment and Couple Violence: The Role of Communication Patterns and Relationship Satisfaction. In J. Simson and W.S. Rholes (Eds.), *Attachment Theory and Close Relationships* (pp. 317-352). New York: Guilford Press.

Saunders, D. (1992). A Typology of Men Who Batter: Three Types Derived from Cluster Analysis. *American Journal of Orthopsychiatry* 62(2), 264-275.

Schore, A. (1994). *Affect Regulation and the Origin of the Self.* Hillsdale, NJ: Lawrence Erlbaum Associates.

Shapiro, F. (1995). *Eye Movement Deprocessing and Resensitization.* New York: Guilford Press.

Sharpsteen, D. and Kirkpatrick, L. (1997). Romantic Jealousy and Adult Romantic Attachment. *Journal of Personality and Social Psychology* 72(3), 627-640.

Slade, A. (1999). Attachment Theory and Research: Implications for the Theory and Practice of Individual Psychotherapy with Adults. In J. Cassidy and P. Shaver (Eds.), *Handbook of Attachment* (pp. 575-594). New York: Guilford Press.

Smedes, L. (1984). *Forgive and Forget.* San Francisco: Harper & Row.

Smith, D., Furlong, M., Bates, M., and McLaughlin, J. (1998). Development of the Multidimensional School Anger Inventory for Males. *Psychology in the Schools* 35(1), 1-15.

Smith, J. (1999). *ABC Relaxation Training.* New York: Springer.

Sperling, M. and Lyons, L. (1994). Representations of Attachment and Psychotherapeutic Change. In M. Sperling and W. Berman (Eds.), *Attachment in Adults* (pp. 331-348). New York: Guilford Press.

Spielberger, C. (1999). *Manual for the State-Trait Anger Expression Inventory-2.* Odessa, FL: Psychological Assessment Resources.

Spielberger, C. (2001). Relationship between Anger-In and Suppressed Anger. Personal Correspondence.

Stearns, P. (1994). *American Cool.* New York: American University Press.

Steinberg, L. (2002). *Adolescence,* Sixth Edition. New York: McGraw-Hill.

Strauch, B. (2003). *The Primal Teen.* New York: Doubleday.

Tafrate, R. (1995). Evaluation of Treatment Strategies for Adult Anger Disorders. In H. Kassinove (Ed.), *Anger Disorders: Definition, Diagnosis and Treatment.* Washington, DC: Taylor and Francis.

Tangney, J. and Dearing, R. (2002). *Shame and Guilt.* New York: Guilford Press.

Tavris, C. (1989). *Anger: The Misunderstood Emotion.* New York: Simon and Schuster.

Teicher, M. (2002). The Neurobiology of Child Abuse. *Scientific American,* March 68-75.

Tivis, L., Parsons, O., and Nixon, S. (1998). Anger in an Inpatient Sample of Chronic Alcoholics. *Alcoholism: Clinical and Experimental Research* 22(4), 902-907.

Toseland, R. and Rivas, R. (2001). *An Introduction to Group Work Practice.* Boston: Allyn and Bacon.

Tucker, N., Stith, S., Howell, L., McCollum, E., and Rosen, K. (2000). Meta-Dialogues in Domestic Violence-Focused Couples Treatment. *Journal of Systemic Therapies* 19(4), 73-89.

Volavka, J. (2002). *Neurobiology of Violence,* Second Edition. Washington, DC: American Psychiatric Publishing.

Walfish, S. (1990). Anxiety and Anger Among Abusers of Different Substances. *Drug and Alcohol Dependence* 25(3), 253-256.

White, G. and Mullen, P. (1989). *Jealousy: Theory, Research, and Clinical Strategies.* New York: Guilford Press.

Wickham, E. (2003). *Group Treatment in Social Work.* Toronto: Thompson Educational Publishing, Inc.

Wilson, S. (2001). Attachment Disorders: Review and Current Status. *Journal of Psychology* 135(1), 37-52.

Index

Page numbers followed by the letter "f" indicate figures; those followed by the letter "t" indicate tables.